Freudians and Feminists

New Perspectives in Sociology
Charles Tilly and Scott McNall
Series Editors

Freudians and Feminists, Edith Kurzweil

Exceptions Are the Rule: An Inquiry into Methods in the Social Sciences, Joel H. Levine

FORTHCOMING IN 1995

Criminological Controversies, John Hagan, A. R. Gillis, and David Brownfield

Postmodernism, David Ashley

Immigrants in America's Future, David M. Heer

Work and Labor Markets, Chris Tilly and Charles Tilly

Rise and Demise: The Transformation of World Systems, Christopher Chase-Dunn and Thomas Hall

Contact Westview Press for information about additional upcoming titles.

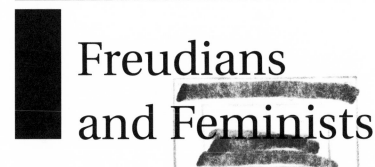

Freudians
and Feminists

Edith Kurzweil

Westview Press
Boulder • San Francisco • Oxford

New Perspectives in Sociology

Copyright © 1995 by Westview Press, Inc.

Published in 1995 in the United States of America by Westview Press, Inc., 5500 Central Avenue, Boulder, Colorado 80301-2877, and in the United Kingdom by Westview Press, 12 Hid's Copse Road, Cumnor Hill, Oxford OX2 9JJ

Library of Congress Cataloging-in-Publication Data
Kurzweil, Edith.
    Freudians and feminists / Edith Kurzweil.
        p.   cm.—(New perspectives in sociology)
    Includes bibliographical references and index.
    ISBN 0-8133-1420-8 (hc.).—ISBN 0-8133-1421-6 (pb.)
    1. Psychoanalysis and feminism.   2. Feminist psychology.
3. Feminism—History.   4. Freud, Sigmund, 1856–1939.   I. Title.
II. Series: New perspectives in sociology (Boulder, Colo.)
BF175.5.F45K87   1995
150.19′52′082—dc20   94-39464
                                                                                              CIP

Printed and bound in the United States of America

 The paper used in this publication meets the requirements
of the American National Standard for Permanence of Paper
for Printed Library Materials Z39.48-1984.

10   9   8   7   6   5   4   3   2   1

Contents

Conclusion 187

Preface

In this book I continue to explore the influence of Freud's ideas, which I traced in *The Freudians: A Comparative Perspective* (1989b). But this time I concentrate on the consequences of the belief in psychic liberation on the consciousness and lives of Western (mostly American) women. I focus on those components of psychoanalysis that have been important in influencing feminist thought and thus have helped enhance women's status and enabled them to enter a variety of occupations and professions that until twenty-five years ago were closed to them. Hence I am extending my earlier argument that traces the ebb and flow of the application and incorporation of Freud's ideas, and their effect, on a succession of feminists and their opponents—as well as the impact of feminist concerns on the theories and therapies of psychoanalysis.

To that end it is necessary to constantly keep in mind that Freud firmly believed that human nature is universal and, at the same time, that each individual's life has its unique history. Thus I start out by relating Freud's assumptions to his zeitgeist and his reactions to some of the mores and beliefs of fin de siècle Vienna. I then go on to summarize his major ideas about the female personality and to outline the evolving theories and their innumerable transformations up to the present. Essentially, I demonstrate the specific contexts in which feminist movements arose and functioned and why these sometimes enthusiastically endorsed Freud's concepts and at other times relegated all of psychoanalysis to the dustbin of history. Still, whether feminists tried to answer Freud's question, "What does a woman want?" or laughed at the notion of penis envy as a product of fin de siècle Vienna, they all eventually addressed the biological differences between the two sexes. I look at the ways feminists have come to terms with these differences and at the consequences of their assumptions and solutions.

I could choose no more than some examples among the myriad works about the female psyche by Freudians and feminists, and by their supporters and detractors in academe, to typify the succession of trends and emphases. My sociological training itself led me to focus on why at certain moments specific theoretical or therapeutic details became attractive and why some of these soon were discarded. Therefore, I read many of the thousands of contributions by psychoanalysts on questions of therapy in order to assess them in relation to general, social concerns. But I stayed away from therapeutic issues themselves and from those that deal with the ultimate role of therapy primarily to help patients adjust to or change their lives. I put aside psychoanalysts' speculations about social influences on the psyches of their "cases" and feminists' allegations that some Freudians set out to adapt their patients to patriarchal conditions.

When I began to analyze my data, I found strong differences among feminists who kept their feet on empirical ground (the First Wave) and those who in one form or another followed up on Jacques Lacan's "rereading" of Freud (the Second Wave). Together these two stages of the American feminist movement helped alter not only the lives of women but the entire social fabric.

Inevitably, I had to confront the growing influence of modernism and so-called postmodernism on both Freudians and feminists and the consequences of both "movements." Because of the current popularity of my subject in the humanities and among publishers, I had to narrowly limit my topic, to leave out many writers as well as topics sparked by the women's movement, such as the impact of psychoanalysis on gay and lesbian studies, on issues of legal rights, and on abortion.

Some feminists will deem this book too evenhanded, and others will criticize me for my sociological slant. Some Freudians will look in vain for "therapeutic" considerations. However, I wrote on this topic because I am partial to both the sociological and the Freudian view and because I am frustrated by the tunnel vision of some of the advocates of feminism and by the hermeneutic bent of some Freudians. That is why I have aimed to be polemical, to open up debates among so-called traditionalists and postmodernists as well as among the members of different Freudian and feminist groups. Ultimately, I hope that my readers will pay more attention than previously to the ways in which both psychoanalytic and feminist principles have become ubiquitous and have furnished us with many by now accepted values. That these values themselves continue to fluctuate in response to cultural fashions has become a truism. But the moments when intellectual trends shift, and the specific winds that propel them, are determined not only by the social construction of reality by feminists and Freudians but also by the degree to which they are judged central or marginal by their fellow citizens. This intricate interaction, which reaches to all of intellectual activity, is the subject of this book.

I want to thank the editors of Westview Press, Dean Birkenkamp and Connie Oehring, for their expert assistance; the series editors, Scott McNall and Charles Tilly; and the anonymous readers for their comments on earlier versions.

I could not have written this book without the help of the librarians at the Freud Archives, Library of Congress, Washington, D.C.; Maria Arkagelitis at the Brill Library of the New York Psychoanalytic Institute; and the late Eric T. Carlson at the Oskar Diethelm Historical Library at the Payne Whitney Psychiatry Clinic, New York.

Edith Kurzweil

Introduction

In this book I trace the ambivalent relation between psychoanalysis and feminism, which has existed almost from the beginning, when Freud's thought promised, among other things, to help emancipate women. Subsequently, the two movements, together or in opposition, were among the most dynamic mainsprings of modern society. But as their theoretical underpinnings matured in response to intellectual questions and their communities clamored for political guidance, they evolved along national and local lines. Here, I address primarily their American trajectory. But in order to highlight specific cultural influences, I also go into relevant French theories and German practices. Thereby, I expect to alert my readers to some of the taken-for-granted and parochial assumptions about Freud's ideas and thus to indicate different theoretical paths and reinvigorate debates that have turned unnecessarily stale.

The speculative nature of psychoanalysis itself legitimates its proponents' and opponents' flights of fancy, the confusions between reality and fantasy and between scientific and therapeutic explanations of psychological phenomena. The political nature of feminism justifies the often hyperbolic calls for active involvement and the consequent exaggerations of women's psychological dilemmas in order to score points and achieve political ends. Although psychoanalysis and feminism function in different spheres, the psychoanalytic views of a few women gave feminism inordinate boosts whenever their insights into psychic mechanisms freed women to compete in political arenas. Feminist advances, however, have not directly bolstered the psychoanalytic movement. Yet the two activities have grown up like a pair of Siamese twins, unable to exist apart from each other for long—progressing, regressing, or treading water almost in tandem.

I perceive feminism as women's demand for equal rights with men in all economic, political, social, and personal spheres. And I am convinced that these ends can be furthered with the help of insights from Freudian theories. However, I have serious doubts that elaborating on feminist theories that have been adapted from earlier French formulations and that in recent years have found their niche in American universities will ultimately benefit the majority of women. Thus I argue that the straightforward feminism of the First Wave—which, among other things, led to the passage of Title IX of the Education Amendments of 1972—boosted women's liberation and altered the fabric of American society. And while explaining the complicated theories of the Second Wave, I show that these formulations become increasingly marginal to the practical and complex problems facing both liberated and not-so-liberated women in their everyday lives.

Because psychoanalysis is one of the central ideas that changed the thinking of our century (the others are Marxism and Darwinism), I keep pointing to its rising and ebbing impact on feminism as psychoanalysts kept extending and revising their theories of drives and narcissism, of personality structure and object relations, in the hope of creating a radically better world that would help free individuals from their unconscious conflicts. In the process, women increasingly were to become unshackled. But whenever psychoanalysts have come up against—mostly unconscious—resistances to change, feminists have been among those who resisted psychoanalytic insights. This tension becomes clearer when we juxtapose it with specific cultural phenomena and customs, as shown by the impact of innovative French psychoanalyst Jacques Lacan and German psychoanalyst Alexander Mitscherlich. That is why comparing the distinct role psychoanalysis has played in France and Germany to our taken-for-granted American context leads to new insights into the construction of knowledge, including feminist knowledge, in response to local situations and into the fickle ways foreign concepts become familiar and are (partially) adapted.

In my task I have to take account of a number of complexities: From its inception, psychoanalysis has been therapy, theory, philosophy, and metapsychology all at once. Progress in each of these areas inevitably meant that all the other areas had to be recast, so psychoanalysts had to function in a theoretical state of flux. Feminists have had to navigate in their culture, to challenge specific discriminatory habits, and to break down the boundaries of sexual domination by the men they lived with or decided to abandon. These men themselves were brought up in the political order other men had created. Thus to further women's freedom, feminists and most psychoanalysts had to deal with and rethink the philosophies that were in vogue and to build on the realistic (legal) options open, or about to open, to women. Only by adapting their thinking and ideals to existing institutions could they promote their ends. For instance, the women who in 1907 had to contend with Fritz Wittels's argument that women's psychic makeup prevented them from turning into competent physicians could not possibly envision the debate on the advantages of women over male obstetricians that would rage in the 1970s and 1980s. Freud sided against Wittels, but the zeitgeist did not allow for as strong a rebuttal as contemporary Freudians might advance. Yet then and since then women have faced the cultural and interest-based resistance to equality that was founded, at least partly, on the fact that women always (or at least for some time to come) are the ones to bear children. To the extent that women too had internalized these attitudes, they revealed their Janus-faced existences.

All along, both feminists and psychoanalysts have addressed sexual differences, but the ways in which they expected to resolve, minimize, or disregard these have reflected not only their professional training or political aims, but their cultural milieus. Sometimes, they concentrated on personal or social therapies; at other times, they advanced political solutions; at yet other times, they assumed that better collaboration by sociologists and psychoanalysts might penetrate to the core of the individual's psyche in order to pinpoint when and how infants' social experiences determine their future lives.

Because neither feminism nor psychoanalysis can be separated from its immediate surroundings, postmodern theories that allegedly deal with both conscious and unconscious matters, especially in their French incarnations, and which do not allow for closure have in recent years been offered up as answers to these riddles. But postmodernism is yet another enigmatic theory (or a congeries of theories its proponents disagree on) that when superimposed on psychoanalytic and feminist ones multiplies the problems. When we add to these complications the relativism and subjectivism that are at the heart of postmodernism and the myriads of political ends postmodern theories are expected to serve, or at least to explain, the complexities seem insuperable and further muddle the problems they set out to solve. This is what happened when some American feminists incorporated Lacanian innovations, which in turn were responses to "French structuralism" in the native movement.

As we know, the feminism that started in the 1960s was primarily political and social. It looked to psychoanalysis only later. Postmodernist thought then was peripheral, although its controversial mode and its refusal to synthesize differences into uniform solutions or to "privilege" history converged with feminist aims. However, postmodern opinions tended to go against notions of progress (as assumed in modernism and its promises of continuous technical advances), and feminism presumes that women will prevail and, ultimately, will reach true equality with men. Feminist theory, states Evelyn Fox Keller, "has provided us with an instrument of immense subversive power. And along with this provision comes a commitment: nothing less than the reconstruction and deconstruction of knowledge" ([1991] 1993, p. 189). I do not question the commitment to feminism. On the contrary, I share it. But I am arguing that the extent to which recent feminist theory (knowingly or unknowingly) is based on Jacques Lacan's, Michel Foucault's, Louis Althusser's, and

Jacques Derrida's deconstructions, it is built on the shifting sands their theories rest on. Consequently, political outcomes are bound to remain elusive.

In this book, I explore some of these issues by showing how a succession of disparate psychoanalytic concepts were inserted into feminist debates: When they furthered women's autonomy they helped further the movement. But at times they fueled a backlash. This happened when literary feminists in universities who were more and more divorced from psychoanalytic practice took the lead. They tended to concentrate on such abstract Lacanian notions as "desire" and to forget that Lacan, even in his seminars, kept referring to what he had learned from interactions with analysands; their own free associations increasingly were extracted from literature alone.

The early women analysts around Freud tried to come to terms with their own neuroses and soon were caught up in the clinical and theoretical means to liberate all women. Moreover, as they were mining their own and their patients' unconscious, they turned into respected professionals. While attempting to answer Freud's query, what does woman want? they functioned on the levels of their male colleagues. (Later on some women psychoanalysts came to regard these women as role models.)

In tracing feminists' rapprochements with psychoanalysis, I begin by outlining the origins of psychoanalytic feminism of the 1920s and end up with its current theoretical constructions in order to clarify the symbiotic and ambivalent relationship between Freudians and feminists, and the reasons they sometimes stand shoulder to shoulder and other times face each other across an unbridgeable abyss. For their associations and dissociations, like weather vanes, always are subject to political winds; to the prestige each group happens to enjoy at the specific moment; and to viable, local, and institutional alliances and divisions.

In America, we tend to lump feminism with the other liberation movements that began in the late 1960s, particularly with the civil rights movement and with the anti-Vietnam and radical student activities. Although all activists then pursued parallel as well as particular ends, they were predisposed to model themselves more or less on the type of struggle Marx had envisioned for the working classes.

In Chapter 1, I show that the psychic liberation Freud envisioned appeared to offer yet another dimension to that struggle and that Freud's early women disciples were attracted to psychoanalysis because they expected to hasten the progress of the women's liberation they already were engaged in. Actually, fin de siècle Vienna, and later on Berlin, were hotbeds of cultural and political radicalism; so feminism, psychoanalysis, and a variety of socialist policies were feeding each other. Heated arguments among intellectuals were not about the viability of any of these movements but about how to attain their ends as quickly and painlessly as possible. To that purpose, Freudians explored the ways in which biological factors and psychic development influence women's roles and behavior, their place in family and society, and the effect the repressive conditions of their lives may exert on their bodies—either in terms of the evolution of the human species or in terms of personal growth. Already then, psychoanalysts were arguing violently about the relevance of Freud's concepts: Did "penis envy" consign women—possibly irrevocably—to an inferior role? Does the little girl's sexual development really parallel the little boy's? How absolute are the psychic consequences of the separation of the sexes? I outline Freud's debates with Karen Horney (the first woman to challenge Freud on the fate of the Oedipus complex), Helene Deutsch (who did so in a much milder form), and Melanie Klein (she focused on the impact of the mother on her newborn infant) and on much of the research and speculation their ideas engendered. That Freud's analysands Marie Bonaparte and Eugenia Sokolnicka started the psychoanalytic movement in France and that Sabina Spielrein advanced it in Russia indicate that psychoanalysis treated women as equals even if not all psychoanalysts did so. After Freud's death, two women, Melanie Klein and Anna Freud, ended up vying for the leadership of the worldwide movement.

Essentially, Chapter 1 is a summary of Freud's and his followers' understanding of the female psyche and the sharp verbal and written exchanges and speculations the women's contributions provoked. These contributions evolved from Freud's *The Interpretation of Dreams* (1900a), from "Three Essays on the Theory of Sexuality" (1905d), and from the subsequent works by both Freud and the disciples. (Then, these were artists, writers, psychologists, and teachers as well as doctors.) I end the chapter by showing that these psychoanalytic investigations helped introduce nonauthoritarian pedagogical methods to teachers (primarily in Adlerian versions) in nearly every one of Vienna's private and public schools and provided strong support to the Social Democratic forces in government as well. (Psychoanalysts and most psychologists will be familiar with the material in this and the next chapter.)

In Chapter 2, I discuss the concepts of some of these women psychoanalysts and indicate that after they moved away from Europe, they were more concerned with understanding their new culture and the English language than with feminism. But they all thought of themselves as practicing feminists. In America, they joined existing psychoanalytic organizations, and they researched and expanded the methods of training and therapy that followed from Freud's structural model. Because the native American psychoanalysts were expected to have medical degrees, those Europeans and the women among them who were doctors soon enjoyed exalted professional recognition. Indeed, the women helped develop the ego-psychology theories, which after 1945 would sweep Europe as well, and the many so-called deviant theories of the nonmedical Freudian émigrés. Horney once more set the example. She "defected" from the New York Psychoanalytic Society because she considered ego psychology too narrow, and she advocated therapeutic methods that focused on her patients' present lives in order to understand their pasts rather than the other way around. Her defiance of institutional authority and her ability to stand her ground, however, evoked the image of the superliberated woman. Helene Deutsch's books about the differentiation between *motherhood* and *motherliness* were widely debated in the late 1940s. Although in the culture at large feminism was not a priority at the time, the women psychoanalysts' contributions to the war effort and to views on the socialization of children, were qualitatively and quantitatively equal to those of their male colleagues. Thus when feminism again came to the fore these women would be held up as examples.

In Chapter 3, I discuss the fact that psychoanalysis entered the mainstream during World War II and that, at least indirectly, it was responsible for the explosion of all sorts of other therapies and for the therapeutic society we currently inhabit. Sociologists such as Talcott Parsons (and those he trained at Harvard's new Department of Social Relations) cooperated with leading psychoanalysts to better understand human motivation and social formation and, in the process, further helped establish the therapeutic climate in which psychoanalysts were looked upon as gurus.

In the 1950s families happily moved to the suburbs. But by 1963 Betty Friedan's *Feminine Mystique* struck a chord in middle- and working-class women who were suffering from suburban domesticity—which Freudian psychoanalysts allegedly had been supporting. By the late 1960s, some of these women spearheaded the feminist movement on the heels of the civil rights movement. Although at first feminists (wrongly) blamed psychoanalysis as the culprit that spawned patriarchy and with it the earlier quiescence of women, by 1973 women psychoanalysts, psychologists, and writers began to demonstrate that the women's movement could benefit from the thought of Karen Horney, Helene Deutsch, and Melanie Klein, as well as from that of the younger women who were linking psychoanalytic ideas to hormonal, chromosomal, and embryological research, to psychological studies of traits and bisexuality, and so on. New avenues for investigation opened up into the genesis of femaleness, gender roles, and all sorts of cultural influences. Investigators expected to unravel the impact "culture" may have on "nature."

Chapter 4 begins with a summary of the themes of a few of the popular feminists in the early 1970s—such as Germaine Greer, Kate Millet, and Pauline Bart—who were blaming Freud for most of the abuses of patriarchy and chauvinism. They also were expanding on the influences of, for instance, Masters and Johnson's studies of sexual practices, which by proving that women could have multiple orgasms opened up new views of female sexuality. Already in 1974, Dolores Klaich was informing feminists that Freud had been friendlier to lesbianism than run-of-the-mill feminists because he had stated that it "was not *necessarily* a neurotic illness" and that Helene Deutsch had reported on the successful analysis of a lesbian patient (Klaich, 1974, p. 68). But while women psychoanalysts kept pursuing this path, feminists were increasingly defining sexual behavior more broadly. They publicly explored the consequences of all sorts of conceptualizations of nature and nurture and soon psychoanalysis began to be separated from patriarchy as such and to be perceived by some as a possible cure for patriarchy. By then the ethos of the liberation movements had been catapulted by affirmative action laws and outspoken women and had captured the center of the culture. The media increasingly supported these movements, and publishers printed and promoted women's books. But because none of the women as yet had explained why women continued to remain in subordinate roles even as more opportunites had opened up, psychoanalysis, however reluctantly, was brought back in.

Nancy Chodorow then began to investigate why even the most emancipated women continued to mother their daughters in the way they had been mothered. She rediscovered Horney and Deutsch, Klein and other object-relations theorists (they focused on early mother-child relations), and a number of Europeans such as Juliet Mitchell, Janine Chasseguet-Smirgel, and Alexander and Margarete Mitscherlich, all of whose radical premises appeared to match her own. Subsequently, Chodorow criticized some of the Europeans' notions, along with those of (superficial) American feminists, and demonstrated that Freud's judgments about women belonged to *his* time but that psychoanalysis belongs to *ours* as well. Jessica Benjamin challenged Chodorow from inside the movement by stressing that the girl's wish for autonomy and agency is not so much a defensive reaction to males as an identification with her mother. And Carol Gilligan explored women's voices as these develop in infancy in response to mothers who, according to Freud, have been deprived of a clear-cut Oedipal resolution ([1982] 1993, p. 7). At the end of the decade, literary scholar Kate Stimpson and psychoanalyst Ethel Person brought out an issue of the feminist publication *Signs, Women: Sex and Sexuality* (1980), containing the best arguments by the most serious feminists, including psychoanalytic contributions; and

Jean Bethke Elshtain (1981) chided feminists for having (falsely) attacked Freud for misogyny. Freudian thought no longer was non grata within feminism, but because by then feminists had to catch up with an enormous and internally polemical body of work, they were as likely to start reading a follower of Lacan's as of Freud's or Horney's. This general widening opened the door to feminists in all disciplines. Among them, the literary scholars were the most successful in influencing other feminists: They introduced the debates that had been raging in Paris among French feminists. Elaine Marks and Isabel de Courtivron (1980) brought out the first selection of French women's writings.

By 1980 most of these Parisian authors were abandoning their original ideas and were becoming therapists. Their typically French rhetorical style, however, was being transplanted to American soil: In its new idiom it promised a deliverance it could not deliver and thereby roughly ended what Christine Sommers (1992) and I call the First Wave of feminism and ushered in the Second Wave. In order to understand the underlying assumptions of this Second Wave, it is necessary to grasp the premises of Lacan's rereading of Freud, which is more attuned to his seminars on the language of psychoanalysis than to his clinical work. This explains, at least in part, why in America Lacan's thought has come to be at home in universities rather than on couches and why it so frequently is *mis*read and *mis*understood.

In Chapter 5 I put Lacan's clever and purposeful obfuscations into their intellectual and cultural context—that is, into the debates among the other so-called French structuralists of the 1960s and 1970s. (The others are Michel Foucault, Claude Lévi-Strauss, Louis Althusser, and Roland Barthes.) They all claimed to champion radical causes, including feminism. Lacan inspired the theories of such French feminists as Luce Irigaray, Julia Kristeva, and Hélène Cixous, who have been the primary psychoanalytic mainstay of the Americans' Second Wave. Lacan's distinction between a phallus (it structures the relation between the sexes) and a penis (it defines the terms) opened the floodgates for various psychological and cultural fantasies. And his puns and alliterations, such as *nom du père* (name of the father) and *non du père* (father's authority), and his humorous asides about *jouissance* (rapturous pleasure) for a while provided food for serious inquiries by psychoanalysts, philosophers, and general intellectuals in France. But by the time his ideas had entered into the talk of American academics, the French had exhausted them: Lacan's heyday was past. (He died in 1981.) However, even though most of his French feminist disciples had abandoned his theories, their discussions on perversions, homosexuality, and bisexuality, as well as the insertion of Lacanisms into Freudian "mainstream feminism," kept sparking novel theoretical formulations among their American admirers.

Chapter 6 deals with the various ways American feminist critics began in the 1980s to import and explore these French theories. Unlike their colleagues in history, sociology, anthropology, and the other social sciences, many professors in departments of literature of the Second Wave eschewed empirical inquiries and, unlike the Freudians (including Lacan), ignored the fact that psychoanalysis had been mandated to keep its links to therapy and that both Freud's and Lacan's theories always claimed some direct relevance to cases—their own or those of their disciples. Instead, academics now invented uncountable links to unconscious elements in literature, and they constructed imaginative theories of the unconscious that were attuned to the "postmodern" sensibility. In the process, they presumed to have access to privileged knowledge and, over time, won over many feminists who wanted to keep up with the latest developments and who felt that they too could contribute to the pseudophilosophical twists and turns of Lacanian lore. By then, Michel Foucault's archeological, historical discourse; Roland Barthes's epigrammatic, literary constructions; and Jacques Derrida's philosophical deconstructions and embellishments and exegeses on them took a decidedly American turn. American feminists warmed to their French female counterparts—beginning with Kristeva's *About Chinese Women* ([1974] 1985), Irigaray's *Speculum of the Other Woman* ([1974] 1985), and Hélène Cixous and Catherine Clément's *The Newly Born Woman* ([1975] 1986)—around ten years after their original publications. The Americans expanded on the speculations about the relations of women to their bodies and to the unconscious fantasies these trigger in psychoanalytic and other discourse and from them drew rather direct parallels to women's struggles and to the class struggle. Of course, these struggles don't directly reflect unconscious fantasies and are largely verbal. It is easy to get carried away and to ignore the fact that Kristeva, for example, has maintained for a number of years that the unconscious cannot be politicized, since this confuses (conscious) political and (unconscious) psychic resistance.

Chaper 7 provides a German interlude in order to demonstrate by a very specific example that the application of Freudian thought to feminism is culture-bound. Here, I summarize the state of psychoanalytic feminism in Germany, which ever since the end of World War II has followed an entirely different drummer. Influenced by the Freud-Marx syntheses of the Frankfurt School (including those of émigrés Erich Fromm, Herbert Marcuse, Max Horkheimer, and T. W. Adorno) and by Freudian psychoanalysts, Alexander Mitscherlich convinced his compatriots that psychoanalytic therapy alone might rouse their fellow Germans to liberate their psyches from the Nazi past. Because this assumption cast psychoanalysis as a radical activity, it became the theory par excellence for the German left. Psychoanalyst Margarete Mitscherlich, in fact, was the first prominent German feminist. Essentially, psychoanalysts in Germany followed most of the American ego psychologists' therapeutic practices. But they also engaged in joint research with sociologists and psychologists and were especially attuned to their patients' social milieu. In their resulting "socioanalysis" they paid more attention to Freud's universalist notions than did many American or French Freudians.

Given the individual and social memories that "by necessity" were driven into the unconscious after 1945 and if, as Alexander Mitscherlich asserted, Germans had to make these memories conscious in order to again join humanity, socioanalysis made sense. Margarete Mitscherlich's (1985) thesis that German women too had accepted Nazi doctrines and had been implicated in the Nazi crimes, even as they had been victims of their husbands and of Hitler's male followers, further extended this doctrine. Consequently, German psychoanalytic feminists eagerly continue to mine their own, their patients', and their society's unconscious by more or less classical Freudian methods while adding whatever other social ingredients they deem useful. In the process, they expect to be emancipated as Germans and as women.

In Chapter 8, I once again go into the American feminist theories of the Second Wave. By 1990, this theorizing appeared to have cut loose from its former moorings in women's social conditions and in the name of postmodernism gave rise to ever more imaginative and amusing interpretations of literary and social texts that are meant to shock. Because these have gotten too convoluted and inventive to be intelligible to the average reader, I explain a number of strands among them. Most of these theories tend to assume that the unconscious is a replica of the social world or of the feminists' own psyches. More recently, their center has shifted to lesbian feminism and gay studies.

I am not writing about all of feminism or about any of its specific branches but only about its contacts with and claims of descent from Freudian (and this includes Lacanian) thought. However, I maintain that abstract solutions to social problems and inequalities tend to include excessively lofty assumptions and to a great extent derive from the deeply implanted postmodernist credo that theory as much as practice will solve our dilemmas. (This may well be an unacknowledged remnant of Althusser's search for "theoretical practice"—itself a very selective reading of Marx's texts.) In any event, the belief that we will be able to create a better society is deeply imbedded in the assumption of feminist theory, and the Second Wave of feminism has come to dominate the humanities in many universities. In the process, it often has been forgotten that theory ought not to be separated from practice and that talk about politics does not equal political action—even though it may incite it. Yes, Lacan encouraged his feminist disciples to say what they pleased, to "let their unconscious speak." But the French did not take their talk all that seriously: The love of hyperbole, of equating the sound of words with their meaning, was a soon-to-be-forgotten game. In France most of these game players did not claim direct political validity for their theories, but in America the theories often were taken at face value.

The overall success of feminism itself, I believe, has derived from changes in laws on divorce, abortion, human rights, affirmative action, and so on that resulted from the First Wave of feminism, which still continues to function in the political realm. Psychoanalysis has figured in this equation inadvertently insofar as it prepared the emotional ground with the assumptions that all of us are bisexual, that by altering unconscious response patterns learned in infancy individuals' lives can be improved, and that the proper socialization of little girls will produce liberated women.

In this book, I focus only on the components of theories that address the evolving psychological nature of women in their environment, and especially on the women psychoanalysts who have contributed to our understanding of the cultural conditions that are more (or less) hospitable to the encouragement of sexual and emotional equality. That psychoanalysis has evolved and has lost many of its earlier promises complicates the issues exponentially, maybe hopelessly. So, as I touch on theories that are constructed to explain yet other theories, readers often may wonder how many more dancers can possibly fit onto the proverbial pinhead as they multiply, fall off, get on, and jostle each other. Because this presents problems for the uninitiated, I stayed away from the most complicated of the countless exegeses by both Freudians and feminist scholars. Instead, I have attempted to give the flavor of the discussions among psychoanalytically oriented feminists and Freudian women analysts. I have focused only on those of their notions that continue to be cited and debated.

That Freud himself was a product of modernism and that Lacan is said to represent postmodernism makes my task especially complex. Often both of their ideas of psychoanalysis are incorporated by psychoanalytic feminists without such distinctions. And if, as both Freud and Lacan assumed, the unconscious is individual as well as cultural and is therefore timeless, then we cannot regard psychic matters as modern, postmodern, or traditional or as anything else that is temporally bound—whatever label we pin on our era. And Freud and Lacan placed the individual—man and woman—at the center of art and social life.

Furthermore, they both linked the analysis of fictional characters and literary figures and thereby justified the application of psychoanalytic thought to what happens to women as well as to men. But the perceived shift from modern to postmodern conditions—which are said to call into question everything modern—does create new problems. Because of the legitimate and imperceptible fusion in the unconscious of time and space, of fantasy and reality, it is difficult to maintain a practical application of psychoanalytic thought to feminist practice.

My own view is an extension of my argument in *The Freudians: A Comparative Perspective* (1989b), where I demonstrated that every culture creates the psychoanalysis it needs. Here, I maintain that feminists fashion their means of liberation in response to their local, intellectual surroundings. I support the application of Freudian and Lacanian ideas to the extent that they link up with actual women's needs and desires and thereby help foster women's autonomy. But I am critical of fanciful, abstract constructions for which advocates claim political currency but which ultimately will be proven beside the point and unfeasible: These are built on ideological quicksand and thus may endanger the enormous strides that (variously oriented) feminists have made. The postmodern project dilutes the focus on issues surrounding the present-day, real-world needs of women—especially those outside the university—and the focus on their need to continue building in a clear, directed way on the equality achieved in earlier decades.

Psychoanalysis is on the decline everywhere: The discovery of the unconscious has proven more elusive than Freud at first assumed; the therapy has become too expensive emotionally and financially. But this does not mean that it will not survive as the clinical forerunner of quicker and simpler therapies, as a means of training the best of clinical practitioners, or as the actual (unconscious) liberating force for women. However, the declining use of psychoanalytic therapy is yet another cultural phenomenon rooted in the individual and the cultural unconscious and in political and institutional conditions that are beyond the scope of the present inquiry.

1 The Early Freudians' Views of Women

At the turn of the century, *women's* liberation was a by-product of *human* liberation, and psychoanalysis was to be the principal means of attaining personal freedom. Freud had spent many years writing his first psychoanalytic publication, *The Interpretation of Dreams* (1900a), in which he advanced the principles of his new doctrine. As we know, he then was as bent upon convincing his fellow physicians that they would be able to cure their hysterical (women) patients by talking to them as he was to prove that such interventions would be in line with advanced, scientific tenets. To be listened to at all, he also had to present psychoanalytic ideas in the terms of the then acceptable intellectual discussions. These were dominated by psychologists and philosophers who in a variety of ways were attempting to explain by means of scientific cosmologies the psychic underpinnings of an inordinately eroticized yet innately repressed society.

Freud, of course, shared his contemporaries' conceptualizations and philosophers' customary ways of dividing the world into dualities such as nature/culture, sea/land, liquid/solid, gemeinschaft/gesellschaft, capital/labor, male/female. Historical progression was taken for granted; and so were generalizations about little girls that derived from psychological assumptions about little boys. So after he had become convinced that the Oedipus myth is universal and that the boy's first desires are for his mother, he also could expect that the girl's are for her father (1900a, p. 257). Moreover, even though Freud was not religious and did not believe that Eve had sprung from Adam's rib, the society he lived in certainly was organized as if this were the case. And no one seriously questioned the sexual division of labor or the division of privilege, although the mostly liberal philosophers expected to eliminate these divisions. In this context, Freud's notion of the bisexuality of both men and women went against both the scientific and taken-for-granted assumptions of most of his contemporaries. Humanists, laypeople, and scientists were shocked at the idea that innocent children had knowledge, however unconscious, of sexuality and at the possible psychosomatic consequences of its repression. Thus they all were bound to deny the validity of psychoanalytic presumptions.

The handful of followers who chose to take Freud seriously and to explore his views also were living with the unexamined dualisms. They too did not question that men and women were different in every conceivable way. The (widely dispersed) disciples were too busy establishing psychoanalytic enclaves and defending these against detractors. That not a single woman joined Freud's Wednesday Society between 1902 and 1909 was not due to discrimination but to the fact that no woman applied. After all, the University of Vienna allowed women to enter only in 1897.

On April 21, 1909, at the Seventy-sixth Wiener Psychoanalitischer Verein (WPV), Dr. Margarete Hilferding presented the paper "Propaganda Among Physicians" and thereby was the first woman to qualify for membership in the Freudians' circle. (Dr. Sophie Erismann had been at the Salzburg congress of psychoanalysts in 1908 and belonged to the Zürich Society until 1914, and Dr. Maria Gincburg [later Oberholzer] was already studying with Jung in 1909.) She was officially elected to join on April 27, 1910, by "twelve yeas and two nays" (Nunberg and Federn, 1967, 2:499). The nays belonged to Dr. Fritz Wittels and to another one of the three people (most likely Isidor Sadger) who, on a previous occasion, had wondered whether it was advisable to welcome women. By then, Wittels's biases were legend. Already on December 16, 1908, he had presented a paper questioning women's innate intellectual powers on "scientific" grounds: Going beyond (or undercutting?) Freud's (1905d) assumed parallel between male and female sexuality, he had argued that women were inferior because their thinking was rooted in "converted sexuality" (Nunberg and Federn, 1967, 2:83). Freud questioned this supposition indirectly by contending that the sexual life of men was accessible to research but that of women was "still veiled in an impenetrable obscurity" (Freud, 1905d, p. 151). He did not convince Wittels. However, this loaded issue was intrinsic to the larger purposes of a number of psychoanalysts. Alfred Adler's sharp response made that clear. He attacked Wittels's assumption that psychoanalysis by itself would revolutionize thinking and thereby facilitate the transition to a truly socialist society. He accused Wittels of underestimating women and of "sharing the attitudes of the philistines" (Nunberg and Federn, 1967, 2:91)—the uncultured who were the bane of *all* intellectuals, including psychoanalysts.

Another time, Wittels dug in his heels even further. He presented a rather questionable, anthropological thesis about the unconscious meaning of menstruation and concluded, this time over the objections of most of the participants, that women who are feminists originally wanted to be born as men. Adler repudiated him in explicitly Marxist terms and maintained unequivocally that women's fate arose from patriarchal and property relations:

> Whereas it is generally assumed that the framework of present relationships between men and women is constant, Socialists assume that the framework of the family is already shaky today and will increasingly become so in the future. Woman will not allow motherhood to prevent her from taking up a profession; motherhood may either remain an obstacle for some, or else it will lose its hardship. (Nunberg and Federn, 1967, 2:352)

Although Adler was not exactly prophetic about the future of socialism, he certainly foresaw the changes that would occur in the relationship between the sexes. He articulated clearly not only the opposing opinions among the early Freudians but those among intellectuals and politicians.

Undoubtedly, none of the men around Freud were feminists. But all of them were going against the grain; all of them were disdainful of the philistines among whom they lived; all of them shared utopian visions; and they expected psychoanalysis to free society not only from psychological but from every other repression. In other words, they were idealists who, together, were striving to liberate humanity with the help of their new science in the making.

Viennese Women

Since men's psyches could not be explored without considering their relation to women, particularly to their mothers, women ipso facto were part of the Freudians' subject matter—even though men alone participated in the formulation of early hypotheses. The women who soon would join them were emancipated, going against Vienna's zeitgeist. (Among the things expected of women was being coquettish and flirtatious while remaining chaste.) Freud himself remarked more than once that society was subjugating woman to man in every sphere and making impossible demands of her. Commenting on his own translation of John Stuart Mill into German (in 1880), he stated that even Mill had "overlooked the fact that a woman cannot earn a living and raise children at the same time." At a meeting in 1909, he concluded that "women as a group profit nothing by the modern feminist movement; at best a few individuals profit" (Nunberg and Federn, 1967, 2:351). Wittels had been nearly alone in actively opposing female membership, and gradually more women were entering the group.

Alfred Adler, along with other members of this group (among them Wilhelm Stekel, Margarete Hilferding, and Karl Furtmüller), agitated for changing social conditions, for severing the chains of the existing order so that feminism would be able to thrive. (Nevertheless, Freud did not notice the contradiction in the fact that he encouraged his youngest daughter, Anna, to become a teacher rather than a doctor.) Unlike Adler, who proseletyzed for his watered-down psychoanalytic theories and coupled them to his Marxism, Freud assumed women would automatically be liberated. Consequently, Adler played a larger role in the Austrian left than the Freudians and had more impact on the Viennese educational establishment, which urged all of the city's school teachers to adopt Adlerian ideas.

In 1911, Adler started the Verein für Freie Psychoanalytische Forschung (VFPF), which was to put psychoanalysis at the service of socialism. Freud, however, advocated patience and focusing on individuals' liberation through psychoanalysis. This disagreement triggered the first split within the original circle. But not all the women were led to separate from Freud. The records indicate that those of Freud's followers who stayed in the Wiener Psychoanalytische Verein, though less intently supporting revolutionary activities, nevertheless were on the political left.

At the Weimar Congress (an international meeting of pyschoanalysts) in September 1911, the year of the break with Adler, the picture of forty-one participants includes eight women: All of them are seated in the first row (Jones, 1955, 2:86). The name of one is omitted, and only one, Emma Jung, is a wife, though she too later on would become a (Jungian) analyst. Beatrice Hinkle, who came from America, is missing in this picture. Lou Andreas-Salomé, who had been Rilke's and Nietzsche's lover and already in 1900 had written and spoken publicly on the intricate elements of eroticism, was studying with Freud and became his lifelong friend. She sat at the center of the picture, in front of Freud and Sandór Ferenczi, the Hungarian disciple whose contributions would stress clinical empathy, including physical contact, over abstract theory. (His ideas currently are being reintroduced by American psychotherapists.)

Even though the early Freudians made no special effort to attract women to their movement, they readily accepted those, such as Hermine Hug-Hellmuth, who wanted to join. By 1912, this schoolteacher had written a number of papers on child analysis, among them "Analysis of a Dream of a Five and a Half Year Old Boy." The boy in the analysis was her sister's illegitimate child, whom they were bringing up together. Influenced by psychoanalysis, Hug-Hellmuth raised him permissively, particularly after the death of her sister. When this nephew, Rolf, reached adolescence, he apparently was unable to take frustration and engaged in all sorts of asocial behavior. Eventually Hug-Hellmuth, in desperation, put him into a home for delinquents. In 1924, he escaped and broke into her house to steal money once again. When Hug-Hellmuth screamed, he panicked and strangled her.

In 1913, Hug-Hellmuth published the first of seven daring papers, "On Female Masturbation," in the *Zentralblatt für Psychotherapie*.[1] There, she noted that neither male nor female physicians ever talked to their female patients about their habits of masturbation, or even about how to avoid stimulating their infants' erotogenic zones while taking care of them, and that male physicians and psychologists tend to overemphasize the frequency of girls' masturbation and their female colleagues take its absence as "a special immaculateness" (Maclean and Reppen, 1991, p. 220). Hug-Hellmuth differentiated among masturbatory acts and their accompanying fantasies (some of them included past experiences with men) according to age, psychic experiences and autoerotic activities away from the genital zones and their varied replacement in later life. Because she requested that none of her writing be disseminated after her death and her analyst and friend, Isidor Sadger, saw to it that this wish was granted, Hug-Hellmuth's contributions on both children's and women's sexuality were being forgotten until recently. Clearly, she qualifies as a feminist.

Later, as I will note further on, some of the women who joined Freud, such as Marie Bonaparte, Eugenia Sokolnicka, and Sabina Spielrein, ended up playing major organizational and intellectual roles; and Anna Freud and Melanie Klein eventually vied for overall leadership of the movement. There were also indirect influences on women. Freud's argument against sexual repression appealed, for instance, to Emma Goldman, a revolutionary and defender of free love. According to her, in his lectures at Clark University in 1909, Freud presented proof that repression cripples the intelligence of women (Hale, 1971, p. 22). But this sort of broad-based influence on the larger culture cannot be substantiated directly or definitively.

Nellie Thompson, a historian, carefully examined the early records to locate all the persons who turned to psychoanalysis between 1902 and 1930. She found that overall, 653 individuals belonged to psychoanalytic organizations, of whom 133 (about 20 percent) were women, and that a higher proportion of women remained lifelong members (79 percent as opposed to 70 percent of men). Moreover, Thompson noted that between the second and the third decade of the century, the number of women who joined the international movement more than doubled (from 39 to 92), and the number of men remained stable (from 221 to 219) (1987, pp. 393–394). This leads to the conclusion that psychoanalysis was more open to women than other professions—either because, like other not-yet-established movements, the Freudians welcomed whatever support they could garner or because, along with Freud, they felt that they had better listen to women in order to help Freud find out "what woman wants." Inevitably, the women psychoanalysts bared their unconscious, opened it up to scrutiny, and were eager to better comprehend the obstacles that prevented all women from achieving equality with men.

Responses to Freud's Evolving Theories

In general, Freud was more flexible than his male followers, more inclined to admit what he did not know and to offer tentative hypotheses he expected them to explore—some of which he felt at liberty to reject or at least alter at a later date. But because he too was a product of his time, albeit an exceptional one, it should not surprise us that he postulated the masculine as the cultural and sexual norm and then defined the feminine in the same terms as a sort of appendage. However, long after his first full depiction in 1900 of the oedipal conflict, the linchpin of psychoanalyis, he reiterated in "The Ego and the Id" (1923b) that what was true for the boy followed for the girl. Even though he synthesized his earlier findings, Freud restated that the processes surrounding the dissolution of the Oedipus complex were "precisely analogous" in boys and girls. (Yet his preanalytic as well as many of his subsequent clinical observations were based on work with female hysterical patients.) In a footnote to the "Three Essays on the Theory of Sexuality" in 1905, he went out of his way to make clear that he did not mean to equate "masculine" with "active" and "feminine" with "passive":

> Activity and its concomitant phenomena (more powerful muscular development, aggressiveness, greater intensity of libido) are as a rule linked with biological masculinity; but they are not necessarily so, for there are animal species in which these qualities are on the contrary assigned to the female. … In human beings pure masculinity or femininity is not to be found in the psychological or biological sense. Every individual on the contrary displays a mixture of the character-traits belonging to his own and to the opposite sex; and he shows a combination of activity and passivity whether or not these last character-traits tally with his biological ones. (1905d, pp. 219–220)

In "Some Psychical Consequences of the Anatomical Distinctions Between the Sexes" (1925j) Freud elaborated on the fact that for both sexes, the child's first love object is the mother and that the ambivalences due to bisexuality inherent in both sexes are expressed in early childhood and then reactivated in all later love relations. Certainly, one could deduce that his interpretations of this process are as dependent on social as on biological elements. According to Freud, the boy starts out by loving his mother (a member of the opposite sex), and during the oedipal phase, when this attachment is sexualized, he first begins to fear his father as the unbeatable rival and then identifies with him. This transition allows him to preserve his heterosexual love and to hope for a wife and children of his own when he is grown up. For the girl, however, the task is more difficult: She too begins by being attached to her mother (a member of her own sex) but must shift to loving her father. And while she is learning to identify with her mother and finding out that she must abandon her as her love object and move toward her father, she also realizes that she will never have a penis. This recognition (in conjunction with other factors) may make her "wish" for one or deny that she doesn't have one. But when she has realized that this is the universal condition of being female, "she begins to share the contempt felt by men for a sex which is the lesser in so important a respect ... and insists on being like a man." She knows that her mother "sent her into the world so insufficiently equipped," and this knowledge may emerge in fantasies, in jealousy toward a sibling, and in a curtailment in masturbation (the small clitoris cannot compete with the superior penis) (1925j, p. 252). This is why the little girl enters the Oedipus complex by wanting a child from her father and perceives her mother as a rival and why there is less impetus for her to dissolve this complex—and to develop a strong superego.

Clearly, these (unconscious) events are experienced as a series of defeats and are bound to be the mainspring for feelings of inferiority and defeatism and of fears of conflict, struggle, and competition. Thus, the theory gets grounded in a biological determinism that does not allow for the enhanced chances psychoanalysis itself was to open up for women.

All in all, the question is not only whether Freud relied too strongly on biological parallels to other species at the expense of sociological determinants but whether women can be socialized in a way that leads to more equitable results. Among Freudians the concept of bisexuality did remain central. Soon, none of them questioned the fact that each sex carries the biological characteristics of the other. Consequently, research into bisexuality went hand in hand with research into the sociological aspects of the personality formation of both girls and boys. Because it is the repression of early sexual instincts that plays havoc with our unconscious and that triggers the onset of neurosis, psychoanalysts conducted thousands of inquiries into the unconscious of the adult patients they attempted to cure and also published thousands of clinical and literary contributions. Some focused on specific moments of preoedipal, oedipal, and postoedipal development; others dismissed the oedipal period as central; and a few said that the Oedipus complex was Freud's own neurosis. But the deepest roots of the human unconscious, both male and female, ultimately have remained hidden.

Outside the Freudian camp (in both intellectual and therapeutic fields), people have picked up selectively on whatever notions contained in Freud's or his disciples' oeuvres they happened to appreciate. American feminists, who until the mid-1970s condemned Freud for his concepts of castration and penis envy, since then have made amends by championing components of these conceptions, although they have often been incorporated into more of the literary rather than the clinical theories. But at first, Freudian men and women analyzed literary works to gain insights. And the original disputes about the genesis of women occurred in the 1920s.

In *The Interpretation of Dreams* (1900a), Freud essentially relied on his self-analysis, on his associations to dreams, daydreams, wishes, experiences, and literature that were derived from his own unconscious. Therefore, psychoanalysis often has been rejected as an artifact of Vienna at the turn of the century. However, Freud himself was a composite of his Jewish origins and of the masculine ethos rooted in patriarchy, so his unconscious inevitably was molded by these social forces. And because, with a few rather debatable exceptions, most known societies have been dominated by men (in one form or another), I go along with those feminists who believe that psychoanalysis—that is, the inquiry into conscious and unconscious mental mechanisms—is the best means of inquiring into the formation of male/female identity and, eventually, of bringing about the psychological conditions that might usher in social equality. Therefore, I am putting aside the objections of anti-Freudian feminists and dealing only with the discussions by feminists who have attempted to apply psychoanalysis to the liberation of women which, incidentally, was what Freud did in his "Studies on Hysteria" (1895d).

The 1920s Debates

Freud and his disciples agreed that the castration complex is caused not only by biological factors but by psychological and social ones as well. Yet at their meetings they focused, for the most part, on male castration and continued to conceptualize female development in relation to it. Karl Abraham, who was with Carl Jung at the Burghölzli clinic in Zurich and afterward started psychoanalysis in Berlin, was the first to object and to seriously elaborate and expand on the consequences of the biological differences on psychic formation. He wrote an essay, "Manifestations of the Female Castration Complex," that began by stating that "the psychological phenomena which we ascribe to the so-called castration complex of the female sex are so numerous and multiform that even a detailed description cannot do full justice to them" because the interaction of psychological with biological and physiological processes are so exceedingly complicated (Abraham, [1920, 1922] 1974, p. 109). By then, he could fall back on the information he and his colleagues had gleaned from the psychoanalytic patients they had treated. They all had noted that either consciously or unconsciously, "many women have repressed the wish to be male" because boys are allowed more freedom, are permitted to choose their profession, and are not subjected to so many restrictions in their sexual lives. When looking into the social reasons for the differences, he remarked that girls feel at a disadvantage when, at a certain stage of development, they notice that their "external genitals" are inferior to those of boys. Many women have not successfully repressed or sublimated this feeling of disadvantage and thus suffer from a "castration complex" that arises during the narcissistic period of development—a time when every child "wants to keep what it has and to get what it sees" (p. 111). When the little girl realizes that she never will have a penis (or the advantages boys are privy to), she reacts with *envy*—"a typical expression of the sadistic-anal developmental phase of the libido" (1925j, p. 111).

Abraham, in the by then typical way of moving from social to unconscious, psychological phenomena, demonstrated this point by recounting the experiences, fantasies, and dreams of a young patient who envied her brother. He went on to show, by recounting the trajectory of her analysis, how her "original so-called 'penis-envy' was replaced in the first instance by envy of her mother's possession of children" and later on by reconciliation to her own sexual role and that of men (Abraham, [1920, 1922], 1974, p. 114). Abraham's clinical generalization, like so many others, was based on too small a sample, and it related directly to the state of psychoanalytic theory at the time. By 1920, Freud had moved from his so-called topographical theory, which essentially divided the psyche into its unconscious, preconscious, and conscious components, to his works on narcissism ("Introduction to Narcissism" [1914a], "Drives and Their Vicissitudes" [1915c]), which were more hospitable to subsequent elaborations of the genesis of female personality.

Abraham pointed out that in Freud's essay "The Taboo of Virginity" (1918a), he contrasted the normal outcome of the castration complex, which is said to be in accord with the prevailing demand of civilization, with the "archaic" type (Abraham, [1920, 1922] 1974, p. 115). Abraham went on to describe *neurotic transformation* (which he found to exist also in tribal societies) and to argue that such a transformation might end up in the girl's (often unconscious) fantasy to possess a male organ, or in the refusal of the female role, and in a repressed desire for revenge on the privileged man (p. 117). He illustrated this theoretical issue with patients' dreams and experiences and their adjustments to the accompanying anxieties. However, Abraham also outlined two specific outcomes of the castration complex besides the normal one: "the homosexual type and the archaic (revenge) type" (p. 117). (Much later, French women psychoanalysts such as Janine Chasseguet-Smirgel [(1970) 1971] and Joyce McDougall [(1978) 1980] would return to this hypothesis.)

Abraham accepted the overall relation Freud postulated between perversion and neurosis. But he now generalized to two neurotic types among women: "They are the 'negative' of the homosexual and sadistic types ... [among men and] contain the same motives and tendencies, but in repressed form" (Abraham, [1920, 1922] 1974, p. 117). Abraham then went on to enumerate a variety of causes and manifestations of women's *frigidity*, which he connected to the unconscious wish to be male and which he found to be accompanied by feelings of inferiority and by female-passive instincts. He did not pass judgment on these women. However, his conclusion that neurotic women whose libido has been displaced from the genital to the anal zone ultimately will transfer these attitudes to both their sons and daughters must have led many women to feel anxious—especially if they were frigid with their (typically unfaithful Viennese) husbands. Certainly, they would not consciously (or unconsciously) have wanted to negatively interfere with their children's psychosexual development (p. 134).

Basically, Abraham's lengthy paper not only synthesized Freud's understanding of women up to 1920 but opened up the dialogue that led Freud to reformulate his premises in 1925. Abraham outlined the many ways in which women may express their castration complex through "wishful" or "vengeful" behavior, and he gave detailed examples culled from the memories and dreams of his female analysands. Some of his women collaborators were eager to explore the issues further. They were enthusiastic psychoanalysts and were working with patients in the adjoining clinic. Among them were Karen Horney, Helene Deutsch, and Melanie Klein, whose ideas have inspired successive generations of feminists. Like Freud, Horney was legendary for distrusting every accepted wisdom throughout her life. Deutsch, allegedly his favorite student and analysand, played a leading role in reconciling his oedipal theories with her astute observations of women patients and with her own femininity and vital desires. Klein was the daughter of an overbearing mother and an ineffectual father. And she had overcome her tendency to fall into deep depressions while in an earlier analysis with Freud's most charming follower, Sándor Ferenczi. All three women now were being analyzed by Abraham. This meant that he could extrapolate from their upsurging memories and feelings as these were rising to consciousness. Clearly, the reformulations about women's psychology arose from the material these budding women analysts were discovering about themselves while working with Abraham and from their own inner conflicts.

Karen Horney: A Sea Captain's Daughter

Karen Horney, the daughter of a domineering German who had terrorized her while she grew up and who even tried to keep her from going to medical school, fought her father tooth and nail. In the process she developed inner strength. She had been thinking about how women deal with their sexuality long before she went public with her first paper, "On the Genesis of the Castration Complex in Women" ([1922] 1924). Her disagreements with Freud were stronger than those Abraham offered, and she argued with Abraham as well. For some time, Horney did not step outside the bounds or think of breaking away. She made her case from within the Freudian camp. Yet she ridiculed the "assertion that one-half of the human race is discontented with the sex assigned to it. ... [This is] decidedly unsatisfying, not only to feminine narcissism but also to biological science" (p. 51). And she suggested alternate explanations to Abraham's, based on the perception of girls. Although she agreed, for instance, with his observation that at some point all little girls desire to "urinate like boys," she suggested that their fantasies may just as readily be due to their feelings of omnipotence: to their envy of the jet of urine a boy passes; of his ability to satisfy his sexual curiosity by watching himself urinate, or of his ability to show off his genitals and thus to know them better than girls ever are able to. In other words, she intimated that there may be objective reasons for envy. Furthermore, Horney found that "little girls *are* at a disadvantage when it comes to gratifying their masturbatory urges" or having their mother accept these urges during the pregenital period. She went on to note that those of her patients who bore "the stamp of the castration complex ... had fantasies of rape [committed] ... by father images [such as uncles and other older men] ... and clung to the fiction that this primal feminine fantasy [was] real" (pp. 55–56).

In other words, Horney confirmed the existence of the Oedipus complex but set out to get beyond those implications that would perpetuate women's inferiority. Instead, she emphasized that "*the desire to have a child* (from the father)" is just as far-reaching as male activity and also is embedded in the two-fold relation to the "penis-envy" complex (Horney, [1922] 1924, p. 58). She agreed with the notion that the maternal instinct receives "unconscious libidinal reinforcement" from the desire for a penis—a desire that originates during the autoerotic period. But when the little girl experiences her disappointment in relation to her father, Horney went on, she renounces not only her claim upon him but also the wish for a child (p. 59). Horney said that this emotional regression is (in accordance with the familiar equation) accompanied by fantasies she had during the earlier anal phase and thus by the former demand for the penis. But for Horney, "that demand is not simply revived, but is reinforced with all the energy of the girl-child's desire for a child" (p. 59).

Horney was every bit as "scientific" as Freud: She bolstered every one of her points with examples from work with patients. She argued that the young girl displaces her envy of her mother, who is able to bear children, onto her brother, who has a penis; identifies with her father; and regresses to a pregenital phase that helps stir up "a powerful 'penis-envy' that then remains in the foreground and seems to dominate the whole picture" (Horney, [1922] 1924, p. 60). Horney concluded that the root of the castration complex in women is due to identification with the father and engenders a more or less marked tendency to homosexuality when it dominates. Therefore, "the basic fantasy of having suffered castration through the love-relation with the father ... is of typical and fundamental importance" (p. 63).

Horney rejected Freud's assumption that women repudiate their womanhood because of their "penis-envy" alone. Instead, she held that it conditions the *forms* of the castration complex. This does not preclude a deep and wholly womanly love attachment to the father: Envy leads to the girl's revulsion toward her own sexual role only when the Oedipus complex results in grief (Horney, [1922] 1924, p. 64). By comparing the female neurotic to the male neurotic, who identifies with his mother and whose fear of "castration ... corresponds exactly to the female neurotic's desire for the penis" (p. 64), Horney laid a cornerstone for theoretical equality.

Freud accepted Horney's major point by stating that "when the girl's attachment to her father comes to grief later on and has to be abandoned it may give place to an identification with him and the girl may thus return to her masculinity complex and perhaps remain fixated in it" (1925j, p. 256). But he did not basically alter his views of female sexuality. Horney, however, went on to investigate. In "The Flight from Womanhood: The Masculinity-Complex in Women as Viewed by Men and by Women" ([1926] 1974), she noted that psychoanalysis, itself the creation of a male genius and furthered primarily by male disciples, inevitably evolved a model based on masculine psychology and that the recent extensions of the concept of penis envy to the phallic phase further exemplified male preoccupations. She found theoretical support outside psychoanalysis in the work of sociologist Georg Simmel. He recently had demonstrated that all of civilization was based on masculine dominance and that the very standards by which the values of male and female nature were judged (by both men and women) inevitably were biased. Accordingly, Horney argued convincingly, psychoanalysts too had been measuring the nature of women by masculine norms. To bolster this point, she cited Ferenczi for having formulated an "extremely brilliant genital theory" (p. 175).

Basically, Ferenzci maintained that the ultimate meaning for both sexes in coitus is in the desire to return to the mother's womb. The man can reenact this scene in the act of sexual penetration. But Horney maintained that the woman has other potentialities of pleasure, for example, in the act of birth, that perhaps are denied to the man (Horney, [1926] 1974, pp. 175–176). She went on to say that she had been "most surprised to find an intense envy of pregnancy, childbirth and motherhood, as well as of the breasts and of the act of suckling" in her male patients (pp. 176–177). This led her to infer that women's anatomical disadvantage exists only at the pregenital levels of organization. Later on,

> the difference between the outcome of the male and the female Oedipus complexes seems to me in average cases to be as follows. In boys the mother as a sexual object is renounced owing to the fear of castration, but the male role itself is not only affirmed in further development but is actually overemphasized in the reaction to the fear of castration. We see this clearly in the latency and prepubertal period in boys and generally in later life as well. Girls, on the other hand, not only renounce the father as a sexual object but simultaneously recoil from the feminine role altogether.
>
> In order to understand this flight from womanhood we must consider the facts relating to early infantile onanism, which is the physical expression of the excitations due to the Oedipus complex. (p. 180)

Horney then noted that it is extremely difficult to determine whether the girl, in the early phase of her genital development, has organic vaginal sensations. Thereby, she questioned the notion that the clitoris serves the same—obviously inferior—purpose as the boy's penis (p. 181).

In addition, Horney found that the (unconscious) motives for women's flight into the male role could account for translating her genital anxiety into male terms and for turning fear of vaginal injury into fantasies of castration. After all, when she exchanges the anxiety regarding the punishment she expects from the negative perception of her anatomy for the concrete wish to be a boy, she gains by this conversion. Moreover, she desires the penis as a proof of her guiltlessness (Horney, [1926] 1974, p. 182).

Horney again shifted back to the girl's social circumstances by citing Simmel, who at the time was investigating the impact of modernity on individuals. Due to external conditions, men were considered more important and were always in stronger and superior positions: "It is one of the privileges of the master that he has not constantly to think that he is master, while the position of the slave is such that he can never forget it" (Horney, [1926] 1974, p. 184). Horney ended by saying that the masculine character of our civilization has made it easier for men than women to sublimate their natural desires (in work and other achievements). This has become a cliché, but in 1926, Horney was taking a step away from Freud. She continued to value and employ his major concepts but injected a decidedly feminist twist into them and thereby enlarged the Freudians' theories and discussions.

Helene Deutsch's Psychology of Women

Helene Deutsch did not believe that women were trying to flee femininity. Nor did she look beyond psychoanalytic theory in her search for the answer to woman's subjugated role or passivity. Instead, in "The Psychology of Women in Relation to the Functions of Reproduction," which she presented at the international meetings in Salzburg in 1924, she burrowed deeper into the obvious differences and minute details of male and female sexual development by examining how boys and girls perceive and (unconsciously) respond to biological change in themselves.

Deutsch essentially confirmed Freud's ideas and thus did not upset her (male) Freudian colleagues in the way Horney did. As she set out to explain "how the change in the valuation of a person's own genital organ takes place and how this relates to the functions of reproduction," she offered a highly theoretical framework of female maturation through all its phases (Deutsch, [1924] 1974, p. 148). Deutsch's complex theories are based on the oscillation of libido (energy) that is said to regress in very specific and yet variable ways. Thus they are not easily grasped by people unfamiliar with both psychoanalysis and physiology. Basically, Deutsch explained the infant's psychological moves into ever-higher stages of development, in lockstep with biological growth. Unlike Horney, Deutsch did not stop to illustrate her points with patients' experiences; nor did she draw on sociological or other more popular notions to garner support. So both the later popularity of Horney and the relative neglect of Deutsch were to a large extent due to not only Horney's explicit and Deutsch's no more than implicit feminism but also to the fact that Horney made her ideas accessible but even Deutsch's (later) cultural arguments were somewhat divorced from her clinical concepts and thus could be more readily dismissed.

In 1924, Deutsch, like all psychoanalysts, expected to find out when, how, and for what reasons neurosis begins; when, how, and for what reasons *women* succumb to hysterical symptoms. And like them, she planned to remedy the situation by intervening in adults' lives through psychoanalytic treatment and in infants' lives by raising them without neuroses. To that end, Deutsch dissected every developmental phase beginning with the first—the oral and autoerotic—which she found to be devoid of narcissistic, ego, and outside attachments and yet, through the process of weaning, to leave traces of a narcissistic, unconscious wound. She maintained that because oral sucking activity brings gratification, it also leads to discovering the mother's breast and to its being the first object of attachment. Initially, Deutsch went on, the infant experiences the mother as a part of its own body and invests this relationship with large doses of narcissistic libido that later on, via the penis, becomes the energy of the sexual drive. (*Libido* also is used in a more general sense to refer to the energy of the death or aggressive drive, which may or may not be the same as the sexual drive.) The ramifications of the little girl's perceptions, and their accompanying libidinal attachments (via tender love for her father and pleasurable gratification at her mother's breast), led Deutsch to equate "in the ... (unconscious) the paternal penis with the maternal breast as an organ of sucking, and later with her conception of coitus" (Deutsch, [1924] 1974, p. 149).

Deutsch completely accepted Freud's notion of the girl's primary aim as passive: In the sadistic-anal phase, for instance, the girl either perceives coitus as a sadistic act or identifies with her mother's masochistic habits; in the phallic phase, the clitoris, which Deutsch said attracts massive doses of libido to itself, relinquishes its functions to "the 'feminine' vagina only after strenuous and not always decisive struggles" (Deutsch, [1924] 1974, p. 149). By accepting the clitoris as a penis substitute ("it is inferior to its masculine counterpart, ... [and] lacks the abundant energy of the penis"), Deutsch also reaffirmed Freud's progression from the clitoral to the vaginal phase as normal (p. 150). That is primarily why subsequent generations of feminists have not found Deutsch's contributions too useful or have denounced her as conformist or even as antifeminist.

Deutsch, however, was the first Freudian to truly investigate the later phases of female growth. For instance, she found that the process of menstruation "exercises an eroticizing and preparatory influence upon the vagina"; that the infant's passive, sucking mouth at the breast "actively takes possession" so that libido is drawn from the whole body; and that in the unconscious, the infant equates the penis with the breast and then with the sucking activity of the vagina. This identification of the vaginal functions with the penis, held Deutsch, allows for the "perfect unity of being" in coitus; and because the vagina also is an organ of sucking and incorporation, it not only becomes the receptacle of the penis but also of the child (Deutsch, [1924] 1974, p. 153). She supported these claims with references to Freud's thinking on the instincts of sadistic destruction, to Ferenczi's concept of "maternal regression," and to

Otto Rank's assumption that women actively repeat "the trauma of birth" in the act of giving birth (p. 152).

Deutsch also analyzed the process of pregnancy as (psychological) preparation for childbirth—as the flow of libidinal relations between mother and fetus that feeds the mother's secondary narcissism, which manifests itself when object relations that previously had been placed in the service of the ego are being superimposed upon its primary form. At the same time, Deutsch continued, the mother experiences the child as part of her super-ego through a process of sublimation, or it triggers her own (repressed) ambivalent conflicts during her (early) libidinal development. To penetrate to the roots of the "typical" difficulties, and the many disquieting frames of mind pregnant women and young mothers often experience, she analyzed their typical dreams. She ended up by diagnosing, somewhat lamely, that if it weren't for women's bisexual disposition and for the clitoris with its masculine strivings, women could so easily master their existence. This throwaway ending provided yet more fuel to Deutsch's critics who emphasize only her conventional notions and to those who dismiss psychoanalysis as using the biological models that dominated *all* research at the beginning of the century, models they often blame—erroneously—for the beliefs in masculine superiority.

Whereas in her 1924 essay Deutsch thought that the traumatic aspects of feminine development could be overcome through motherhood, in "The Significance of Masochism in the Mental Life of Women" (1930), she was somewhat less sanguine. For she now wondered what was happening to the energy attached to the clitoris after it takes the place of the penis. She related femininity to reproduction in order to better explain women's sexual inhibition and frigidity and assumed that impulses to masturbate, which are masculine-sadistic, may arouse feelings of guilt. These, in turn, may lead the girl to blame her mother for the loss of a penis. She then reiterated Freud's view in "Anatomical Distinctions" (1925j). However, she went further by converting the loss of the penis to the masochistic fantasy of castration (rape) by the father. Deutsch said that this "anatomical destiny," also, is independent of masochistic reactions of guilt. And frigidity occurs when the little girl does not convert to the passive attitude, when the clitoris does not want to relinquish its pleasures to the vagina. Deutsch maintained that psychoanalysts must help some women to remain masculine but that these women then pay for it by giving up sexual pleasure. And she ended by maintaining that modern women per se are more masculine and that the accompanying frigidity is more neurotic. That is how Deutsch explained not only the persistence of the feminine castration complex but also the girl's infantile move toward femininity—which both Freud and Deutsch believed coincided with her identification with her mother. For this reason as well, later feminists did not take readily to Deutsch and perceived her as identifying with the inferior role of women.

Melanie Klein: Unconscious Child-Mother Interactions, or Object Relations

Melanie Klein's view of the difference between boys and girls drew the wrath of both Freud *and* feminists: She located the inception of neurosis long before the onset of the Oedipus complex, and she did not directly address feminist concerns. In "The Psychological Principles of Early Analysis" ([1926], 1975), Klein argued that oedipal tendencies appear when the child is frustrated while being weaned, at the end of the first year or at the beginning of the second one, and that these tendencies are reinforced by the anal frustrations that accompany toilet training. A year later, at the congress in Innsbruck, in "Early Stages of the Oedipus Complex" ([1928], 1975), she spoke of the fears due to the anatomical differences between the sexes. Abraham had located oedipal guilt in the early anal-sadistic phase and Ferenczi had situated it in "sphincter-morality." Klein, however, went further back and held that it begins at the initial stage of the oral phase—stirred up by the anxiety in a sort of pregenital superego. (Some years later, Anna Freud made the defenses against this anxiety the linchpin of *her* theories.)

Essentially, Klein focused on the infant's curiosity, which is frustrated because the infant cannot yet speak, and found that it expresses this frustration in hate. The child, whose oedipal tendencies already are in place, she said, craves to appropriate the contents of the mother's body (the object); this craving arouses feelings of guilt in both sexes up to the anal-sadistic phase. At this point, Klein theorized, the boy turns his mother into a love object and fantasizes that she will punish him for wanting to rob her body of its contents—first, of feces; then, during their femininity phase, of babies and breasts; and later, of his father's penis, which he imagines her to have "taken in." Thus he is afraid she will punish him by castrating him. The girl, according to Klein, has genital impulses *before* the successful move from oral to genital libido, during the first arousal of these impulses. The genitals' oral receptive aim, she summarized later on, influences *the girl's turning to her father* (Klein, [1928] 1975, p. 192). And although Klein did not contradict either Freud's, Horney's, or Deutsch's views that the girl turns to her father when she realizes that she lacks a penis, she argued that the deprivation of the breast is the primary reason for this event. And because of her conflicted and fearful relation with her mother, who inevitably continues to frustrate her, Klein went on, the girl may not be able to overcome her sadistic fixations on the mother object. In that case, her ability to be a good mother later on will be limited. Klein equated the girl's anxiety about becoming a good mother with the boy's fear of castration.

Ernest Jones was attuned to Klein's theories in his "Early Development of Female Sexuality" (1927), the paper he presented in Innsbruck. Essentially, Jones argued that there were more subtle transitions between the oral and oedipal stages than so far had been acknowledged and that castration is not the cessation of sexuality. Instead, Jones postulated that castration produces anxiety that has different consequences in men and in women. And he addressed the genesis of homosexuality in great detail. Freud rejected most of Klein's and Jones's suggestions. The components he retained were included in his "Female Sexuality" (1931b).[2] (Eleven years later, Klein's theoretical challenge culminated in the controversial discussions of 1942–1944 between Melanie Klein and Anna Freud—who by then had emigrated to England and taken on Freud's mantle. She became the theoretical leader until her death in 1982.)

The Lasting Legacies of Horney, Deutsch, and Klein

Since the early 1970s, feminists have often returned to the theories of Karen Horney, Helene Deutsch, and Melanie Klein. As I note in Chapter 6, Nancy Chodorow, though concentrating mostly on their later contributions, to some extent also addressed their early formulations when exploring the reasons for women's more or less submissive, or at least less-dominant and -dominating roles, and when questioning why even radical feminist women tend to reproduce the mothering they themselves received and why their children, even in the absence of fathers, tend to perpetuate traditional behavior patterns. But these were not the questions of the early women analysts. They were immersed in the issues of *their* times, when *women's* liberation was considered a by-product of *human* liberation, when the essential split (and its resolution) was perceived to be between capital and labor rather than between men and women.

Because Freud developed his psychoanalytic method by analyzing hysterical women, by extrapolating from their treatment and then generalizing to *all* women in order to emotionally free them, investigations into the origins of women's psyches were closely linked to those of neurotics and psychotics and to those of group behavior. But the study of children, in whom behavior can be observed, as it were, in incubo, would be especially useful. Although liberated women such as Maria Montessori and Genia Schwartzwald (Freud admired the innovative and nonauthoritarian methods they established in their progressive schools) did not directly further psychoanalytic practices, their activities contributed to the acceptance of psychoanalysis in Vienna; the introduction of psychoanalytic principles into the school system, primarily by Alfred Adler and *his* disciples, did so as well. In retrospect, we realize that the analysis of children became the most fruitful source for the general and theoretical advances of Freudian thought, as well as for feminism. And both of these areas were dominated by women.

Still, whether or not the early women analysts are now included in the roster of feminists, they were emancipated women who espoused feminist ends. After all, at a time when most women took care of their families and households, they were teachers, psychologists, and physicians. Since women alone were thought able to take care of children, it seemed natural that those who became doctors would turn to pediatrics and to child analysis: They were aware of children's behavior as a matter of course and automatically applied their analytic skills to their observations. In Vienna, in addition to Hug-Hellmuth, Sabina Spielrein—a young Russian woman who had been one of Jung's first patients and his mistress and who went to Freud for analysis in order to free herself of this inadvisable involvement—joined Freud's circle in 1912. She, too, did not explicitly profess feminist principles but exemplified them. She took social equality of the sexes for granted. Among the 133 women who—however briefly—joined the movement before 1930, Marie Bonaparte, Jeanne Lampl-de Groot, Therese Benedek, Sylvia Payne, Josine Müller, Clara Thompson, Grete Bibring, and Annie Reich sooner or later would make lasting contributions and would psychoanalyze women patients to further feminine development. But the early debate, as Thompson (1987, p. 400) summarized, ended with Freud's "Female Sexuality" (1931b). It resumed under different circumstances, after the European psychoanalysts had moved to Anglo-Saxon countries. In England, Anna Freud and Melanie Klein would compete for the conceptual leadership of the movement, thereby acting out feminist aims though not always articulating them. In America, which became the mainstay of psychoanalysis (by 1945, 65 percent of the members of the International Psychoanalytic Association had become "American" [Kurzweil, 1989b, p. 204]), Helene Deutsch more or less walked in Freud's footsteps, and Karen Horney pursued a more interpersonal theory. In England, Melanie Klein's observations of mothers and infants initiated the focus on object relations—today's central, clinical theory. In practice, they all were living feminist lives. Their structure-oriented theories were not equally useful to feminism. Thus these would rise and fall in line with the popularity of feminism and with the viability of later psychoanalytic theories such as Lacanian, Kohutian, Sullivanian, Rogerian, and derivations from them all. In sum, the early women psychoanalysts generalized from themselves, from therapy with their women patients, and from literary works to help liberate not only women but their entire society. To that end, they rehoned their psychoanalytic lenses and reconceptualized and refined Freud's insights. They argued passionately among themselves in order to penetrate to the origins of psychic development and its links to sexuality, to fantasy, and to biology. And their debates have lived on.

2 The Freudian Feminists Cross the Atlantic

When Freud's female disciples came to America, they no longer focused too directly on the scientific aspects of feminine development. In 1932, Karen Horney was invited to the United States by Franz Alexander, a Hungarian with whom she had worked at the Berlin clinic. (He had gone to Chicago in 1929 to train psychoanalysts.) But the atmosphere in America was very different: In Berlin spirited theoretical disputes had lasted long into the night, often in coffee houses and nightclubs, and psychoanalysts had been in touch with intellectuals and writers. In Chicago (and the rest of the country), psychoanalysis was inserted into medicine, so that it was more narrowly professional and fairly insulated. Alexander started a psychosomatic institute to broaden its base. The shift in interest, which itself was caused by the new milieu, apparently caused Horney and Alexander to disagree on the cultural direction and clinical guidance of psychoanalysis. After about a year and a half, in 1934, Horney left for New York. There, she joined the training institute of the New York Psychoanalytic Society. By then, Helene Deutsch was about to settle down in Boston and Melanie Klein was already installed among the London intelligentsia in the Bloomsbury circle and was analyzing the children of the British Freudians.

Actually, when Horney burst upon the American scene with *The Neurotic Personality of Our Time* (1937), she was responding to American culture and to the variety of values held by native citizens. The other women analysts as well, after leaving the cradles of psychoanalysis—that is, Vienna, Berlin, and Budapest—no longer emphasized the questions of female development, or of femininity, that had preoccupied them before their sea change. Instead, they observed their new colleagues through their psychoanalytically refracted lenses, along with the Anglo-Saxons around them. And they compared the varieties of people they now met to those in their former avant-garde settings and looked at the different histories and traditions that had formed them and at their neuroses. In part, the émigrés wanted to make sense of their customs and mores because they wanted to fit in, and in part they wanted to assess the impending events in Europe more objectively—that is, the rise of Hitler, of fascism, and of the dangers facing relatives and friends in the impending war.

Karen Horney responded to America when she introduced *The Neurotic Personality* primarily by disclaiming interest in particular neuroses or neurotics. Instead, she asserted, she would focus on "the neurotic's actually existing anxieties and the defenses he has built up against them … [insofar as these] are generated not only by incidental individual experiences, but also by the specific cultural conditions under which we live" (1937, pp. vii–viii). Throughout the book, Horney used the masculine pronoun: "He" who behaves contrary to the prevalent norms of his culture and who thereby arouses anxiety within himself is her neurotic. Whereas, for instance, the normal Jicarilla Apache is expected to be mortally frightened by the approach of a menstruating woman, such fear, noted Horney, would be neurotic in Western cultures. And if a mature and independent woman were to consider herself "a fallen woman, unworthy of the love of a decent man because she had a sexual encounter, she now would be suspected of neurosis," but it was not so a few decades before (p. 15). After giving scores of such examples, many of them culled from fascinating anthropological investigations—some by Ruth Benedict in *Patterns of Culture* (1932) and by Margaret Mead in *Sex and Temperament in Three Primitive Societies* (1935), authors who themselves were informed by psychoanalysis—Horney again praised Freud for his unrivaled insights into the functions of the unconscious but then urged taking "a definite step beyond Freud … though only on the basis of his revealing discoveries" (p. 20).

Basically, Horney argued that neuroses must be traced back to their start in infancy, but she insisted that character disturbances also spring from cultural expectations. For instance, she stated that even though we all want to be liked, the neurotic depends disproportionately on affection and approval and his inner insecurity is overwhelming (Horney 1937, p. 36). Horney then went on to translate psychoanalytic concepts into homey terms, to question whether the Oedipus complex arises in every child or is provoked by definite situations (p. 82). She outlined the conditions that make a child repress its hostility—helplessness, fear, love, or feelings of guilt—and explained in detail how specific anxieties take hold. The very familial tone and the accessibility of her arguments led the American intellectual public to believe that she had psychoanalytic recipes that would teach them how to immunize their children against neurosis, against turning into unhappy, neurotic adults.

We might deduce that the very fact that Horney's neurotics were not gendered, that they were androgynous, indicates a pro-feminist stance. I rather think that she had put her feminist concerns on a back burner: The index had no "women" category, and feminine psychology was summarized on two pages, when she stated that more women than men use love as a bribe and that

> for centuries love has not only been women's special domain in life, but in fact has been the only or main gateway through which they could attain what they desired. While men grew up with the conviction that they had to achieve something in life if they wanted to get somewhere, women realized that through love, and through love alone, could they attain happiness, security and prestige. (Horney, 1937, pp. 139–140)

Thus Horney blamed the plight of women largely on cultural conditions and on the habits brought forth by patriarchy.

Horney, of course, knew Freud's theories by heart. She noted that her colleagues now were focusing less on unconscious guilt feelings than he had. But if these are *not* the central dynamics of neurosis, or not the only ones, she now suggested, Freudians ought to change the assumptions underpinning their clinical techniques: They ought to stop assuming that unconscious guilt feelings cause a "negative therapeutic reaction," that the inner construction of the superego inflicts self-punishment, and that self-inflicted suffering is due to moral masochism, to a need for punishment (Horney 1937, p. 258).

However, in her following book, *New Ways in Psychoanalysis* (1939), Horney once more tackled the psychic manifestations of neuroses and explained them more sociologically. "Character neuroses," she stated, "are molded by early experiences to an extent hitherto unthought of" (p. 33). Freud had rooted them too thoroughly in biology, she chided diplomatically, and thus had based "psychic differences between the two sexes" on anatomical ones (p. 38); had incorporated the dualistic thinking of the nineteenth-century philosophers; and had dichotomized instincts and ego, femininity and masculinity. Horney advised psychoanalysts to concentrate instead on the corollary oppositions of greediness and possessiveness—which they call "oral" and "anal"—because they are embedded in early experiences. And she noted that parents who knew about psychoanalysis and indiscriminately had accepted the libido theory and the Oedipus complex had become inhibited from spontaneously responding to their children: Some had gotten scared of exciting them sexually; others had become overindulgent or overprotective. And they did not realize that by refraining from meting out deserved punishment they unwittingly were hiding their active interest in the child, were depriving it of warmth, and thereby were failing to convey that they were reliable and sincere people (p. 86).

That Horney increasingly shifted the blame for neurosis from individual psychic development to environmental factors was bound to upset those Freudians who were in the process of exploring "ego psychology" to construct ever more complex models of the human psyche and to generalize from these to society at large. In fact, the members of the New York Psychoanalytic Institute, led by such émigrés as Heinz Hartmann, Ernst Kris, and Rudolph Loewenstein, did not take to Horney's teaching. Neither would Anna Freud: Both in England and America her emphasis on defenses as the motor force of neuroses, as set forth in "The Ego and the Mechanisms of Defense" (1936), increasingly was moving to the theoretical center. The subsequent split around what were unreconcilable, hypothetical assumptions, as we will see further on, had to end up in Horney's separation from the ego psychologists. Actually, Horney's defection resulted from her deeply held intellectual convictions and from the fact that her colleagues were equally convinced that ego psychology alone would be able to advance psychoanalytic knowledge. They all felt they had the clue to the methods that would uncover unconscious materials and to perfecting the clinical practices they considered best suited to this endeavor. But Horney held her ground and did not allow herself to back down.

Horney's Break with Ego Psychology

By definitively rooting neurosis in social customs and norms, Horney inevitably addressed the unchallenged and unexamined acceptance of masculine superiority. By blindly asserting the primacy of the phallus in libidinal development, she stated, Freud had condoned it. Furthermore, by rooting female maturity in the move from clitoral to vaginal pleasure, Freud had blamed the female's failure to mature on biological factors. Horney, however, argued that in such a model the sexual instincts inevitably are bound to remain mired at a "feminine, immature stage" and that this immaturity subsequently must dominate the repressed penis envy (Westcott, 1986, p. 59). Such a theory, objected Horney, is fatalistic because the repercussions of the concept of penis envy reinforce the conditions that caused it in the first place—and in so doing reinforce the earlier repressed unconscious and conscious anger. According to Horney, that was what her analytic patients were telling her, what she was gleaning from the manifestations of their intrapsychic conflicts.

Horney's break with the New York Psychoanalytic Society was *not* due to male chauvinism as some have assumed; that was not why, in 1941, she set up her own and rival organization, the Association for the Advancement of Psychoanalysis (AAP). Her biographer, Susan Quinn, reported that Horney's relation with the New York Freudians already had started on the wrong foot when they asked her to fill out an application for membership upon her arrival. This implied that they did not know of her reputation as a training analyst in Berlin and in Chicago. Still, after being "accepted for active membership by transfer" on April 30, 1935, she got along with them; and she soon *was* allowed to teach candidates (New York Psychoanalytic Society, hereafter NYPS, *Minutes,* 1935).

In general, the basic problems over anyone's admission to the New York Psychoanalytic Society revolved around the medicalization of the discipline, around an earlier resolution by the American Psychoanalytic Association to accept only medically trained persons, and not around gender. Women who were doctors and who also had had an analysis were admitted. In 1936 and 1937, for instance, Clara Mable Thompson, Phyllis Greenacre, and Ruth Loveland joined. This also was when psychoanalysis began to flourish, when European Freudians started to arrive as the Nazis came to power in one country after another. Of these, too, except for a few celebrities, only doctors were accepted by the New York Psychoanalytic Society and by the American Psychoanalytic Association: These included Ruth Mack Brunswick, Edith Jacobson, Frieda Fromm-Reichmann, and Annie Reich, all of whose contributions were later on examined in connection with new feminist theories.

Gradually, as the membership grew, questions of whom to admit to practice were being superseded by questions of what to teach as it became ever clearer that those who trained the analysts had the power of shaping the future of psychoanalysis through the influence they could wield over candidates. This was what started the conflict with Horney. Many senior members were upset when, in October 1939, she presented "The Emphasis on Genesis in Freud's Thinking: The Influence of the Genetic Viewpoint on Therapy and Practice, Its Value and Its Debatable Aspects." This paper was discussed by psychoanalysts on both sides of the divide, by Drs. Sándor Lorand, Clara Thompson, Ludwig Jekels, Abram Kardiner, Gregory Zilboorg, Bertram Lewin, and Paul Federn. Still, the members of the Educational Committee of the New York Psychoanalytic Society, after many deliberations, recommended removing Horney as an instructor: They disapproved of her inordinate influence on students. Much maneuvering ensued, with open appeals and countless behind-the-scenes meetings of moderates who recommended greater emphasis on scientific matters in order to reduce political hostility. Horney, however, insisted on her right to teach *her* psychoanalysis: "A democratic organization should balance one group (including students) against another" rather than insist on a rigid curriculum (NYPS, 1940). Lawrence Kubie, then the president of the society, in a letter to his former analyst in London, Edward Glover, reported, however, that Horney had rallied students around her, that they no longer were getting a balanced training, and that Horney's teachings were too watered down, not clinical enough. He became her major public adversary. The following confidential letter, dated March 21, 1940, from Kubie to Wittels (he had argued against allowing Horney to teach) throws light on the controversy. It indicates that the New York Freudians focused on institutional and theoretical questions rather than on feminist ones:

> With you, I regret the fact that Dr. Horney presented so sweeping a version of her views to the general public before giving them, piece by piece, to the Society.
>
> With you, I also regret the fact that the subject matter of her two evenings in the Autumn did not bring into clear focus the more drastic of her theoretical deviations. For this, however, I can see many possible reasons, without jumping to conclude that Dr. Horney was insincere.
>
> Also I feel with you, that it is unwise and undesirable to have any individual teacher so influence any group of young students as practically to exclude from their training a full contact with contrasting points of view. Not because of anyone's malice, but from a series of natural causes, just such a situation has in fact grown up in these last years; and has given rise to the embarrassing and pathetic open "confessionals" to which you refer. But even more significantly, it has given rise to a one-sided and disastrous warping of the students' training. It is to correct this situation and to prevent its recurrence in the future, that the amendments to our training regulations which are now being considered by the Society were introduced by the Educational Committee. I hope that the Society will see the wisdom and necessity of these amendments at our next meeting on March 26th.
>
> And I hope particularly that the group that constitutes at this moment a small divergent minority will realize that these amendments will have a protective as well as a restrictive value, and for them as much as for the rest of us; because if we can make sure that every student gets an adequately rounded training, then we need not fear his contact with any teacher, no matter how divergent that particular teacher may be. This seems to me to make possible and to insure true academic freedom in our Society, insofar as it is possible to insure this by any rules and regulations.
>
> This brings me to my point of serious disagreement with you. I am basically opposed to any form of "purge" in a scientific organization. I feel completely with Voltaire in this matter, and would defend the right to teach of those with whom I disagree profoundly, provided only that they are experienced and gifted teachers, able to inspire students to think for themselves, and able to move students to enthusiasm. In my opinion, no such drastic steps as the one which you describe are either necessary or desirable, as long as our members accept in good faith the authority of their Educational Committee—an authority which does not attempt to limit what they believe or even what they teach, but which does insist on prescribing a balanced diet for every student. If, however, a teacher should claim under the slogan of "democracy" the right to limit a group of students to any one set of ideas, and should therefore refuse to abide by the decisions of the Educational Committee as approved by the Society, then such a teacher would certainly have to be deprived of teaching functions. I am hopeful, however, that no such situation will arise. (NYPS Archives, 1940)

Horney answered Kubie on the following day:

> I have taken cognizance of Dr. Wittel's letter and of your reply. Since the matter has gained a certain publicity, I would request that an opportunity be given at the next meeting for an open discussion, particularly of the points mentioned in your letter. (NYPS Archives, 1940)

This was the first of many meetings that took place. Male and female members were on both sides of these curricular debates. But positions hardened. The discussions during March and April 1941 were full of charges and countercharges—of alleged intimidation of students, of undue influence, and even of slander. These culminated in the vote on April 28, 1941, to demote Horney from instructor to lecturer. Even the moderate Dr. Daniel Levy's warning against "the wisdom of such a course in view of the Schilder grievances" went unheeded (NYPS, *Minutes*, 1941). (Paul Schilder had been a psychiatrist and regular member of the Vienna Psychoanalytic Society but had not been analyzed. Thus the New Yorkers denied him admission but, after much back and forth, rescinded their rejection. He had recently died.) On May 1, 1941, Horney resigned, along with five other members and fifteen candidates.

According to Susan Quinn, Horney was viewed with suspicion because she was involved with Erich Fromm, a nonphysician and former member of the Frankfurt School who was practicing psychoanalysis; because her friends were the leaders of the Washington-Baltimore group— Harry Stack Sullivan, Clara Thompson, and William V. Silverberg— whose psychoanalytic preferences focused on interpersonal relations, and who recently had moved to New York (Quinn, 1987, p. 286); and, at least to begin with, because Sandór Radó "never had gotten over Horney's attack on his paper on female castration anxiety at the meeting of the American Psychoanalytic Society in 1933" (p. 288). Wittels's well-known prejudice against women doctors and psychoanalysts also probably played a role.

In any event, Horney confronted her colleagues on two major points: (1) the orthodox ego-oriented psychoanalysis of her colleagues was culture-bound rather than universal and (2) it often was more productive to address a patient's present in order to understand his or her past rather than to begin with insights into this past. Both of these themes dealt with psychoanalytic theory and clinical technique. Neither was directly political, although the fact that women as well as men would be liberated proceeded from an egalitarian ethos. However, as a former student put it, Horney's going against the increasingly rigid rules for students and against the new curriculum, which apparently was foisted upon them by Kubie (in part to counteract Horney's influence), appeared to be a political act. And the students appreciated an ally who would challenge the increasing lip service to psychiatry by psychoanalysts and who effectively could confront Kubie, whose suave and adroit manner allowed him to dominate—particularly during his presidency of the society.

Horney's Association for the Advancement of Psychoanalysis got off the ground immediately and successfully with lectures at the New School for Social Research, the promise of an affiliation with the New York Medical College at Flower Fifth Avenue Hospital, and the publication of the first issue of the *American Journal of Psychoanalysis* (Quinn, 1987, p. 354). Horney's success upset the members of the New York Psychoanalytic Society. On July 15, 1941, Kubie informed his colleague Adolph Stern that he "resent[ed] the fact that the misleading statement which was circulated by Dr. Horney and her associates in resigning from the Institute has been allowed to go unanswered. ... We should consider also the advisability of filing [a refutation] with the American Psychoanalytic Association, and write to the New York Medical Week and even to the lay press" (NYPS, 1941).

On October 14, 1941, a special meeting of the New York Psychoanalytic Society was called to discuss the resignation of five members and fifteen candidates and the rumors surrounding those resignations and to draft a statement of refutation. Ultimately, society members prepared a statement for wide dissemination. They claimed, among other things, to be the only organization for training in psychoanalysis chartered by the University of the State of New York. But Horney's lawyers challenged this point, and it had to be partially retracted. In any event, both psychoanalytic societies vied for credibility; animosities increased; no one forgave and no one forgot; and differences about psychoanalytic practice were translated into personal vendettas as well as psychoanalytic theories, clinical concerns, and accounts of the history of the split—but none of these differences were over feminist issues.

Helene Deutsch Moves Center Stage

The women analysts who remained in the fold continued their research within the paradigms of ego psychology. On the whole, they did not enter the battle against Horney, although Phyllis Greenacre, in a handwritten letter to Kubie, indicated that she thought the entire conflict might have been handled with less confrontation. And their scientific papers did not directly address feminist issues, although I have been told that in their practices they encouraged their female patients to free themselves of the customary subjugation to men. Among these Freudian analysts was Helene Deutsch.

Just as in Vienna, Deutsch continued to elaborate on Freud's original concepts. She did not stray far enough ever to be requested to leave the fold. With Grete Bibring, another émigré from Vienna, she helped establish the Boston Psychoanalytic Society and then its institute. Soon after Deutsch's arrival, she began to concentrate on the impact of the much freer (than its European counterparts) American society on modern women. The two volumes of *The Psychology of Women,* which Deutsch published in 1944 and 1945, reach beyond Freud insofar as she ranged over what she saw as the major stages in women's lives. Essentially, she observed that women respond to the needs of their society by bearing children. She found the girl's infantile identification with her mother to enjoin her to be passive and masochistic—traits that get reinforced when her receptive vagina welcomes the active penis. Moreover, "her service to the species impels her to assimilate her feminine masochism and her human anxiety" (1944, p. 277). Deutsch concluded that feminine sexuality acquires its masochistic character as women learn to harmonize the masochistic and narcissistic elements within their psyches (1944, p. 278). By addressing the influences of the oedipal stage on subsequent development, Deutsch continued to stress its central importance, but she then endowed its aftermath with a flexibility Freud might have denied. In other words, in 1945, Deutsch argued that how women deal with motherhood depends as much on their social class and on the stage of societal development and needs—on their role in, for instance, settling the American West or settling down in the suburbs—as on their biological and psychological makeup. This alleged inclusiveness of the repercussions of the oedipal drama made it more plausible but less meaningful, and more palatable and less threatening to the intellectual public. Thus Deutsch offered the American Freudians' version to parallel Horney's public appeal.

Reiterating the then much-discussed theory of anthropologist Robert Briffault, a partisan of the matriarchal theory of social origins, Deutsch maintained that some of the emotional relationships between mother and child are so deep and primitive that they transcend all social and individual differences. Because the infant's first link is to the mother, she stated, "a certain stage in the development of the mother-offspring relation seems to be the prototype of the first social organization" (Deutsch, 1945, p. 5). But instead of focusing primarily on what this means to boys and girls as they grow up, Deutsch quoted another anthropologist, Bronislav Malinowski, who had found, for instance, that in Melanesia women's inclination to abandon themselves to their motherly instincts from the moment of conception is supported by the society around them. She now asked: "What is the psychology of a mother living in a social order in which this harmony between social custom and biologic factors does not exist?" (p. 12). Drawing on psychoanalysis, she explained some of the concealed phenomena of physiological and psychic processes.

Deutsch sharply distinguished between *motherhood* (the sociological, physiological, and emotional relationship) and *motherliness* (the emotional phenomena related to the child's helplessness and need for care) (1945, p. 18) and then outlined how motherhood in the *feminine* woman influences the "harmonious interplay between narcissistic tendencies and masochistic readiness for painful giving and loving; ... [and how] in the *motherly* woman the narcissistic wish to be loved, so typical of the feminine woman, is metamorphosed ... [and] transferred from the ego to the child or its substitute" (p. 19). She conceded that distinctions between sexual and reproductive instincts are extremely debatable. So are instincts to preserve the self and the species. But she exemplified how these instincts form the basis of the human personality and end up being embedded not only in the need for reproduction but in the beliefs and mores of specific religions and societies. And she proceeded to outline the ramifications of the psychic problems encountered in connection with the sexual act, conception, and pregnancy. Following Freud, Deutsch noted, for instance, an analogy between oral intake and the receptive sucking function of the vagina in coitus, and she stated that "in pregnancy all the ideas and fantasies of childhood and puberty that are connected with oral intake and expulsion often are revived through the physiologically determined proneness to nausea" (p. 136). She went on to relate psychosomatic manifestations to the revival of infantile hostility, fear, and other violent feelings. But fears and (unconscious) misconceptions about pregnancy can result in functional disturbances, Deutsch contended—in pseudomotherliness, spurious pregnancy, pseudocyesis, and sometimes anorexia nervosa (p. 204).

Insofar as earlier psychic mechanisms that keep resurfacing can be understood at all, only psychoanalytic insights into the unconscious, maintained Deutsch, can relieve their inhibiting manifestations and their symptoms. By connecting early emotional adjustments to their reappearances in relation to motherhood and motherliness and by stressing postoedipal experiences and expectations as crucial, Deutsch went beyond Freud. She kept distinguishing also among relatively young mothers, older ones, and those who were still in puberty; among stronger and weaker sexual and motherly instincts at various stages; and among the relative impacts of new medical advances. However, as the techniques for relieving pain during childbirth improved, Deutsch noted, they subverted "the dynamism of feminine psychic life" insofar as the new mother renounced "the experience of birth and the ecstasy of the first contact with [her] child" (Deutsch, 1945, p. 268). In other words,

Deutsch argued that the intensity of motherhood is weakened in modern society. Childbirth itself, Deutsch said, had become a masterpiece of masculine efficiency, so that women were unwittingly freed to take part in activities that used to be men's prerogative. Thus such medical advances helped wipe out sex differences.

All along, Deutsch brought in the relevant biological data. For example, she relied on comparisons between motherly and unmotherly attitudes shown by a large array of animal mothers, on these mothers' organic relationship to the fetus, and on the varying shocks of birth for both mother and offspring. In her chapter on mother-child relations, she argued that mothers must cut the umbilical cord. Here, she diverged from Freud's contention that "the only thing that brings a mother undiluted satisfaction is her relation to a son, ... [who can] gratify everything that has remained in her of her own masculinity complex" (Deutsch, 1945, pp. 320–321). Instead, she found that some mothers transfer their (unconscious) aggressive, envious hatred of men to their sons, emasculate them, and drive them into passive, feminine orientation. A daughter's identification with her mother, however, usually degenerates into hostility only later, during puberty, continued Deutsch. This tends to leave the mother feeling abandoned; the masculine woman, however, "tries to make her [daughter] into a man" (p. 322). Deutsch, more than other Freudians except for Melanie Klein, considered the mother-daughter relationship as the most enduring one—as the relationship that is preserved from birth to death:

> It is erroneous to say that the little girl gives up her first mother relation in favor of the father. She only gradually draws him into the alliance, develops from the mother-child exclusiveness toward the triangular parent-child relation and continues the latter, just as she does the former, although in a weaker and less elemental form, all her life. Only the principal part changes; now the mother, now the father plays it. The ineradicability of affective constellations manifests itself in later repetitions. (Deutsch, 1944, p. 205)

Clearly, Deutsch's direct deviations from Freud's writings are minimal. But by 1976, Nancy Chodorow would single out the previous passage to point out that the mother remains the primary internal object to the girl. In 1944, however, Deutsch's foremost concern was not feminism: In part, it was the perfection of clinical psychoanalytic theory from the ego-psychology perspective; in part, it was the construction of a social-psychoanalytic theory to rival Horney's. In fact, her books did bring psychoanalytic insights to the attention of a larger public and did help to keep the classical Freudians in the running against Horney's group, as well as against those—Abram Kardiner, George Daniels, Daniel M. Levy, and

Sandór Radó—who had split off to pursue cultural-anthropological issues more directly. (They founded the Columbia Institute for Psychoanalytic Research and Training in 1942.)

Psychoanalysts Help the War Effort

Deutsch's focus on motherhood showed that cultural questions were compatible with the methods of ego psychology even though the "culturalists" had stolen their march. In fact, during World War II, *all* psychoanalytic camps were involved in larger, societal questions, specifically in efforts to win the war. They contributed in a variety of ways, thereby disseminating psychoanalytic credos and practices. Among the classical Freudians, Walter Langer (1972) provided a psychoanalytic portrait of Hitler at the suggestion of Colonel William J. (Wild Bill) Donovan, the future director of the Office of Strategic Services (OSS); Kurt Eissler (1960) did a psychoanalytic study of eight American soldiers to predict what personality types would make the best leaders during impending battle; Heinz Hartmann (1944) collaborated with the Harvard sociologist Talcott Parsons to better understand social interaction, and he was among the psychoanalysts and social scientists who in 1944 at a high-level conference in Washington, D.C., advised the American government on how to deal with the Germans after the end of the war. And Karen Horney's Committee on the War Effort, in its *Bulletin,* suggested ways of encouraging the population to support the war effort, to learn, for instance, to feel *helpful* rather than *helpless.* None of these endeavors were feminist in any way. But at the time it was taken for granted that women were as important as men in winning the war: They joined the armed forces, and they were taking over "men's work" in offices and factories as the men went into battle. In view of the threat posed by a German victory, feminist activities seemed irrelevant.

Still, the break with Horney signaled a new theoretical turn. For *all* Freudians began to accept more fundamentally that socialization is one of the most central elements in the formation of the human psyche, or at least one of its ingredients. Among them, some shifted their attention to women as mothers. René Spitz, another émigré from Vienna, treated severely disturbed children at a foundling home, focusing on what happens to children deprived of maternal care, maternal stimulation, and love and on the effects of severe isolation. (Both he and Anna Freud in London investigated how best to respond to children orphaned by war.) He found that war-orphaned children don't have much resistance to disease and tend to die young and to suffer from all sorts of eating disorders. Thus it did not take long for mothers to be blamed, by their absence, for the neuroses of their children. Nor did it take long for nonpsychoanalysts to use such findings *against* mothers, and against women generally, particularly against their participation in the labor market.

Psychoanalysts and other health professionals pursuing all sorts of psychological inquiries delved deeper into questions of adaptation; policymakers who had their own (legitimate or illegitimate) agendas increasingly quoted these studies to push for both minor and major legislation. Later on, their assumptions spurred inquiries into the impacts of differing general cultural influences on individual mothers. After the fact, the overall antifeminist climate frequently, though incorrectly, was blamed on the Freudians; those who had had their theoretical disagreements with Freudians were thus cast in a more positive light. Although this perception up to a point may have been warranted, the differences among the psychoanalysts were theoretical and institutional: Neither the Freudians nor their "defectors" had any direct input into domestic policy. Nor did they single-handedly formulate the family ethos of postwar America.

However, psychoanalytic ideas as such did enter the mainstream, and the impact of specific mothering on the mental health of the young did supply the rationale for a number of traditional attitudes. Thereby, a new sort of confusion arose: Feminists blamed psychoanalysts for discriminating against women rather than blaming the political forces that were using and institutionalizing the psychoanalysts' findings to keep women at home. By the end of the 1960s, however, feminists pointed to entrenched habits and inequalities, and a number of politicians started to represent feminist interests when it suited their purposes. Of course, psychoanalysts often were pulled into the fray, sometimes as expert witnesses in lawsuits. But this happened only after psychoanalysis had become fairly well established.

Still, in the 1940s, the presence of women analysts itself appeared to prove that women were gaining equality—even when these analysts did not focus on the psychology of women. But because doctors alone were accepted in the institutes affiliated with the American Psychoanalytic Association, and no more than 6 percent of medical students were women, few young women were able to join. Thus women belonged to the less prestigious institutes and within these were subject to the inevitable discrimination by their male colleagues, which, in turn, seemed to be a cultural reflex. The distinction of women like Horney and Deutsch, and the popularity of their books, helped counteract the fact that only some women psychoanalysts were thriving. Among the early Freudians, however, an inordinate number of women *had* climbed up the hierarchic ladder, and their theoretical works were taken as seriously as those of their male colleagues. Essentially, the women who were accepted into their institutes had an equal chance to contribute. They did so, and as Nancy Chodorow found when interviewing some of them in the 1980s about what it had been like to get into their profession, most of these women indicated that they had thought of themselves as feminists and had not felt much—or any—discrimination against women psychoanalysts (Chodorow, 1989, p. 203).

Anna Freud's Ego Psychology Versus Melanie Klein's Object Relations

A similar situation developed in London. There, questions of feminism did not arise. Psychoanalysis itself was dominated by two women— Anna Freud and Melanie Klein—and as I was told, they were pleased when prominent men became affiliated. The animosity between these two leaders has been discussed endlessly in psychoanalytic circles, and it is nearly impossible to find any neutral comments.[1] But everyone seems to agree that already in 1927, Anna Freud and Melanie Klein had clashed on the technique of child analysis and that Ernest Jones, who dominated the British group and was the last survivor of Freud's inner circle, at first had sided with Klein but also had not wanted to go against Freud's daughter. Whether Anna was her father's daughter and thus responded to intellectual disagreement as if it were a personal attack, as the Kleinians said, or whether Klein's work was not psychoanalysis but a substitute for it, as Anna Freud pronounced (Hughes, 1989, p. 22), is not at issue here: Intellectual leadership and professional competition within the international movement were at stake rather than ad hominem attacks—or feminism.

Both women based their (competing) theories on their therapeutic work with children. Anna Freud maintained that as long as a child was dependent upon its parents—that is, until the superego is internalized enough to deal with actual parental authority, around the age of five— there could be no viable transference and therefore no psychoanalysis. Klein, however, held that the child's ego emerges from the earliest projections and introjections—that is, from the feeding experiences that begin at birth. Then, object relations (between mother and child, which Klein postulated as the bedrock of *all* future psychic responses and interactions) are being formed and begin to impinge on both healthy and neurotic development. Thus Anna Freud regarded preoedipal children as different beings from adults, and Klein maintained that the earliest (unconscious) perceptions of the mother are decisive in how the child will get through the Oedipus complex.

Because Anna Freud asserted that therapy was not viable before a child was between four and five years old and radical theories of social change—most of these vaguely derived from Marxist premises—argued that permanent social change needs fundamentally altered psyches, her thrust on the analysis of psychic defenses was deemed conservative. Consequently, subsequent generations of feminists did not consider her contributions of direct interest. But Klein's focus on object relations, precisely because it promised a better understanding of the unfolding, and as yet unformed, social and psychic mechanisms—and thereby the possibility of interfering in them—sometimes was picked up as a developmental theory that might induce a basic transformation of the unconsciously triggered emotions that influence all of our thoughts and actions.

Both Anna Freud and Melanie Klein focused on the differences between masculine and feminine development to construct theories that would guide the methods for psychoanalytically treating male and female neurotics. Each was convinced her own approach was best. Neither was an active feminist. Nor would either of them, if asked, have been against feminism or feminist aims. However, in the late 1970s and early 1980s, Klein's object-relations theory gradually moved to the center of psychoanalytic thinking. Because, as noted in Chapter 6, some feminists made part of her thought the linchpin of their own theories, the main presumptions must be outlined briefly.

Klein's focus on the conflicts and anxieties that infants experience during their early feedings led her to differentiate between two main processes of development in narcissistic neuroses. And because she also found such neuroses to be more prevalent insofar as these manifested the inner-directed, self-involved concerns of the baby boom generation growing up in the 1960s—concerns that themselves were evidence of the impact of psychoanalysis on the culture—Klein's concepts gained in actual relevance. Basically, she postulated that the infant assumes a paranoid-schizoid position when its persecutory fears are very strong and a depressive position when it begins to differentiate between itself and the mother and realizes that it both loves and hates her. However, if an infant cannot work through the paranoid-schizoid position, Klein argued, it may fail to reach the depressive position, which may regressively reinforce the fears of persecution and, in some cases, induce psychosis—that is, schizophrenia. In line with the principle that these events occur in response to experiences related to feeding, Klein spoke of "putting things outside" and of "taking them inside"—experiences that, in terms of the ego and of psychosomatic connections, are translated into mechanisms of projection and introjection. Again, these are psychic mechanisms that are neither masculine nor feminine but ungendered.

In *The Psychoanalysis of Children* (1932), Klein purported to also base her work on Freud's juxtaposition of the love and death instincts. But whereas Freud postulated this dualism as an expression of the castration fear and thus as an adjunct of the Oedipus complex, Klein held that mourning reactivates the most terrifying, primitive experiences. She observed these reenactments in her patients, along with the reparative and restitutive mechanisms that she found to be based on the infant's initial perceptions and subsequent internalizations of love, hate, and sadism and of good and bad objects; and she examined why and how separation from a loved one (particularly during mourning) reawakens the early unconscious fantasies that originally gave rise to paranoid feelings and manic defenses. When summarizing Klein's basic thoughts, Hanna Segal, who is both one of Klein's most ardent followers and a political activist, once more focused on the infant's responses to its mother's breast:

> The love, care and food received from the mother stir in the infant two opposite reactions: one of gratification leading to love, a primitive form of gratitude, the other of hostility and envy, based on the realization that the source of food, love and comfort lies outside one's self. Those feelings are not related to the physical feeding only. For the gratified infant ... idealizes the breast and experiences it as a fount of love, understanding, wisdom and creativity. ... Envy of the breast is stirred by gratification ... but can also, paradoxically, be stirred by frustration and deprivation. (Segal, 1979, pp. 139–140)

Inevitably, arousal of these feelings during therapy brings about a "negative therapeutic reaction" that, according to Klein, must be countered by the proper technique—a technique based on much direct interpretation. She was certain that the sooner the analyst in the transference relation spoke to her or his child patient about the deepest disturbances, the easier it would be for this child to recall them. To this end, it was imperative that the therapist learn to distinguish among envy, jealousy, and greed in order to help reintegrate the patient's split-off envy. But the ego psychologists were increasingly opposed to premature interpretation; Klein's technique not only went against Anna Freud's clinical convictions but against those of *all* classical Freudians. And I must note, once again, that Klein spoke of children and of infants. Only in her views of the Oedipus complex did she differentiate between boys and girls. According to Klein, the latter do not fear castration but a retaliatory assault on their own bodies, on their internal genitals:

> Her fears concerning her genitals are especially intense, partly because her own sadistic impulses are very strongly directed towards her mother's genitals and the erotic pleasures she (the mother) gets from them, and partly because her fear of being incapable of enjoying sexual satisfaction serves in its turn to increase her fear of having had her own genitals damaged. (Klein, 1932, p. 195)

Klein's conclusion that the girl, prompted by her dominant feminine instinctual components, turns to her father and his penis indicates that she transformed the Oedipus complex into a sort of secondary phenomenon. In the process, she added to the voluminous discussions about what happens to the Oedipus complex. But her treatment of the psychology of little girls did not (consciously or directly) contribute any more to subsequent feminist agendas than did Anna Freud's or Helene Deutsch's.

Conclusion

Soon after World War II, on both sides of the Atlantic, Freudians embarked on complex child studies, many of them financed by government agencies such as the National Institute of Mental Health. Some of these, among them the laborious and extremely intricate observations of children by Margaret Mahler and her associates (1975) on separation and individuation, did teach us much about the genesis of object relations but at the same time seemed to imply that a mother's behavior is the most decisive factor in her child's future mental health. So did the studies conducted at Yale University, which to a large extent hinged on Anna Freud's teachings. Although the psychoanalysts themselves, for the most part, did not draw instant and pejorative conclusions, the general public got the impression that psychoanalysts were acting as a sort of educational police. This perception made it easier for legislators to justify the erosion of women's participation in the workplace after the war and for this public to further perceive psychoanalysis as conservative. (To what extent the immediate postwar euphoria about buying the little house in the suburbs with its accompanying washing and other domestic machines contributed to the subjugation of women remains unclear.) However, women psychoanalysts continued to be emancipated role models for some, even though they did not address feminist issues any more than did other women. In 1963, Betty Friedan's *Feminine Mystique* publicly exploded the myth of blissful, suburban domesticity, and women once again publicly dared begin pushing their aspirations to equality.

Inevitably, women psychoanalysts soon got into this fray and offered their expertise. Their ideas were both rejected and partially accepted by feminists in sociology, anthropology, psychology, and other fields. The ensuing polemics, and their intellectual and cultural roots, are discussed in the remainder of this book. Still, we must keep remembering that the polemics themselves brought new issues to the fore. Consequently, old concepts were being reformulated as ego psychology was being decentered by some and invalidated by others. For instance, whether Freud's early hypothesis of infants' seduction is based on reality or fantasy—which remains problematic throughout his works—becomes an important issue only when questions of child abuse are central, social issues. And whether psychoanalysis is based on biology is important to, for instance, Frank Sulloway, who casts it as a science, and anathema to Lacan, who locates it in language and symbolism. These issues as well, though not directly feminist ones, are present or absent in feminist discourse depending on where and when they are being addressed.

3

From the Quiet 1950s to the Storm in the 1960s and 1970s

By the end of World War II, Freudian notions were being bandied about in the culture. Although feminism then was at a low ebb, it was assumed that psychoanalysis, though far from popular, could free repressed women to lead relatively emancipated lives. This is not to say that in the 1950s middle-class women were not going into analysis unless they were exceedingly unhappy, were unable to deal with aspects of their marriages, or had general feelings of malaise. But as this practice became increasingly acceptable, more individuals sought emotional help, which in turn ushered in the therapeutic society we now take for granted.

Some blamed the Freudians for having masterminded the shift in Americans' dominant beliefs. Even though it always had been taken for granted that men were superior to women, this assumption appeared to be reinforced by the Freudian notion that going against it would increase women's unconscious guilt. The media echoed this interpretation. Nevertheless, intellectuals, artists, and other educated people went into psychoanalysis either because they felt blocked in their work or assumed that their thinking might be flawed without its potential benefits. Such acceptance by the avant-garde helped psychoanalysts make inroads into the culture. And the messages of sociologists, psychologists, psychometrists, and other social scientists did so as well. Moreover, after World War II women stayed home and bore children for reasons that had nothing to do with the psychoanalysts.

In 1945, when Viola Klein published her historical overview *The Feminine Character,* she gave "The Psycho-Analytical Approach: Sigmund Freud" twenty pages, just over 10 percent. According to Klein, biologist Havelock Ellis, Viennese philosopher Otto Weininger, experimental psychologist Helen B. Thompson, and psychological testers L. M. Terman and C. C. Miles had had the largest impact—along with historians Mathias and Mathilde Vaerting, anthropologist Margaret Mead, and sociologist W. I. Thomas.

Klein, a psychoanalyst but not an explicit feminist, trusted that in due course women would be liberated. She wrote this book in order to point to the increasing conflicts women were faced with in modern society.

51

Sociologist Karl Mannheim, in his preface, praised Klein for her synthetic approach to the social sciences and for "coordinating results drawn from various fields of knowledge" (Klein, 1945, p. xiv). When this book was reissued in 1971, Janet Zollinger Giele, a historian and sociologist, stated in her introduction that due to institutional changes *role sharing* had become a more central problem than *role conflict*—as Klein had concluded. By then, demarcations of roles, role sets, role changes, and so on not only had become central to sociology but were accepted and understood by most people. And these concepts did not originate with the psychoanalysts.

I could argue, of course, that the notion of *role,* one of the cornerstones in Talcott Parsons's theory of social structure, did incorporate Freud's conception of the personality, including its unconscious dimension, and that Parsons himself was influenced by the leading ego psychologists Heinz Hartmann and Ernst Kris, with whom he collaborated in the 1940s when formulating this element of his social system. However, the analysis of roles—which function on the conscious level and are simple to grasp—role conflicts, role sharing, role coordination, and so on could be interpreted to subsume the unconscious. Still, it was not this aspect of Parsons's systems theory that deligitimated his sociological structures in the late 1960s. He was scorned by rebellious students who attacked every nonrevolutionary theory as reactionary and as furthering the status quo. They advocated Marxist views that focused on the polarization of the capitalist and working classes and expected the victory of the proletariat. Furthermore, they dismissed Parsons as elitist, as accepting the traditional division of labor without questioning it. That he used an abstruse vocabulary to explain even the obvious made him an object of derision.[1] Similar accusations soon were leveled at the psychoanalysts: They were elitist; spoke of "him," whom they cast as the dominant member of the family, and did so in abstract language. Consequently, the earlier, hopeful attempts to create a common conceptual language for the social sciences that was to define sociological problems in terms of their psychological meaning and vice versa (Hartmann, 1950, p. 90), attempts that had united sociologists and psychoanalysts, now were held against the analysts.

The violent and often vicious attacks on Freud and Freudians in the late 1960s were not coming from feminists alone but were part of larger cultural forces. In the mid-1940s, cooperation among disciplines had been held out as the new and superior way of comprehending our social world and as a means of overcoming the fragmentation that had occurred in the wake of the stepped-up professionalization accompanying modernization and industrial advances. When such understanding did not ensue, the advocates who tried to explain conceptually what was going on around them were blamed for the phenomena rather than for their inability to properly comprehend the accompanying social ills and the fragmentation. The psychoanalysts' early promises to cure neuroses had not been kept: They had not been able to perform miracles or even to uncover the roots of the ever more elusive unconscious. (In France this promise was being renewed via the so-called structuralisms.) In America, where a mix of populism, media hype, and high jinks always gets inordinate attention and where the public routinely shoots the messenger when it doesn't like his or her message, few people stopped to recall that Freud, whatever his patriarchal hangups, had stated that women succumbed to hysteria because their sexuality was being strangled.

Already before World War II, partial and watered-down versions of psychoanalytic concepts gradually had filtered down into the culture. These had begun to take hold piecemeal, particularly among "experts" on child rearing who, as the culture became more and more child-oriented, were being heeded by everyone. When psychologist Otto Klineberg introduced the "explicitly eclectic" and popular college text *Childhood and Adolescence* (1957) by psychologists L. Joseph Stone and Joseph Church, he was addressing the parents of baby boomers:

> The book has much to offer ... to fathers and mothers who are looking for guidance in understanding their own children. It has been suggested that Americans are so insecure in this respect that they become eager disciples of the so-called experts, and our comic magazines are filled with unflattering references to the "techniques" of the child psychologist. (p. vi)

Stone and Church were "integrating a huge body of facts that ha[d] been accumulated, not only by psychologists but by zoölogists, physicians, psychiatrists, sociologists, and just plain people with a sharp eye for the doings of children" (p. xiii). They did not deal separately with boys and girls except when, rather rarely, a reference to biological factors was called for. No entries for *women, girls, female* or for *men, boys,* or *male* were listed in the extensive index. Basic psychoanalytic ideas were mentioned, by Freud and Erik Erikson, but only occasionally and peripherally. The authors of this book, and many others like them, certainly had more of a direct impact on American society than the Freudians. And they were equally guilty of talking of the child as "he" and of advocating progressive child-rearing methods. What, then, accounts for the fact that the wrath of the student dissenters and of the feminists among them descended upon the Freudian analysts, who in America, as a result of their professional segregation in medical circles, were more or less outside the university while psychologists like Stone and Church were teaching at Vassar College?

What set the Freudians apart, I believe, was their elitist reputation and the extraordinary prestige some of them had garnered as advisers to government circles during World War II (they psychoanalyzed Nazi leaders in order to topple them and advised on reeducating the German population) and as expert witnesses in criminal cases after the war. Their meteoric though transient visibility added to the unease psychoanalysts engendered in a public that assumed they could "read" peoples' unconscious; and a rather large dose of arrogance made them targets for all those dissatisfied with the existing social order. That a few psychoanalysts were hobnobbing with members of the establishment increasingly isolated them all from those who radically criticized this establishment. In contrast to the psychologists, to the majority of sociologists, and to others in the social sciences whose theories probably were as "sexist" as theirs, the leading classical Freudians appeared to be more influential and yet did not apologize for or deny their influence: That a number of them responded, sometimes disdainfully, by analyzing the rebellious students' reactions as manifestations of their oedipal adjustments or as rejections of their (permissive) fathers only reaffirmed their intransigence to these students. Thereby they helped paint themselves into the conservative corner. (That the psychologists' categorization of traits into masculine and feminine actually was permeating the culture and the job market appeared less objectionable, at least at first.)

The concepts of penis envy and the castration complex were easy marks, especially for those who were ignorant of the internal controversies and the reformulations these subjects were engendering among the Freudians themselves. Moreover, these concepts were part of the theory of the unconscious, which cannot be observed in the way we can observe behavior. "Show me an unconscious" or "Show me an id" were demands that already had been stated by vigilant opponents in Vienna. But whereas the early charges took place in a culture that was totally opposed to therapeutic notions, that celebrated behaviorism, and that, at best, began to look into influences of Gestalt while hanging on to all sorts of biological determinisms, including Lombroso's typologies, the 1960s student rebels were themselves products of the therapeutic child-rearing practices of the Stones and Churches as well as of the psychoanalysts. In other words, the students already were the beneficiaries of the permissiveness that psychoanalysis, among other forces, had strongly supported.

By then, the classical Freudians, though in the limelight, had become a vocal minority. In addition to the groups led by Horney, Fromm, and Sullivan, other "simplifiers" of psychoanalysis kept capturing the public mind, so that the average person had increasing difficulty distinguishing among them. Sometimes, the dissensions about therapeutic theories and practices themselves had fueled controversies that enlivened media programs; other times these considerations had introduced further institutional splits. But each new therapeutic fad attracted patients, many of them students. And whatever the motives or the practices and by whatever neo-Freudian faction, these polemics further entrenched psychotherapy and the assumption that it would bring not only self-understanding but self-fulfillment. Thereby the supremacy of psychological analyses and principles was reinforced, and the psychotherapeutic society Philip Reiff (1966) had predicted a few years before was being irrevocably entrenched and was soon dominated by the new cultural assumptions.

The Feminist Movement

In the late 1960s at the height of the black liberation movement, women suddenly began to get together and to seriously address the inequalities and injustices most of them had taken for granted. By the early 1970s the message of women's liberation had spread from the universities to their surrounding communities and had reached almost everyone around the country. It did raise the consciousness of women. They pointed to the sex-typing of jobs, to discrimination in pay scales that ranged from the lowest to the highest levels of occupations, and to the fact that many professions were as good as closed to women. Thus women began to organize politically, to form pressure groups that eventually changed some laws and opened opportunities for women in the professions, in fire departments, post offices, the military, and so on. And they agitated in order to be remunerated at the same rate as men for their work outside their homes. The followers in the movement practiced the radical, confrontational politics that had led to the success of the (California) free speech movement, the civil rights movement, and the other liberation movements: The feminist movement was their precocious offspring. Under the circumstances, it was inevitable that the 1960s feminists did not start out with a precise program. But after amassing information on example after example of discrimination—on access to education, jobs, and professions and on underpayment and exploitation—they pooled their experiences. Each woman told her own tale.

Betty Friedan already had exploded the myth of the alleged bliss of suburban domesticity. *The Feminine Mystique* (1963) would not have had such enormous success had it not touched a nerve in nearly every middle-class woman in her thirties or forties (according to sociological inquiries in America, over 75 percent considered themselves middle class) who, though loving her children and enjoying the convenience of modern household appliances, felt that life and opportunities were passing her by, were being blocked. And each of Friedan's readers who had nodded agreement while reading and who could add ample evidence of her own discontent was a potential champion of a feminist revolution. Some of these women actively joined the civil rights movements out of liberal convictions. To begin with, such "volunteer work" did not subvert the existing ethos or threaten their husbands' assumed superiority. But while working for blacks' voting rights in the South, for better living conditions in the ghettos in the North, and for integrating the schools, women were coming into their own; they realized that they were able to act just as the suffragettes had before them and that by organizing they could wield political power.

When some of these women first started to speak of liberating themselves, they were letting off steam, were telling each other about their own complaints. However, in order to get redress for the many griefs on their long list of mostly justified discontents, which they soon realized were pervading the society, they needed to band together more formally. Thus they had to launch an association—the National Organization of Women with affiliated local chapters and special groups. Now, they were obliged to think through what they expected to achieve, where their potential members and allies would come from, how to ensure democratic procedures, and whom to put on the executive committee. In the process, women were having the sort of spontaneous rap sessions they soon would institutionalize to sensitize them to their innate repression, and they were formulating the general guidelines of the movment, what some would call its ideology. Before long, they organized and succeeded in changing divorce laws and gained access to every profession, including male-type occupations such as policing and driving taxis and trucks. In sum, they were entering the political arena.

In their heated discussions, women realized almost at once that the enormous range of discriminations needed to be separated into those at home and those outside the home and that they had to get to the roots of them all and to find out why women always were at the bottom rungs of whatever ladder they expected to climb. Graduate students, young professors, and older ones who until then had taught at most as adjuncts did much of the research. The sociologists and historians among them documented the legal and structural inequalities; the Marxists, and they were increasing in number in every discipline, proved that it all was due to capitalist and imperialist domination; the psychologists found the sources of discrimination in psychological repression and began to question the conclusions drawn from stereotyped notions of masculine and feminine traits.

In this ambience, it was no wonder that Freudians, most of whose institutes were not attached to universities, not only were perceived as supporters of the status quo but soon became a major target. Freud was

perceived as a misogynist and his followers as part of the antiwomen ca-
bal of American psychiatry. One article after another would start with
"Freud said that penis envy and the castration complex are universal
phenomena, and that is why ... " and would go on to explain everything
from a husband's control of finances and the car to wife-beating and
philandering as having been furthered by the psychoanalytic ethos.
(That psychoanalytic theory postulated homosexuality as a sickness—
because Freud had maintained that mature sexuality ends up as heterosexuality—had not yet become a central topic.) In any event, no one
then recognized that in a psychotherapeutic society it was inevitable
that psychological phenomena would be used to explain cultural ones
and, as indicated earlier, that Freud had become the symbolic whipping
post for the many psychological schools that opposed psychoanalysis.

Freudians' and Feminists' Rapprochement

Some of the feminists who had been attacking the so-called Freudian establishment—that is, the classical, medical analysts belonging to the
New York and the American Psychoanalytic Societies and their affili-
ates—themselves were psychoanalysts and doctors. But they had joined
one or another of the dissident Freudians in the 1940s or 1950s because
they preferred to pursue one of the cultural paths Karen Horney's (1937,
1939), Erich Fromm's ([1942] 1960), and Harry Stack Sullivan's interpersonal theories had offered as alternatives to the so-called American classical, ego-oriented approach. Yet they had not rejected Freud. Among
them, Jean Baker Miller sought to articulate a new psychology of
women. She put together a collection of disparate articles, *Psychoanalysis and Women* (1973), by psychoanalysts who in various ways had extended Freud's ideas on the subject. Each of them tackled women's subjugation from a different perspective and attempted to examine why
males have been dominating females throughout history.

By 1973, in conjunction with black liberation or, as some would say, on
its coattails, women had nominally gained equal right of access to jobs
and education. Feminists then had to concentrate on finding means of
helping women to take advantage of new opportunities, to concretely
fight for the possibilities that had opened up. Among psychoanalysts,
the descendants of Horney, Clara Thompson, and their followers had
been doing research on feminist topics for some time.

Miller started out by recapitulating Horney's "The Flight from Womanhood" ([1926]) 1974) and "The Problem of Feminine Masochism"
(1935). Miller refuted Sandór Radó's (1933) assumption that a genetic factor guides sexual development into a masochistic channel, as well as
Helene Deutsch's notion of female masochism. And she pointed out that

long before Kạte Millet (1970), Alfred Adler demonstrated that "both sexes had fallen into a morass of 'prestige politics' which robs them of candor and deprives them of love and happiness" (Miller, 1973, p. 39). Instead, she upheld Clara Thompson's thesis that the underprivileged position of women leads them to rationalize feelings of inferiority and to use the penis as the symbol of superiority and that the derogatory attitude toward female sexuality (her genitalia are not clean, she does not accept her sexuality in its own right) is a reflection of the culture. And she reprinted a friendly refutation by Frieda Fromm-Reichmann, who put the primary blame of faulty women's cultural attitudes on the general devaluation of procreation and on men's unconscious fear of women.

In this inclusive search of her *new* psychology of women, Miller reminded her readers that Gregory Zilboorg (1944) had not strayed from the basic Freudian concepts (he did not leave the New York Psychoanalytic Society) and yet had relied on evidence from biology, embryology, and anthropology to demonstrate that women's changing psychological attitudes are manifested in fashion (they flaunt or disguise femininity or announce equality with men through their clothes) and in literary works (Miller, 1973, p. 95). Nevertheless, he also had supported "traditional attitudes by pointing to woman's organic, psychological, and cultural inadequacy" (p. 102) and had pointed to the androcentric bias that persisted after Freud's death, so that no one had reexamined women's so-called passivity and activity in relation to cultural changes. In other words, Miller highlighted the contradictions that needed to be addressed.

Furthermore, Miller brought in "newly emerging evidence," beginning with Mary Jane Sherfey's findings in *The Nature and Evolution of Female Sexuality* ([1966] 1972). Sherfey cited embryological research to show that there is no initial anatomical bisexuality or equipotentiality in the human embryo, that it starts out as female and that differentiation (by the action of fetal androgen) takes place between the sixth week and the third month of fetal life. This lack of early hormonal differentiation, Sherfey hypothesized, "renders women more sensitive to hormonal conditioning in later life, especially to androgens ... [that] could evolve to enhance [her] sexual capacity" (Miller, 1973, p. 136). Masters and Johnson as well, she went on, did not notice any distinction between vaginal and clitoral orgasm; they had observed that the clitoris, labia minora, and lower third of the vagina function together during coitus and that women are capable of many orgasms. Therefore, suggested Sherfey, just as in primates, women's sexuality occurs basically through selective adaptation; orgasmic experience increases with more of it; in the distant past sexual insatiation may have facilitated evolution; and with the rise of modern civilization woman's hypersexuality has been curtailed because it would have interfered drastically with her maternal responsibilities (p. 139). Consequently, Sherfey speculated about the biological and physiological influences that might have impinged during the past seventy-five million years on the evolving culture, and she ended up with theories like those in Freud's "Totem and Taboo." But here Sherfey was less convincing, and soon her entire enterprise faded away. Just the same, its popular appeal added to the force of the movement.

Mabel Blake Cohen ([1966] 1973) analyzed the data from psychological studies of masculine and feminine traits. Traditional masculine and feminine role expectations, she found, had perpetuated the socialization of boys and girls into taken-for-granted behavior—brave and strong boys and passive and weak girls. She then linked these expectations to psychoanalytic findings by Erikson on identity, by Sullivan on effects of interpersonal experiences, and by Hartmann on the active, adaptive functions of the ego. She found that both middle- and working-class couples and their children's personal and sexual identities from birth through childhood and adolescence to the maturational process as young parents were being socialized into incompatibility (Miller, 1973, p. 167). However, in her psychoanalytic study of fifty couples, whom she divided according to typologies of marital adjustment, Cohen found that "the more maladjusted subjects had had a history of greater tension and conflict in their childhood homes and had more difficulties in their marriages [whereas] ... problem-free women had come from harmonious childhood homes and were happily adjusted in their marriages, with feelings of affection and security. ... [They] were mature, competent, and quite free of conflicts about femininity" (p. 169). From this data she concluded that the accepted dichotomies between activity and passivity and between independence and dependence were not the parameters of masculine and feminine development but (unfortunately) were the sex-typical behavioral expectations embedded in the culture (pp. 181–182).

With the help of other essays written on the subject elsewhere, Miller brought diverse findings together to demonstrate that we have to adjust our traditional Freudian reading glasses when looking at female growth, that biological factors have to be examined in relation to the changing cultural matrix. She also found that recent changes in mores (girls may be more competitive and autonomous during adolescence and thus become more self-confident) have allowed women greater freedom in taking both social and sexual initiatives (Miller 1973, p. 225). Judd Marmor, who later would show that homosexuality is something other than just a stage toward mature development, found that Freud's doctrines were flawed because they not only flowed from his surroundings but also were the logical outcome of his theory of superego development. And

Marmor pointed out that Erikson's thesis, based on the anatomical differences between the sexes—"women are prone to be more concerned with 'inner space' ... [and] men with 'outer space' ... due to 'the existence of a *productive inner-bodily space* safely set in the center of female form and carriage'"—is wrong (p. 229). The task of the analyst, he summed up, is to comprehend changes within the culture and to treat his female patients accordingly, to make them aware that they now have choices that in Freud's Vienna did not exist. Ruth Moulton, who focused on the concept of penis envy alone, arrived at the same conclusion. She added that the therapist who wants to help her patient overcome the negative concept of womanhood must believe in woman's positive potential.

Robert Stoller wanted to refute those who continued to insist that biology is destiny. By extrapolating from studies of patients whose genitalia did not correlate with their designated sex, he investigated how the sense of femaleness develops. He related girls' views of themselves to how their parents were rearing them and found that so long as parents believe that their infant is a female, the core of feminity will develop regardless of the state of chromosomes or genital anatomy. For this reason Stoller concluded that, contrary to Freud, "both sexes [do not] pass through the early phases of libidinal development in the same manner" (Miller, 1973, p. 277). He supported this position with data from studies brain physiologists had undertaken with laboratory animals and from John Money's "natural experiments" on the structure of (female and male) chromosomes in which Money studied infants and children who were born with genitalia that were not unequivocally male or female and who had been assigned one sex and then resocialized into the other (p. 282).

The rest of the essays in Miller's volume suggested possibilities for establishing the psychic equality that would engender future social and sexual equality. Miller concluded that the women's movement already had proven that the one-sided woman of helpmate and mother is depassé; that new knowledge has increased the ability to unravel confusions among social, biological, and psychological factors that hinder full growth; and that women's natural psychological instincts are not violated when they begin to broaden their lives (Miller, 1973, p. 387). Insofar as the accepted nature of women is a reflection of social structures, she concluded, it will alter in relation to changes in this structure if women take a hand in the process. Altogether, these contributions pointed the way to a Freudian psychology of women that was in tune with feminist goals.

Miller ended on an optimistic note: In the future love and sex no longer will remain separate, and men and women will cooperate differently once we focus on the fact that in modern society women, on the average, give birth to only two children (who are expected to survive to old age). She pointed out that many psychoanalysts no longer perceive psychological problems as rooted in sexual suppression (as Freud did), but in thwarted needs for growth, creativity, and full communion with others. And because psychoanalysis has the potential both to promote conformity and to create conflict within the established order, Miller urged her colleagues to pursue primarily what they can do better than everyone else: support individual values, expression, and self-determination. Her colleagues, we recall, were those psychoanalysts and doctors who believed that "culture" has a decisive impact on "nature."

A selection of articles by Freud and some of his early disciples, and invited comments on them, put together by writer and editor Jean Strouse followed on the heels of Miller's volume. The contents of the contributions and sentiments overlapped. Strouse featured the long-forgotten essays on femininity by Freud, Karl Abraham, Helene Deutsch, Carl Jung, Marie Bonaparte, Clara Thompson, and Erik Erikson, in part to invigorate the increasingly stale interactions in consciousness-raising groups, in part to make anti-Freudian, uninformed feminists realize that they might be reinventing the wheel.

Juliet Mitchell, an English literary critic who became a Freudian analyst, started off by explaining that Freud's "Distinctions Between the Sexes" (1925j) (see Chapter 1) not only was a response to Abraham's thesis but also expressed the views of a patriarch who was suffering from an already chronic cancer and who now wanted to "gather his scattered observations on the *different* psycho-sexual history of boys and girls" (Strouse, 1974, p. 32). From a Lacanian perspective, which in America would not be introduced until a few years later, she argued that Freud's Oedipus complex was a manifestation of the importance of the *father* in *patriarchy*.

Novelist Elizabeth Janeway chided those who dismissed Freud as a male chauvinist and called attention to his ambiguities of language, particularly in his discussion of cases. She pointed out that for Freud the notions of activity and passivity imply, also, social differences: "The female's lack of power and freedom slides into Freud's theorizing by the back door. The lack of a penis implies, denotes, inferiority … [and this] statement cannot be taken seriously *unless it is taken symbolically*" (Strouse, 1974, p. 65). Janeway then applied psychoanalysis to Freud. He lived up to what patriarchal society demanded of him, in action and behavior, and this included putting women into their traditional role: "If he did not rebel against the social structure, how could they?" (p. 68). And since even Adler, the radical socialist, did not imagine that his female patients' "masculine protest" could change their lot, how could

Freud do so? (p. 69). However, concluded Janeway on an upbeat note, if as a result of ongoing social changes mothers' positions change, then their daughters' will too.

Margaret Mead, who had argued that differential socialization among Malaysian tribes had proven definitively that passivity and activity are not genetically but socially induced traits, commented on Freud's 1933 summation "Feminity." She reviewed his position sympathetically and placed the entire discussion into the cultural context. Mead noted that it was time to redefine male-female relationships and the role of marriage and to examine whether anatomy really is destiny. She was alarmed at the "extreme statements, of the tit-for-tat order ... [triggered by Sherfey's thesis in a *New York Times* article] that assumes because 'women can achieve five to six sexual climaxes to a man's one, if continuously stimulated they can reach over fifty' this means that 'obviously women were not designed for monogamous or polygamous marriage'" (Strouse, 1974, p. 103). Instead of celebrating these possibilities as one would have expected, Mead wondered whether "in spite of any theory of penis envy, Freud's insistence that anatomy is destiny may not, in some deeper (cultural) sense, be true" (p. 104). She went on to speculate whether the failure to bear a child may not bring on other (negative) psychological or physiological consequences; whether interfering in the repetitive cycles of reproduction, of menstrual cramps, pregnancy, delivery, and menopause might not "transform human beings into beings who are incapable of the primary love and loyalty for kith and kin and country"; and whether women, as Freud assumed, may not be psychologically different from men after all in a very fundamental and as yet unfathomable way (pp. 104–105).

Joel Kovel, a practicing psychoanalyst, was working on yet another cultural synthesis of Freud and Marx. He began by "reconsidering" Abraham's view of the castration complex (see Chapter 1) by questioning whether there is such a thing as normality. According to Abraham, argued Kovel, "the castration complex is sexual madness internalized and made unconscious" in both men and women (Strouse, 1974, p. 139). Kovel expected to correct the situation by coordinating social critique with psychoanalytic understanding (p. 141).

Marcia Cavell recapitulated Helene Deutsch's *Psychology of Women* (1944) to explain why she thought Freudians had become a prime target of the women's movement: Deutsch had accepted women's passivity, whereas women must be encouraged in activity. And Robert Coles illustrated how Karen Horney's "revisionism" had become "common sense" and likened her to a misunderstood prophet (Strouse, 1974, p. 187). And after Barbara Charlesworth Gelpi explored Emma Jung's 1931 "On the

Nature of the Animus," Ethel Person evaluated Maria Bonaparte's 1934 paper "Passivity, Masochism and Femininity."

Bonaparte had maintained that the pain inherent in female reproductive functions is compensated for in woman's high degree of erotic pleasure in sexual relations and in her craving for caresses, which Bonaparte attributed to a residue of virility in her organism. However, she went on, a young child witnessing the sexual act perceives it as sadistic aggression by the male upon the female, usually as an oral act as well, and depending upon whether this child is male or female it will interpret (and reinterpret) this early experience in keeping with its own background. The girl may take fright and reject her passive role or confuse it with masochism. Person elaborated on this aspect of Bonaparte's thesis and particularly on the origins of feminine masochism. After summarizing the theoretical agreements between Bonaparte and Freud, Person found Bonaparte's distinctions between masochism and passivity most salient. She bolstered her argument with, for instance, Abram Kardiner's (1959) view that "masochism is an adaptive (though neurotic) technique born in an early interpersonal drama rather than a derivative of instinct" and with Rudolph Lowenstein's (1957) conception that masochism is "a weapon of the weak—of every child faced with the danger of human aggression" (Strouse, 1974, p. 254). However, Person now introduced the concept of gender role identity to allow psychoanalysts to better integrate nonsexual attributes and behavior into their work. She, too, had recourse to Money's and Stoller's findings on psychosexual development—on gender differentiation and on self-designation of maleness or femaleness—but focused on the importance of gender core. Person concluded that the origins of gender differentiation are more complicated than Freud realized. And she felt that Bonaparte's insights still were holding up clinically, even though she had "confused the *meaning* of certain themes which emerge in analysis with their *causality*" (p. 260). (A reexamination of Freud's concept of bisexuality by Robert Stoller was included in this volume as well.)

Ruth Moulton contributed "Clara Thompson's Role in the Psychoanalytic Study of Women." Thompson, an American psychoanalyst, had been influenced by Sullivan (he had avoided Freudian terminology and was convinced of the nonsexual origins of neurosis) and at his suggestion had gone to Budapest to be analyzed by Ferenczi. Thompson's writing is simple, easy to understand. An ally of Horney, she too emphasized women's social conditioning and explored the means of dealing with it psychologically. Moulton cited Thompson's focus on transference and countertransference in the 1950s and her "Femininity" (published posthumously in 1961), which pointed out that "women could have and enjoy many kinds of orgasm and should not constantly compare their responses to those of men" (Strouse, 1974, p. 285).

Erik Erikson was known for his studies of the symbiotic elements of nature and culture after he published *Childhood and Society* in 1950. But later, while observing children building with blocks, he found boys to *erect* towers and *protruding ornaments* in the form of *cones* and *cylinders,* and girls to create *enclosures* that contained people and animals into which others *intruded* (Strouse, 1974, p. 325). Thus he became a feminist target. Strouse, who attended Erikson's course "The Human Life Cycle" at Harvard, reprinted his lecture "Womanhood and Inner Space" (1968) and asked him to reply to his accusers. Erikson maintained that he had been misunderstood, particularly by Kate Millet, who had dismissed his findings as part of "psychoanalysis' persistent error of mistaking learned behavior for biology" (p. 323). Many women's advocates, he now retorted, "as a corollary to the attempt to raise consciousness [are determined] to repress the awareness of unconscious motivation" (p. 322). And he recalled that he had been as surprised as everyone else at the results of his investigations. Moreover, he accused Elizabeth Janeway of embroidering on his study in *Man's World, Woman's Place* (1971) when she noted that "little girls prefer interiors where their dolls serve each other tea, or play the piano," for neither he nor his subjects had drawn such conclusions. Erikson went on to refute yet other reinterpretations and reiterated that he advocated equal opportunity for women but that we must evaluate "negative as well as positive elements in the [unconscious] identity formation of *both* sexes" (p. 332). And he proposed inquiring into a workable division of roles (p. 333). Erikson ended by elaborating on the connections of birth control and abortion to the future of society and by suggesting that one can maintain true genital liberation only by coming to terms with generativity (p. 337) and with the general problem of human survival in the face of inhuman inventions. In the 1970s, this issue was much closer to Erikson's heart than the research on children he had done so many years before.

All in all, both men and women psychotherapists kept in mind the links between psychoanalysis as a cure and psychoanalysis as a theory. But this was not always a useful connection for feminists in a hurry to change society. Whereas the psychoanalytic feminists knew that it is not enough to alter the outer manifestations of inner reality, that permanent change must be internalized, other feminists did not have the necessary patience that, in fact, was counterproductive to then-existing social-political dynamics. In classical Freudian language, psychoanalysts thought feminists were resistant. However, Erikson's larger claims seemed to bridge the gap between psychoanalysts and feminists in universities because they were in harmony with the ultimate aspirations of the movement. Gradually, its radical contingent warmed to Erickson's critique of society and to the liberating promises of his psychosocial criticism. Hence his political convictions ultimately reinstated Erikson in the feminists' good graces just as the movement was looking for new means of reaching a theoretically higher ground that would also have popular appeal.

Broadening the Movement's Point of View

A summary of the psychoanalytic and theoretical themes that were brought to the American women's movement does not do justice to the fervor with which each of them was presented and defended or to the scientific claims most of these precepts advanced. For by 1974, the movement no longer was confined to discontented middle-class women in the suburbs: Both black and white working-class women as well as professional women in law offices and the diplomatic service and in hospitals and universities were having their consciousness-raising sessions. Men were beginning to set up *their* groups to learn to deal with the new ethos of grassroots equality—with having to get their own coffee in the office and their own dinner at home. In all circles, new topics were being introduced: women's increasing assertiveness, allocation of time for work and play, fathering versus mothering, liberated parenting (an altogether new concept), impending divorces, and how to inform children and arrange visitations and finances after a separation.

All of these issues were being aired in the media, and whereas now these subjects have become commonplace, they made splashing headlines when first debated in public. Moreover, the realization that laws needed to be implemented to deal with the newly emerging social ethos and mores led many of the women in the movement to espouse specific political causes on both local and national levels. These burning issues, in turn, necessitated research into existing national and local laws and policies on divorce, child care, women's and children's rights, and so on. The results of such inquiries were of interest to the various other, and complementary, liberation movements. And the search for an overall theory engendered neo-Marxist, class-based analyses, particularly because the larger questions kept pointing to what was wrong with the political structures. Many American radicals in universities, however, did not advocate constitutional changes but went in for ever more abstruse theoretical constructions. At the same time, the feminists among them (my only concern here) increasingly were splitting on what problems to focus on first and on the alterations the larger institutional structures required.

None of the American women psychoanalysts could propose direct remedies to improve the political realm. But their findings were picked up—almost arbitrarily—when they were thought to support a specific political issue. Still, scientific-sounding psychoanalytic opinions about unconscious origins of attitudes and actions tended to be more convincing in courts of law than vaguely presented feelings of dissatisfaction. But except for some of the Marxist works, none of the feminists' theories could address both macro- and microissues, which alone could theoretically integrate the many strands of the movement. Only Juliet Mitchell's *Psychoanalysis and Feminism* (1974) injected a welcome—though foreign—synthesis.[2]

Mitchell was a founding member of the British New Left and was upset that her male colleagues did not take her ideas as seriously as each other's. She was indignant also that they agreed with Frantz Fanon's suggestion that women in the Third World ought not be emancipated until *after* the revolution. She had become intrigued by psychoanalysis while reading the Marxist philosopher Louis Althusser's (1965) critique of ideology in which he assumed, among other things, that Jacques Lacan's rereading of psychoanalysis (see Chapter 5) would allow for the socialization of infants in a way that could eliminate internalizing their parents' bourgeois attitudes and habits (pp. 17–18). (Althusser maintained that unconscious—individual and societal—structures perpetuate the laws individuals live by and thus render these individuals, both men and women, unable to institute change. In the aftermath of the events of 1968 in France, his theories had become increasingly marginalized.) Mitchell adapted Althusser's hypotheses to the liberation of women under capitalism. She argued that women had been kept out of the labor force not because they were physically weak but because they were needed in the family to please men sexually, to bear children, and to socialize them. And as she went through the Freud-Marx literature, she found that feminists were handicapping themselves by rejecting Freud. Her arguments were not internal to the Freudians' discussions or defenses of them but were presented as addenda to radical doctrines. Essentially, she said, leaving out unconscious resistances was hampering feminism.

Mitchell criticized post-1968 feminists for automatically denouncing Freud without putting his ideas within a broader theoretical and ideological context. She enlarged on Freud's theories of sexuality and pointed out that anti-Freudian feminists took his texts too literally (see Chapter 4) and thereby ignored the fact that he invoked unconscious mental processes when speaking of penis envy. And by transposing this concept to the realm of conscious perceptions and decisions, feminists erroneously assumed that Freud had prescribed what was "normal":

They failed to recognize that he used the term relatively, in contrast to "neurotic," "pathogenic," or "psychotic." By quoting from Freud's "Case of Dora," where Freud considered "so-called sexual perversions [as] very widely diffused among the whole population," and from his statement in a 1935 letter to the mother of a homosexual that "it is a great injustice to persecute homosexuality as a crime—and a cruelty too," she proved that he took bisexuality seriously (Mitchell, 1974, p. 11).

When Mitchell got into theories of narcissism she displayed her intimate knowledge of the French discussions not only by pointing to Octave Mannoni's distinction between Freud's *Three Essays*, "the book of the drive," and his *Interpretation of Dreams*, "the book of desire," but by showing that Freud had explicitly denounced biologically based instinct theories—just as every feminist does (Mitchell, 1974, p. 3). Her descriptions of the infant's "megalomanic moment" of narcissism, its search for itself in its mother's expressions, and the beginning of its self again echoed Lacan's concept of the mirror stage (see Chapter 5). And when blaming the current confusions on the inadequate language available to Freud, she relied on Lacan as well as on D. W. Winnicott's clinical findings when she defined *masculinity, femininity,* and *bisexuality.*

But Mitchell also demonstrated the flaws in the theories and practices of two of the most radical psychoanalysts—Wilhelm Reich and R. D. Laing—who had seized some feminists' imaginations. Even though they had become icons to a number of revolution-oriented feminists, neither of them could further feminist ends because they both tried to find a dialectical method of *totalization.* Mitchell placed Reich's ideas in the context of Vienna's iconoclasm, exoticism, and extravagance and of Berlin's bourgeois decadence and working-class wretchedness and demonstrated that Reich finally supported hetero and "healthy" sexuality and that he had not questioned the then accepted ideological underpinning that supported the family and sexual suppression (Mitchell, 1974, pp. 140–141). Ultimately, Mitchell pointed to Reich's conceptualization of neuroses in his ([1933] 1961) "Character Analysis" as too inclusive when, for instance, he first condemned the negative inhibiting effects of the patriarchal family on infantile sexuality, then moved on to glorify the child as the living spirit of Nature (p. 173), and concluded that "Freud discovered the Oedipus complex … but [was] just as far from … a sociological interpretation of the family formation as the mechanistic economist is from a comprehension of sexuality as a social factor" (p. 181). And she found that Reich's crucial misconception of the unconscious as a pool of the instincts is as faulty as his political writings, his sexual politics, his orgonomy, and his prediction that "the duality of sex finally will be submerged in the feminine principle" and that "Nature and culture, man and beast, man and cosmos, man and woman will all discover their so-called 'dialectical' unity" (p. 223).

Mitchell considered R. D. Laing a different kettle of fish: He never wanted to amalgamate Freud and Marx but to render what are considered schizophrenic patterns of behavior intelligible. Basically, Laing postulated that schizophrenia does not exist in isolation but in relationships to other people and then aimed at reestablishing the original social cause of the illness. In *The Divided Self* (1965), he put himself in opposition to psychoanalysis and suggested what *should* be done so that the patient would perceive the analyst as his or her equal (Mitchell, 1974, p. 235). The early Laing purged his existential roots and was free of mystical-religious overtones, argued Mitchell, but the later Laing put them back in (p. 239). And he used the term "science" rather loosely. "In 'Family and Individual Structure,' internalization entails the transference of a pattern of relations from one modality of experience to others: namely from perception to imagination, memory, dreams, phantasies, etc."—which, Mitchell said, differs from conceptualizing the superego as the internalization of parental attitudes (p. 257). Finally, Mitchell concluded that Laing, too, failed to eradicate the social causes of schizophrenia, that he, too, blamed the mother for not letting go of the patient and for forgetting the problematic relationship between mother and child. Mitchell said that the absence of the symbolic father was to be blamed as well (p. 291). Soon, Laing himself would admit the failure of his— much acclaimed—treatments.

Mitchell also called attention to Freud's ambivalence about America, where the popularization of psychoanalysis by nonanalysts (it both annoyed him and provided him with satisfaction [Mitchell, 1974, pp. 295–296]) led to a particular insertion of psychoanalysis into the culture and helped maintain both familiarity and misreadings. For instance, by reading Simone de Beauvoir's *The Second Sex* ([1949] 1952), American feminists had

> compounded certain tendencies within popularized American Freudianism and this combination has had an influence on subsequent feminist reaction to Freud. Thus de Beauvoir, with Sartre, does not believe in the main proposition of psychoanalysis—the unconscious—nor, interested in the person's present existence, does she place much emphasis on his or her infantile past. So, too, does she continue a trend which has been dominant in opponents of Freud, most significantly since Jung: she underplays the importance of sexuality. Many of the factors she criticizes are to be found within later Freudianism, but are counter to Freud. This does not invalidate de Beauvoir's criticism: it *does* mean that the Freud the feminists have inherited is often a long way off-centre. (p. 301)

This misreading, stated Mitchell, meant that women had lost the only means of understanding their psychology. But she did not chide only de

Beauvoir for having subordinated psychoanalysis to existentialism in order to account for the fundamental situation of alienation. She argued just as strongly against Betty Friedan's assumption that Freud's theories were obsolete (Mitchell, 1974, p. 320) and exposed her ad hominem arguments (p. 322). She found that British feminist Eva Figes, in *Patriarchal Attitudes* (1970), did the same thing, although from a more historical and relativist position. She then used Freud's sociological and fairly speculative works—"Civilization and Its Discontents" (1930a), "The Future of an Illusion" (1927c), and "Moses and Monotheism" (1939a)—and brought them together with the letters he wrote to his fiancée many years before (he expected her to be the typical housewife she became) to prove that he was thoroughly bourgeois. Mitchell further pointed out that both Friedan and Figes should have "determine[d] his [Freud's] character in order to interpret his work" (p. 333). And, stated Mitchell, Germaine Greer, a celebrated feminist on both sides of the Atlantic, was disarmingly cavalier about her many mistakes, mixed up psychoanalysis with psychiatry and psychology, and "misconceive[d] Freud's meaning and then endow[ed] this misconception with her own original contribution." For instance, said Mitchell, "Freud did *not* subscribe to the idea ... that one pole was occupied by men, and the other by women" (p. 344). Mitchell noted also that Greer's suggestion that men "with their destructive impulses ... take away from women their natural sexuality and love" was being replicated in Shulamith Firestone's *The Dialectic of Sex* (1972) "in the form of the Male Technological World finally joining in harmony with the Female Aesthetic World" (p. 344). Thereby, added Mitchell, Firestone was "reducing Freud to the social realities from which he deduced his psychological constructs" (p. 347).

By then, de Beauvoir, Friedan, Firestone, and Millet were the established cast of feminist celebrities. Germaine Greer had debated Norman Mailer in New York's town hall and on television, and their faces were recognized by many people. The more outrageous the statement, the more immediate attention it got: Thus psychoanalysis remained discredited while the feminist cause was being advanced.

Near the end of her book, Mitchell summarized Engels's account of women as the first oppressed group and linked it to Lévi-Strauss's analysis of patriarchic rules of marriage in "primitive" societies based on the prohibition of incest and the exchange of women. She then hypothesized that the Oedipus complex may play different roles in different cultures. And she introduced Lacan's interpretation of the Freudian situation of the infant and the child's insertion into the reality of its family during the mirror stage (see Chapter 5). From there, she went on to elaborate his views of the phallus as the basis of patriarchy. But Lévi-Strauss's and Lacan's structuralism were as yet incomprehensible to American feminists and to most other Americans.

Mitchell's book was discussed widely because it was provocative and raised relevant questions, especially about patriarchy: "Under patriarchal order women are oppressed in their very psychologies of femininity. ... [They] have to organize themselves as a group to effect a change in the basic ideology of human society" (Mitchell, 1974, p. 415). By relying on Lévi-Strauss's extrapolations from tribal societies (he said that unconscious mental structures are reachable when analyzing the myths of a society by means of binary oppositions), Mitchell called on feminists to help create new representations in the structures of their own unconscious. By internalizing the new, liberated practices, she assumed that these rather than the traditional (and everlasting) exchanges of women would be passed down. For no society, Mitchell concluded, has yet existed in which "the eternal unconscious [has] shed its immortal nature" (p. 415).

Not much later, the most cogent feminist critique of Mitchell came from Jean Bethke Elshtain (1981), whose focus was on the largely public persona of men and the more private one of women. Mitchell, noted Elshtain, incorporated the private realm into her scheme of things, attacked all structures simultaneously, and thereby deprived individual women of their subjective means of struggle: "She has no notion of a political community, no concept of a citizen ... [so that] there are, finally, neither persons nor politics within Mitchell's abstract Marxist structuralism" (p. 279). And "like her Structures, the Unconscious, rather than a fully fleshed-out person, has agency in the world" (p. 280), ultimately leading to determinism and a lack of self-awareness (p. 281).

Because Elshtain's book came out in 1981, its impact was lessened: Its publication coincided with the introduction in America of the French feminisms inspired by Foucault and Lacan, which soon overtook academic discussions in the humanities. (See Chapters 6 and 8.) Elshtain's focus primarily remained in political theory and thus is not immediately relevant to my focus on the relations among Freudians and feminists.

All in all, in the early 1980s the ideas of Althusser's so-called scientific Marxism, the translations of French feminists' works (see Chapter 6), Lacan's "rereading" of Freud (see Chapter 5), Lévi-Strauss's anthropology, and Foucault's historicism were penetrating more and more into American thought—including feminist thought. This general interest led American intellectuals to widen the context of feminism and to give the movement a new boost. By then, French feminists as well as Juliet Mitchell were practicing psychoanalysts and their feminism increasingly turned to explorations and extensions of classical Freudian paradigms.

4

Feminists' Views of Freud in the 1970s

Like all social movements, American feminism tried to get a foothold in the population at large. At the same time, academic women (and a sprinkling of men) in sociology, anthropology, psychology, English, comparative literature, and history who were learning to examine their disciplines from an entirely new and feminist perspective were neglecting or dismissing psychoanalysis as retrograde and conservative. They did not want to be bothered with intangibles such as the unconscious and thus were investigating where, how, why, and when women had been disadvantaged. They delved into the reasons and proposed wide-ranging remedies for the inordinately prevalent inequities that pervaded the entire society. To begin with, the social sciences and history were in the lead; by the end of the decade, the humanities were catching up. Women in the professions, in law, medicine, and politics, some of whom were being inspired by the academics, also became active. Thus the women's movement soon turned into an interdisciplinary, political endeavor that cut across many of the boundaries of race and class. Anthropologists were quoted by lawyers, sociologists by historians, and medical researchers by professors of French. Thereby the range of empirical inquiries and of theoretical premises was broadened. Ultimately, there were recommendations—some on paper and others on the steps of city halls or the White House—for political action. Links with other liberation movements, that is, black, gay, or ethnic, were being forged. The women's movement explored internal differences in terms of means and ends (including black women's primal allegiance to their gender or their race) while trying to present a united front. *All* their endeavors were geared to the political arena and were aimed to alter the political and economic distribution of power.

Feminists were turned off by expensive and lengthy psychoanalytic treatment, which was not immediately useful for political ends. Impatiently, they dismissed the Freudians as fossils of traditions and as "phallocentric" products of patriarchy. Some went further and blamed the psychoanalysts not only for the fact that the cures Freud had promised had not materialized but for many of the inequalities in society at large.

Feminism Against Psychoanalysis

The handful of Freudian feminists who tried to prove their usefulness to the feminist movement were fighting an uphill battle. Few feminists were willing to listen. They blindly heeded Kate Millet, who in *Sexual Politics* (1970) attacked Freud mercilessly for having shaped feminist discourse, for having indicated the inevitability of male domination. Millet's best-selling putdown served as the bible. Women sociologists investigated myriads of taken-for-granted discriminations in the workplace, the family, and the community. Their books rarely referred to Freud in the index. When they did, it was to malign psychoanalysis. The following statement by medical sociologist Pauline Bart (1974) is typical:

> When I moved from Berkeley to Chicago in 1970, I was struck by two differences: first the omnipresence of shiny, new, enormous American cars, in contrast to the beat-up VW's that dominated the Berkeley scene; second, finding many people who were still in classical psychoanalysis, a treatment modality that, from my West Coast perspective, seemed quaint and old fashioned, like debates over whether or not sociology was a science. Changes in types of psychotherapy are not random but reflect societal changes. Likewise, regional and class variations in acceptance of such changes are also related to sociological factors.
>
> Different psychotherapeutic orientations have different images of man, time focuses, concepts of society, assumptions of cause and effect, and orientations toward social change. These differences clearly reflect different values, hence the major conclusion of this chapter: Value-free psychotherapy is a myth. (p. 9)

Bart's animosity toward the Freudians had much more to do with deinstitutionalizing the mentally ill and with revolutionizing society than with psychoanalysis. In the mid-1960s in response to political pressures from the left and to money-saving schemes proposed by the right, policymakers had agreed that mental patients would be better off in communities and halfway houses than in large federally funded hospitals: They weren't getting the necessary therapy and personal attention, which alone could help them get well. Community mental health centers, it was argued successfully, would cost less and accomplish more than "warehousing." In the course of these policy discussions, psychiatrists and psychoanalysts attached to such hospitals inevitably defended themselves against assaults on their professions; psychologists and social workers, who were more mobile and stood to gain in both status and potential earnings, tended to advocate deinstitutionalization as a human right.

In the ensuing polemics, distinctions of qualifications among the various professions got lost, and when psychiatrists and psychoanalysts referred to the fact that their training was longer, more specialized, and rigorous than that of the others, it was pointed out that the mentally ill (except for those in acute states of schizophrenia, paranoia, or catatonia) needed human contact rather than professional distance. Thereby, psychiatrists and psychoanalysts were perceived as conservative bedfellows, and the radically different approaches to treatment among them was wiped out: They were an elite and ipso facto opposed to the increasingly populist swell.

Bart's statement that values are based on social beliefs had become the sociologists' battle cry: It affirmed that Marx had been correct and Max Weber had been wrong. In fact, these affirmations already had become clichés in the other social sciences as well. Bart's anti-Freudian charges smacked of the prevailing prejudices and served political ends. For instance, she used partial quotes by David Reisman and Herbert Marcuse to assert that "psychoanalytic therapy aims at curing the individual so that he can continue to function as part of a sick civilization 'without surrendering to it altogether'" and concluded that therefore Freud's thought was deterministic (Bart, 1974, pp. 12–13). She bolstered her claim by quoting the report of a lecture by Anna Freud in *Newsweek*: In 1968 Anna Freud had said that the student protests were "mask[s] for concealing personal inadequacies" (p. 13). Rather than ignoring this ad hominem remark, Bart went on to excerpt from a number of psychiatrists' reports in order to show that "psychotherapy is a form of social control and sanity 'a trick of agreement'" (p. 16), still not acknowledging that psychiatric and psychoanalytic methods often are antithetical and that the tension between their practitioners at the time was legend.

That novelist William Burroughs (1959) created a psychiatrist who "is a manipulator and ... an expert in all phases of interrogation, brainwashing and control" and that Ken Kesey's best-seller, *One Flew Over the Cuckoo's Nest,* depicted a psychiatric ward where Big Nurse manipulates patients into cooperating in their own destruction was proof to Bart that whatever was held against Freud had to be valid (p. 16). In retrospect, one must ask not only why Bart wanted to distort in order to refute Freud but why, like lambs, the women in the movement went along. Was it because Bart immediately went on to argue that confinement in America (of Ezra Pound, General Edwin Walker, and Governor Earl Long of Louisiana) was as political as in the Soviet Union—a means of discrediting opponents by labeling them sick? Or was it because the belief that "psychiatric vocabularies ... have an elective affinity with psychotherapeutic quietism" was the acceptable leftist stance? (Bart, 1974, p. 17).

In fact, Bart was discrediting psychoanalysis in order to advance "activist psychotherapy" in community mental health clinics, which by then was being financed by the federal government all over the country and which since then has been spreading throughout our society. By maintaining that traditional psychotherapy was for the "inner-directed man," that group therapy was more appropriate for the "other-directed man," and that a focus on environmental factors such as poverty, voter registration, and code enforcement in housing would help the disadvantaged, Bart did point to social problems that needed redressing (Bart, 1974, p. 19). However, in her argument that these had to be dealt with by health professionals, she did not factor in the *economics* of health care and of jobs.

That such care is come by most cheaply through group therapy, and with nondoctors, is self-evident. But does it really follow that "because the humanistic and democratic values of activist psychiatrists are apparent, it is possible to infer their image of the future ... a world without racism and poverty, a world where the decision-making process is democratized so that individuals have some control over their own destiny"? (Bart, 1974, p. 21). Bart stated that this democratic therapy—in which she included role reversal of patient and therapist and which allegedly kept individuals on "bad trips" out of the hands of doctors as well as away from women's liberation consciousness-raising groups—was "not psychoanalytic." Bart's democratic therapy is social therapy, and as such, it may be valid. But precisely because it is not psychoanalysis, it does not include attempts to alter unconscious structures or, I may add, as a rule conscious ones either. Bart, however, went on to repeat that "Freud's thinking reflected nineteenth-century mechanistic physics, that instead of replacing id with ego, freedom consists of the freedom to express feelings, to get closer to people" (p. 29)—as if that had not been Freud's intent as well.

Bart's utopian vision of loving people who would become happy and free by hugging each other and "dropping out" of course appealed to the zeitgeist. And gradually values changed as the liberation movements—by blacks, gays, ethnic minorities, handicapped people, and so on—moved into the mainstream. At first, *all* of these groups claimed common cause and supported each other in local and national endeavors. It is true that the Freudians were trained to look at the *unconscious* motivations of both participants and social formations. Since such investigations are slow by their very nature, hesitant and introspective rather than oriented to immediate action, the psychoanalysts were useless as allies (even when they sympathized) in implementing rapid political change.

Those Freudians who got involved in aspects of the movement addressed global matters such as the prevention of war and the creation of lasting peace. But these activities were outside their clinical practices and were inspired by radical ideas, by what Bart summarized as psychological politics: Esalen-type therapies to encourage inventiveness; encounter therapy for the man who has everything (Bart, 1974, p. 30); and the enjoyment of casual sex by women who value freedom, spontaneity, intimacy, and creativity (p. 32). Bart noted also that community mental health centers flourished only after there was money to alleviate poverty, after community psychiatry and "psychotherapeutic activism" were government funded (p. 44). But she failed to draw the obvious conclusion that thereby the feminist movement had been assisted. Instead, she went on to speculate that in Soviet psychiatry the environment was more manipulable but in the United States the therapist "must limit himself to focusing on the patient's internal world." Of course, therapists have to consider social ills such as poverty and racism as causes of mental illness. But Bart's successful advocacy of community psychiatry, as we now know, did not improve mental health among the poor. Here, however, I am focusing only on the rejection of psychoanalysis: It did not get a separate entry in the index of the anthology (Roman and Trice, 1974) to which Bart contributed. Freud was mentioned in only two articles: one by Berton Kaplan, who pointed to the psychoanalytic process of "working through" the neurotic links, and another by Paul Dommermuth and Rue Bucher, who recounted that American psychiatry after World War II adopted the Freudian psychodynamic model of treatment.

In one of the best, early collections, *Toward a Sociology of Women* (Safilos-Rothschild [1969] 1972), Alice Rossi's "Sex Equality: The Beginnings of Ideology" has just one reference to Freud. Rossi is fairly specific. She bears quoting for her summary of the zeitgeist:

> Freudian theory has contributed to the assumption of innate sex differences, on which recent scholars in psychology and sociology have built their cases for the necessity of social role and status differentiation between the sexes. Freud codified the belief that men get more pleasure than women from sex, in his theory of the sexual development of the female: the transition from an early stage in which girls experience the clitoris as the leading erogenous zone of their bodies to a mature stage in which vaginal orgasm provides the woman with her major sexual pleasure. Women who did not make this transition were then viewed as sexually "anaesthetic" and "psychosexually immature." Psychological theory often seems sterner and more resistant to change than the people to which it is applied. It is incredible

that the Freudian theory of female sexuality was retained for decades despite thousands of hours of intimate therapeutic data from women, only recently showing signs of weakening under the impact of research conducted by Masters and Johnson and reported in their *Human Sexual Response,* that there is no anatomical difference between clitoral and vaginal orgasm. (p. 349)

Undoubtedly, some Freudians were unable to keep up the value-neutral ethos with their patients, but most practicing psychoanalysts did so. Leading feminists did not have access to the privileged information gained from treatment of patients or to the Freudians' own inquiries into the nature of women's orgasm, "masochism," and the "object relations" women internalize. Most feminist scholarship was based on investigations of liberation through new lifestyles and leaned on radical premises rather than on Marx-Freud syntheses. Gradually, the latter reentered the debates.[1] However, as sex therapists and other experts were investigating the origins of both hetero- and homosexual love from their new feminist positions, some of them sooner or later came to address the questions the psychoanalysts had been asking all along. Occasionally they joined them in research projects.

Attitudes Toward Lesbianism

Advocates of lesbianism turned out to be much friendlier to Freud than the run-of-the-mill heterosexual feminists. Dolores Klaich, in *Woman + Woman* (1974), was the first to point at handed-down and popular misconceptions. In spite of Freud's erroneous distinction between clitoral and vaginal orgasm, she stated, he did not say that "lesbianism was ... *necessarily* a neurotic illness ... [or] that it *necessarily* could be 'cured'" (p. 68), and he maintained that it was rarely possible to convert a fully developed homosexual into a heterosexual or to do the reverse. Freud, she noted, contrary to "the school of psychoanalysis in this country," did not categorically pronounce lesbianism a mental illness or wonder whether it was congenital or acquired (p. 69). Instead, she reminded her readers, he found lesbianism to be rooted in the course of female development: "It may result from an overdose of penis envy, [or] ... may center on a woman's unconscious fear of father-daughter incest which she projects on all men" (p. 71). Freud did not claim to know why this happened to some women and not to others; he suggested to the women among his disciples that they investigate further; and he was neither hopeful of "curing" a beautiful young woman of her homosexuality nor very sympathetic to her rich father (p. 72).

After providing examples of happy and well-functioning lesbians, among them writers such as Freud's friend H.D. (Hilda Doolittle), Vita

Sackville-West, and Havelock Ellis's wife, Siri von Essen, Klaich concluded by recounting the case of one of Helene Deutsch's (latent) lesbian patients. During her analysis she developed a strong transference to Deutsch but was unable to do so with her subsequent, male, analyst. However, she then formed her first successful relationship with another woman—both women were replacing the mothers they had wished for in their childhoods—and instead of continuing to be suicidal or depressed, she turned into a radiant human being (Klaich, 1974, pp. 85–87). Only Americans, Klaich pointed out, try to "cure" homosexuals or consider lesbianism analogous to instability or neurosis (p. 89). She showed that opinions often masquerading as science about its possible origins, "curability," and "effects" were all over the place and that the most promising research was being conducted by endocrinologists who were investigating the distribution of male and female sex hormones and its effect on behavior—both in animals and in humans. Although we still don't know the mix of hormonal, psychological, and behavioral influences that make for sexual preferences, Klaich summarized, science has shown that an individual's sexuality can fall anywhere between the polarities of what *society* considers masculine or feminine behavior.

Phyllis Chesler's book, *"Lesbians": Women and Madness* (1972), in which she criticized Freudians for misunderstanding lesbians and advocated lesbian practices to offset women's domination by males and their sexual repression, was a best-seller. At the time, extremist solutions to social problems were being welcomed as antidotes to America's traditional, puritan morality. No one as yet realized that both conventional mores and those of their opponents, and their inherent biases, increasingly would polarize the society.

The research around these issues was driven by the necessity to eradicate prejudice and its practical consequences as well as by ideology and by the urgency to scientifically refute the prevailing narrow definitions of sexual behavior. The Kinsey Report was both upheld and refuted. And studies such as Mary Jane Sherfey's on the evolution of sexuality and John Money and his coworkers' on transsexuality got women of all feminist persuasions together, often in order to disagree. This research seemed to be scientific and serious and, as yet, was not driven by the political agenda.

Bringing Freud Back In

In the social sciences, the debates over the roots and the impact of sexual differences—nature versus nurture, biology versus environment—gradually began to sound commonplace. For instance, it had become de rigueur to cite the much-touted study by Margaret Mead—who had found that in Arapesh society both men and women are gentle and un-aggressive; that among the Mundugumor both sexes are angry and aggressive; that among the Tchambuli women are brisk and efficient in all endeavors and men are not; and that among the Iamutl both boys and girls first are raised to alternate between being gentle and assertive but that boys, after undergoing severe initiation ceremonies, learn to forget their early feminine-type experiences. (After her death, Mead's data was questioned by another expert on Samoa, Derek Freeman [1983].) In addition, an increasingly vast anthropological literature was proving rather conclusively that feminine and masculine behavior is learned; that in most instances it follows the assigned division of labor between men and women; and that in Western societies, where both girls and boys are taught to be independent and assertive and are praised for achievement, only girls are taught by women alone.

During that time, some of the most militant feminist academics were inquiring why childbirth was no longer being assisted by midwives at home but had become the doctors' purview in hospitals, and they investigated power relations on dates and those among parents and their children. Historical reevaluations ranged from Friedrich Engels's views on the origin of the family in antiquity to the subjugation of women in modern societies, from women's unequal treatment by the law to their status as a minority, from hierarchical interactions in the workplace to the exploitation of women in Third World countries. Empirical inquiries increasingly were linked to theories of capitalism and imperialism. They all came back to the fact that throughout history men had made the laws. Still, as recommendations resulting from some of these (American) investigations were being implemented, a few feminists were beginning to wonder why, in the wake of the now more favorable social and professional climate, the requisite psychological attitudes did not spontaneously emerge.

Thus a number of women started to question their ambivalences toward husbands, fathers, and bosses; the submissive attitudes they still succumbed to even when they didn't have to do so; and the guilt they felt when leaving their children in order to go to work. They asked, for instance, why, as Elizabeth Janeway had predicted, a change in the mother's position in the world did not automatically alter the relationship to her daughter and her daughter's life as well (Strouse, 1974, p. 70).

In other words, some of the most intellectually curious women in the movement looked more closely at the findings that kept blaming patriarchy, social institutions, and structures—and men alone—for the fact that women's psyches were not keeping step with the transformations the feminist movement already had brought about. They had advanced all the neo-Marxist arguments, had managed to eliminate many (though far from all) of the legal hurdles standing in women's way, but so far had failed to engender the hoped-for emotional ease that was to have been a by-product of the increasingly androgenous roles women were expected to assume. As noted in Chapter 3, Juliet Mitchell addressed some of these issues, but from the sort of exogenous perspective the women in the American movement were not yet prepared for.

Already in 1971, when America's leading feminists still were totally opposed to psychoanalysis, Nancy Chodorow, a sociologist, began to tilt her research in that direction when as a graduate student she embarked upon "Being and Doing: Cross-Cultural Examination of the Socialization of Males and Females" (in Chodorow, 1989). She enlarged the anthropologists' debates by adding that girls' socialization is more of a piece, more continuous than that of boys—who are taught by both their mothers and fathers to differentiate themselves from girls and to suppress what are considered feminine traits. In some cultures the feminine is more repressed than in others, and low father-salience, she found, may lead girls to react by adopting masculine behavior, to reject anything feminine.

Chodorow cited psychological studies of behavioral variation by sex and age across cultures to show that young girls tend to prefer more intimacy than boys and to show more dependency; that girls get increasingly more nurturant as they get older; and that boys are more aggressive at all ages. And she held that this does not mean that these differences are biologically determined: They are related to what youngsters actually do, to what is expected of them, and to the type of society they belong to. She held that cultural complexity, household organization, and size of the family group determine child-rearing practices and thus the accepted socialization into sex roles.

Chodorow went beyond the then run-of-the-mill feminist inquiries in the way she differentiated the tasks boys and girls in Western societies must learn while they grow up. Girls are more easily initiated into their adult roles than boys because they watch what their mothers do all along; but boys, especially in urban settings, cannot observe their fathers' work, which is away from home. And whereas boys have to prove their manhood on a daily basis with successes, girls have a (prescribed) goal—to marry and have children—that is more readily attainable: They are trained to "be" whereas boys are trained to "do," to become creators (Chodorow, 1989, p. 33). (She soon was quoted by most feminists.) Chodorow reintroduced Horney's concept of the man's "dread of women," which, we recall, derives from having been brought up by a mother who had total power over him. To compensate, men later on gain power by reserving prestigious activities for themselves. Thus they have trouble according women equal status in the workplace.

But, Chodorow went on, "the threat of femininity is internal as well as external." Thereby, she reintroduced psychoanalysis into the feminist dialogues. Boys' fear of the feminine, she demonstrated, is repressed particularly well in more advanced societies and tends to engender also their assertion of masculinity. Still, "the fear of the womanly power which has remained *within* men [through their early closeness and identification with women]—the bisexual components of any man's personality"—remains an enormous threat. Women, however, develop in a self-perpetuating cycle of female deprecation; girls are reared by mothers who have internalized the negative view of women. This seemed clear among little girls who, among other things, were found to prefer masculine roles more than little boys preferred feminine ones. This preference, cited Chodorow, increases with age from kindergarten to fourth grade, as girls realize more and more that boys get a better deal (Chodorow, 1989, p. 42). "As long as women must live through their children," she concluded, they "will continue to bring up sons whose sexual identity depends on devaluing femininity inside and outside themselves, and daughters who must accept this devalued position and resign themselves to producing more men who will perpetuate the system that devalues them" (p. 44).

Chodorow had participated in a mother-daughter group and had explored the differences that characterize masculine and feminine personality and roles. Instead of focusing on analyses of role training, which had become so customary, she looked at the unconscious qualities of feminine development—at what is obvious to psychoanalysts but disputed by sociologists, such as the child's primary identification with and dependence on its mother, its oral-incorporative relationship to the world, and its push-pull involvement in issues of separation and individuation during the first years of life. While emphasizing the fact that girls identify with their own mothers, she explicitly followed Helene Deutsch, who stated that in motherhood they repeat their own mother-child history and thereby remain bound in a mutually dependent "hypersymbiotic" relationship (Chodorow, 1989, p. 48). (A mother, Chodorow noted, tends to identify less with a son but to push him into a male role that may be unsuitable to his age and undesirable at any age in his relationship to her [p. 49].)

All along, Chodorow's understanding of the oedipal triangle relied more on Deutsch than on Freud, on Deutsch's observation that "a girl wavers in a 'bisexual triangle' throughout her childhood ... now the mother, now the father plays the principal part" (Chodorow, 1989, p. 53). Adult behavior is determined by the quality of these early experiences, but these are not biologically deterministic; and sex-role training in childhood builds upon unconscious development. Translating psychoanalytic concepts into sociological ones and taking women's biosexual experiences into account, Chodorow found that because Western women's ego boundaries are firmer than those in simpler societies, they have more difficulty moving across these boundaries. To explain these ego boundaries theoretically, she delved more deeply into psychoanalytic formulations. She brought in Harry Guntrip's (a British psychoanalyst) distinctions between mature and immature dependence and classified Western middle-class women as remaining in an infantile relationship and women in matrifocal societies—because they continue to maintain definite connections to others—as more mature and more able to receive and give in an adult, independent fashion and to develop a strong sense of self (pp. 61–62).

Because she shifted her focus to unconscious, psychological causes, feminists in the social sciences who until then were in the forefront of the movement criticized Chodorow for her individualistic approach: They blamed the political system, some of its components, or imperialism in general. Thus they either had to oppose Chodorow's scholarship or relinquish some of their own views. All in all, it was as uncomfortable not to chime in with the Freud-bashing and not to get actively involved in radical, political actions as it was to be antifeminist or on the political right. (Attacks from that camp are outside the scope of this book.) Yet recourse to psychoanalytic theory itself was considered reactionary.

At the time, the French discussions had barely been heard, although Chodorow approved of Gayle Rubin, who in 1975 criticized the Marxist-feminist project from Lévi-Strauss's perspective and came up with a "sex/gender system" analysis of society. And in "Oedipal Asymmetries and Heterosexual Knots" Chodorow cited Janine Chasseguet-Smirgel's and Bela Grunberger's theory of the father as "the girl's last-ditch escape from maternal omnipotence, ... [from] the narcissistic relationship her mother (inevitably) imposes on her, but not on her brother" (1989, pp. 71–72).

Then, few French contributions had as yet been translated, mostly because the movement had not yet paid attention and because sociologists primarily were concerned with empirical studies of Third World women and of racism and sexism in America. Still, German psychoanalyst Alexander Mitscherlich's *Society Without the Father* ([1963] 1969) had come out in English, and Chodorow quoted him somewhat out of context in order to prove that when fathers are "comparatively unavailable physically and emotionally" their children suffer (Chodorow, 1989, p. 51). Whereas Mitscherlich referred to *German* fathers who first were away at war and later on refused to tell their children about these experiences and about their participation in Nazi activities, Chodorow talked of American fathers who were gone all day so that mothers who took care of the children had learned to be more independent. And she paralleled the contradictions in the resulting German family relations to those in capitalist societies. Although this point was a bow to the prevailing radicalism, she commented in a functionalist sociological vein that when "divorce rates soar, people flock to multitudes of new therapies, politicians decry and sociologists document the end of the family. And there develops a new feminism" (p. 78).

In the 1960s and early 1970s women advocated access to safe contraception, abortion, and community day care; by 1976 women could legally choose to prevent or terminate a pregnancy. Chodorow then focused on *how* women mother. She criticized, for instance, Nancy Friday, who demonstrated in her bestseller *My Mother/My Self* (1977) that mothers make daughters in their image and then are blamed for whatever problems these daughters encounter throughout their lives, and Dorothy Dinnerstein's *The Mermaid and the Minotaur* (1976) for confusing the infantile fantasy of the mother's "absolute power" with actual maternal behavior (Chodorow, 1989, p. 81). Ultimately, Chodorow showed that all feminist theorists "blame the mother," idealize her possibilities of being perfect and self-sacrificing, or attribute love/hate ambivalences to patriarchy. Instead, she argued that "a theory of mothering requires a theory of childhood and child development" rather than a range of partial (psychoanalytic or sociological) assumptions (p. 95).

Chodorow distinguished sharply between sexuality (biology) and gender (constituted by social, cultural, and psychological phenomena). In *The Reproduction of Mothering* (1978) she still held that male dominance is the prime mover of mothering. After that book, she considered the self as the product of primary emotional relationships. And she began to apply object-relations theory to questions of sex and gender differences and to describe the development of the "I," or the self, during separation and individuation—the way the child learns to differentiate itself from its mother, disrupts the narcissistic relation, and learns to perceive her as separate. The more psychoanalytic she became, the more she moved away from what was getting to be mainstream feminism.

Still, Chodorow, in her essay "Beyond Drive Theory: Object Relations and the Limits of Radical Individualism" (1989), succeeded in explaining how and why the self is much more than a cognitive process, that it incorporates affectively loaded unconscious representations of others (p. 105). She did so by simplifying psychoanalytic language—without simplifying the theory—and relating it to feminist and sociological concepts such as agency, authenticity, and sense of self. Moreover, she elaborated just how feminists can learn from the general inquiry into "differentiation, ... includ[ing] the internalization of aspects of the primary care-taker and of the caretaking relationship, ... [and] attitudes and expectations of mothers and women in general (p. 107).

Along with psychoanalysts Roy Schafer and Robert Stoller, Chodorow rejected Freud's concept of penis envy. But she did agree that "gender identity and the sense of masculinity and femininity develop differently for men and women" (Chodorow, 1989, p. 109). Girls have difficulty in establishing a "feminine" identity because they relate to "a negatively valued gender category and an ambivalently experienced maternal figure." Men "have come to define maleness as that which is basically human, and to define women as not men." If we were to manage a different type of "parenting, and other distributions of power between the sexes," argued Chodorow, women's lives and self-definitions could become more oriented toward themselves, and differences from men would be less salient (p. 112). She ended up by taking a firm stand against those feminists who argue for the notion of an "essential difference" between men and women rather than for an understanding of the differences. In the 1980s, this was one of the central divisions among feminists. Basically, the so-called essentialists did not make allowances for psychologically induced changes in subjectivity and postulated a sort of biological or psychic determinism. But the debate has kept shifting, most recently to oppositions between those who argue that sexuality is partially based on biological factors and those who attribute all differences to environmentally caused gender differences. (Agreement on details, moreover, is rare.)

In response to her feminist critics who questioned Freud's possible contributions to the movement, Chodorow countered that he divorced sexuality from gender and procreation; that he insisted that there is nothing inevitable about the development of sexual object-choice, mode, or aim; that we are all potentially bisexual, active, or passive; that these feelings and fantasies may be shaped by other than biological factors; and that "normal" female development is very costly to women (Chodorow, 1989, pp. 168–169). Against role-learning theory, which is central to sociology and which turns people into *passive* reactors, she maintained that psychoanalysis, by making the unconscious conscious, is a theory of *active* people in spite of the fact that "Freud was sexist" and that his hypotheses have been used against women. And she insisted that antiwomen statements are extrinsic to his theories.

Carol Gilligan, a psychologist, published *In a Different Voice: Psychological Theory and Women's Development* in 1982. While listening to people's voices over the previous ten years, she stated in her introduction, she was struck by the fact that women's voices sounded distinct, differ-

ent from men's. Gilligan does not fit strictly into the Freudian framework. But her reliance on Chodorow's conclusion that "girls come to
experience themselves as less differentiated than boys, as more continuous with and related to the external object-world, and as differently oriented to their inner object-world" engaged her with the feminist-psy-
choanalytic dialogue ([1982] 1993, p. 8). So did her rather negative
(though informed) assessment and inclusion of Freud: He equated the
capacity to love with maturity and psychic health and located its origins
in the contrast between love for the mother and love for the self. And
"relying on the imagery of men's lives in charting the course of human
growth, Freud is unable to trace in women the development of relationships, morality, or a clear sense of self ... [which] leads him to conclude
that they are 'a dark contintent' for psychology" (p. 24). This conception
of human relationships, stated Gilligan, engenders different ways of understanding rights and responsibilities, of the self and of morality, and
could bring about a better understanding of human relationships.

To those Freudian analysts who still wondered what Freud had to do
with feminism and (non-Freudian) female psychology or with politics
and issues of inequality, Chodorow responded that character neuroses
and defenses always develop in relation to others, to social expectations.
She said that because psychoanalysis is based on objective description
but comes out of the transference situation, out of the process of free association and interpretation of it, it is not the value-free science some
(American) psychoanalysts claim. Accordingly, Chodorow advocated
that Freud's value judgments and ad hominem claims about women be
discarded as part of *his* times and that psychoanalysts pay more attention to male dominance on the psychological level as a masculine defense built on fears and insecurity in response to the mother, the first
object-love.

Antipsychoanalytic views, of course, are almost built into sociological
theory. As I argued in "The Uses of Psychoanalysis in Critical Theory and
Structuralism" (1984), in "Macro and Micro Structures in Psychoanalysis" (1987), and elsewhere, a true integration of the two disciplines ultimately is not possible: Psychoanalysts *must* penetrate to unconscious
structures, whereas sociologists *must* analyze only what is empirically
observable. Sociologists who have incorporated psychoanalytic principles into their work, such as Talcott Parsons and Robert Merton, have
subsumed unconscious mechanisms into their concepts of role. Had
such analyses been more useful in bringing about social change, neither
Chodorow nor those who pursued similar theoretical paths in the 1980s
would have had to reintroduce psychoanalysis.[2]

Sexuality and Gender from Various Perspectives

Outside the social sciences, literary works were being examined to better explain why traditional patterns of male and female behavior kept hanging on in spite of the many efforts to break them. In the 1970s in literary studies, both psychoanalysis and antipsychoanalytic theories were explored more fully and less rigidly than before, often with much imagination. However, psychoanalytic criticism flourished in the 1950s and 1960s, most conspicuously that by Lionel Trilling, and this approach now was being lumped with conservatism. Nevertheless, his enterprise, which itself perpetuated endeavors by the early Freudians, encouraged cooperation between literary professors and psychoanalysts. Inevitably, the fact that literature eschews formulas and thrives on talent and originality and that literary criticism interprets writing in relation to the world it inhabits, a society loosened of its former moorings advances ever looser and more ingenious interpretations. It probably is no accident that the best, and most representative, collection of feminist efforts in this genre was coedited by literary scholar Catharine Stimpson and psychoanalyst Ethel Person, both of whom, incidentally, were at Columbia University. The collection was published in the 1980 summer and fall issues of *Signs: Journal of Women in Culture and Society*.

Stimpson and Person assembled materials that continued to be discussed thoughout the 1980s. In their introduction, they took stock of the state of "sex and sexuality" within the women's movement. They found that investigations into female sexuality suffered from both "garish sensationalism and rigid conventionality"; that researchers with egalitarian biases preferred to see male and female sexualities as essentially identical, had shunned differences, and thereby often had masculinized the model of sexuality (Stimpson and Person, 1980, p. 1). Stimpson and Person declared that they distrusted theories of sexuality that are mirror images of the male, that universalize or reify it. Instead, they held that "to understand female sexuality is to explore the power of social constructions of reality and symbolic transformations of what seem to be matters of natural fact" (p. 2). In other words, the editors chose to usher in 1980s feminism by leaving behind the bra-burning and excessively ideological manifestations of the previous decade, not only in order to save the movement from internal chaos and external attacks but to build it up by investigating more thoroughly the values that underpin the matrices of female sexuality within specific contexts and the influences of "erotic desire and gratification, motherhood, the relationship between self-actualization and sexuality, the mutual transformations of sex into metaphor and metaphors into behavior" (p. 2).

In /"Who Is Sylvia? On the Loss of Sexual Paradigms," Elizabeth Janeway asked what femaleness is in Western society. Two pictures have existed side by side, she answered, as symbolized by Mary, the chaste virgin and mother, and by Eve and Lilith, the temptress and the whore. Janeway maintained that these are products of divided minds, of views of self and other that are at war within each woman: "Eve cannot trust Mary, nor Mary Eve" (Stimpson and Person, 1980, p. 7). Janeway elaborated on this idea with examples from the Bible and Victorian literature that romanticize woman as the wife and mother, a romanticization that makes for the oedipal conflict (p. 8) and ends up manipulating women's visions of themselves (p. 9). In the 1980s, however, Janeway said, chastity in women no longer was valued, no longer served a necessary social function as filtered through the belief structure of the male power elite. Thus the Mary myth had dimmed and Eve, "tricked out in polyester ... as the *Cosmopolitan* girl ... . has lost the opposing force that controlled her attraction and her menace" (p. 15). This Eve, stated Janeway, serves patriarchy insofar as she remains a sexual object rather than a sexual being. To find a new paradigm of female sexuality, she concluded, women must discover new ways of interacting that grow out of their own needs in response to changed lives, to present realities (p. 20).

Like Janeway, Alix Kates Shulman, another writer, assimilated social science research into her sweeping essay "Sexual Bases of Radical Feminism," which covered the previous thirteen years. She recounted the denigrations by New Left men; the demonstrations by feminists in 1968—the one against the Miss America Pageant, the Whistle-In on Wall Street (when women made sexual passes at men), the takeover of legislative hearings on prostitution—and the later ones that proliferated like mushrooms. She recalled that in 1970 lesbian feminists began forming separate groups; that the self-help movement encouraged women to examine their own and each other's bodies; that speak-outs on abortion, rape, prostitution, marriage, and motherhood were spreading everywhere and everywhere were attacking the power of men over women. Feminine rebellion against sexual exploitation went from forming antimarriage groups to reordering women's priorities away from the sexual and from advocating life without men to ways of reversing power relations. However, stated Shulman, women had been too optimistic and had underestimated the resistance of antifeminists and the fact that personal solutions to sexual problems obscure the power play inherent in sexual relations (Stimpson and Person, 1980, p. 34).

Shulman did not go into the reasons for this resistance or wonder whether the very extremism of these views and actions might not have caused the decline in the activism of women who *did* want to live with men and realized, either consciously or unconsciously that reproduction *is* a necessity for the survival of the species. In other words, she did not acknowledge the success of the movement: Because equal or nearly equal opportunities for women had been mandated, women now would be competing with each other as well as with men in order to take advantage of these opportunities. A plateau had been reached; the war had been nearly won but the peace had yet to be secured.

From a psychoanalytic perspective, Person attempted to provide the psychological understanding for the road ahead. She argued that before feminists could truly restructure society, they required an inclusive, overarching theory of sexuality and that such a theory would benefit from psychoanalytic insights. With the feminists, Person challenged the popular assumptions that sexuality flourishes when freed of cultural repression and that female sexuality is inhibited (hyposexual) but male sexuality represents the norm (Stimpson and Person, 1980, p. 36). She differentiated carefully between biological sex, gender, sexual behavior, and reproduction and between theories about the nature of sexuality and about sexual motivation. All these theories, she went on, try to explain too much: the motor force behind the desire for sexual behavior; the strength of individuals' sexual impulses; the absence, avoidance, or inhibition of sexuality and its variable intensity; the many erotic stimuli and situations that may trigger them; and the existence of a "sex print"—that is, an individual's resistances to erotic stimuli, the sexual and nonsexual meanings in both sexual and nonsexual behavior, and cultural preoccupations with sexuality (pp. 37–38). In addition, Person pointed out, two major paradigms explain the source of sexual motivation: a biological (libido) theory postulating a fixed sexual drive and an "appetitional" (conditioned) one acknowledging a neural reflex for orgasmic release. Whereas the former assumes that tension will be discharged via sublimation, neurosis, or perversion, the latter considers the pursuit of pleasure to be the motive behind sexuality. But neither of them, Person said, is as satisfactory as the "amalgam of Freud's psychological theory and object-relations theory, which places the appetitional component in a developmental motivational context" (p. 38). Person elaborated on the pros and cons of the first two paradigms and summarized the arguments of their major proponents and opponents. And she argued for an object-relations approach—even though it too is limited by problems of internalization, such as affect, perception, maturational stages, and conflict. In other words, she maintained that object-relations theory could account for the impact of culture on sexuality and that "culture" can explain neither how sexuality influences the development of the autonomous personality nor the variations of personality structure within each culture (p. 46).

Chodorow had reached the same conclusion, although she probably emphasized culture over nature. Person, however, who had had many adolescents on her analytic couch, went on to enumerate their typical fantasies, which reflected both sexual and nonsexual motives. Thus she concluded that sexual liberation and female liberation are separate but that structures of gender and sex print do mediate between sexuality and identity formation—a situation that complicates liberating sexuality from the contaminants of power.

Susan Baker, in "Biological Influences on Human Sex and Gender," reviewed the literature on biological influences on human sex (object choice) and gender (identity and role behavior) from a newly emerging field, psychoendocrinology. Researchers, she reported, had investigated the interactions of biology and environment, beginning with genetic chromosomal patterns and gonadal differentiation and prenatal hormonal environment and anatomical parameters, and then examined possible individual variations after birth. They had found that when female fetuses were exposed to abnormally high levels of androgens there were behavioral-temperamental consequences but that this did not influence the choice of sex objects in adolescence. And she concluded that much more research would be needed on the influence of hormones on specific brain receptors before we may be able to infer how these factors influence the formation of gender identity.

Other contributors to this volume of *Signs* addressed such topics as reproductive rights, menstruation and reproduction, menstruation and behavior, maternal sexuality and motherhood, pornography, prostitution, pregnancy—all of them with an eye on practices in the past and views to the future and all of them drawing on the burgeoning scholarship on these subjects and keeping in mind political ends.

Adrienne Rich, a poet and novelist, for example, argued against what she called the perception of lesbianism by other feminist writers as an acting out of bitterness toward men and went on to explore, mostly via literary works, why feminst scholarship, theory, and criticism are so devoid of understanding of the lesbian existence and lesbians' double lives, which is an acquiescence to institutions founded on male interests. In his review of Masters and Johnson's *Homosexuality in Perspective,* psychoanalyst Arnold Cooper attacked the book as "filled with moralisms, banalities, and tables conveying extraordinarily little information," which rendered the data more than suspect (Stimpson and Person, 1980, p. 288). Cooper had supported their earlier work. But from this research, which he felt was shoddy and culled from an unreliable sample, he found that one could not conclude that homosexuals in general communicate better sexually than heterosexuals, as the authors claimed. Nor could one treat this result as characteristic of homosexuality, since sexual functioning in a laboratory leaves out entire populations whose emotional makeup would make them dysfunctional in such a setting and who would not be willing to participate. In sum, Masters and Johnson, said Cooper, appeared to have carried out research that would find what they wanted to find. (Such polemics, as we will see in Chapter 8, increased in crescendo when, during the Second Wave of feminism, ever more complex theories in lesbian and gay studies, and in film theory, moved to the center and were mixed in with psychoanalytic feminism.) In these 1980 volumes of *Signs,* however—volumes that were, in themselves, the summation of the decade's cultural concerns—women's reproductive freedom and prostitution, menstruation and pregnancy, maternal sexuality and asexual motherhood, compulsory heterosexuality and the sexual bases of power, were the central concerns.

The review by Elinor Shaffer of the first volume of Michel Foucault's *The History of Sexuality* ([1976] 1978) was the only contribution to the *Signs* issues that signaled the coming theoretical turn in feminist pursuits.[3] She pointed out, correctly, that Foucault's inquiry, just like his *Madness and Civilization* (1961), *Discipline and Punish* (1972), and other works, was short on documentation. Foucault maintained that contrary to Freud's observations that sexuality had been repressed, discourse about it had been flourishing and had been converted into a new domain in which power could be displayed and technology employed: People spoke about sex ad infinitum, exploited it as *the* secret. Essentially, Foucault explained sexual practices by making heretofore unmade connections: Emerging knowledge about sexuality in the evolving disciplinary society during the nineteenth century devised the hysterical woman, the masturbating child, the Malthusian couple, and the perverse adult and thereby enlarged the power base of those already in positions of power (Stimpson and Person, 1980, p. 305).

Inevitably, I cannot do justice in a paragraph to the history and analyses Foucault accumulated in this and the following three volumes (he died in 1984 before he could finish this work) or engage in his critics' voluminous discourses. But it is important to recall that his ideas had been neglected in America, although in the late 1970s they were accepted as part of the "structuralist movement," which, among other things, was cast as a boon to the radicalization of society. Then and later, however, Foucault's ideas were picked up piecemeal to the extent that they made the points deemed important by feminist (and gay and lesbian) theorists. (See Chapters 5 and 6.) However, Foucault, too, incorporated psychoanalytic lore and took for granted that it had penetrated to the most intimate as well as the most social of our practices, that it had become ubiquitous. Thus the endorsement of Foucault's theories meant that the unconscious was becoming a subject to contend with. This is not to say that feminists like Bart or Rossi, or other sociologists, would reverse their positions but that other women moved to the forefront of the movement and that some of these would—explicitly or implicitly—espouse Freudian notions from a variety of French structuralist perspectives.

Geoffrey H. Hartman's *Psychoanalysis and the Question of the Text* (1978) was not geared to feminist issues. However, as Hartman announced in his preface, "The emphasis has shifted from producing yet another interpretation, ... to understanding from within the institutional development of psychoanalysis ... what kind of event in the history of interpretation psychoanalysis is proving to be" (p. vii). As the first contributor, Murray M. Schwartz stated, "My topic [is] no less than the possibilities for criticism today. ... I have moments when I hear a babble of critical voices drowning the voices criticism was intended to amplify" (p. 1). Norman Holland echoed this sentiment by asking "how texts correct or limit their own interpretations ... [which] may stem more from personal or communal constructions, myths, or ways of reading than from the text. One needs to consider the whole transaction in which the reader re-creates the literary experience rather than a text supposed to be isolated or 'objective'" (p. 18). From now on, as writing about texts replaced writing about books, the attacks on objectivity snowballed and, among other things, eventually became the backbone of the Second Wave of psychoanalytic feminism but not of psychoanalysts or social scientists and historians.

Still, more of the psychoanalysts' contributions were being discussed; among sociologists, Chodorow was joined by Jessica Benjamin (1978, 1988), Sherri Turkle (1978), Robert Endleman (1981), and myself (1980, 1983 [with William Phillips], 1984, 1987, 1989a, 1989b). But as the center of feminism imperceptibly shifted to departments of literature and French, a new type of academic was spawned, the feminist theorist. These theorists' disregard of empiricism, their love of hyperbole and verbal shock, combined with the political activism all women had learned since the mid-1970s, made it possible for them to take over the direction of many departments in American universities. Soon, they would control professional associations and jobs, especially through the Modern Language Association (MLA), whose publication, the *Proceedings of the Modern Languages Association* (PMLA), already in 1976 "present[ed] a critic speaking of critics as if the trajectories of their careers had displaced the ones they write about" (p. 1).

So although the country was moving to the right under Republican administrations and the backlash to feminism in the country at large was manifested in many a state law against abortion, in the defeat of the Equal Rights Amendment in Congress, and in the appointment of con-

servative judges, the discourse in many universities was being con-
quered by radical feminists and their coalition partners in black studies
(soon to be called Afro-American and then African American studies)
and then in gay and lesbian studies. Some lumped Freud with the
DWEMs, or dead white European males, whom they blamed for all inequalities, and others focused on the language of psychoanalysis in
Freudian, Lacanian, and one or another new garb. In order to explain
what happened, we have to understand why Lacan's reading of Freud
became so congenial not only to feminists who had denigrated Freud
but to the various newly minted offshoots of Lacanianisms and their
American incarnations. Altogether, and without anyone's awareness, the
leftist, cultural unconscious was moving into what later would be called
"politically correct" formulations—which the French never anticipated
or foresaw. With these formulations began what I consider the Second
Wave of feminism, which in its psychoanalytic incarnation no longer
was linking theory and therapy à la Freud, but theory and imagination à
la Lacan.

5 Jacques Lacan and French Feminism

The Second Wave of American feminism relied heavily on Jacques Lacan's rereading of Freud's texts and on publications by his entourage. This shift of focus from Freud's cases to deciphering the way he wrote them up inevitably sparked the imagination of literary scholars. Thus it should not surprise us that in America Lacan's ideas first were explored in departments of literature and that in this environment empirical inquiries of women's concerns by sociologists and anthropologists took a backseat. Moreover, Freudians all along had analyzed literary works and their authors' lives in tandem, and such critics as Lionel Trilling, Erich Heller, and Norman Holland had championed psychoanalytic critiques. In the mid-1970s, some professors of English extended this method to a variety of approaches based on Lacanian concepts. And like those psychoanalysts who increasingly were emphasizing the verbal components of their therapies, American feminists were beginning to probe theories of feminism with the help of linguistic psychoanalysis.

By infusing American ego psychology with analyses based on Saussurean structural linguistics, the emerging feminist theories became inordinately complex and no longer adhered to the proverbial American pragmatism. Lacan maintained that misunderstanding was a necessary component of the language of the unconscious to drive home the fact that even as we uncover some previously unconscious knowledge we already are in the process of adding yet another layer of unconscious content. To account for this process, he advocated that his followers keep decoding the unconscious elements and intermittent perceptions of all dialogues—even though ultimately ambiguities and misunderstandings never can be clarified. In America, these necessary misinterpretations were multiplied by mistranslations and misapprehensions such as Lacan's *phallus* being translated as phallus or penis, his *jouissance* as joy or pleasure.

The difficulty of untangling Lacan's thought is compounded by the fact that, like Gilles Deleuze and Felix Guattari ([1972] 1977), he used some of his own new concepts to postulate innovative unconscious structures—similar to the way Foucault elaborated on some of Marx's and Nietzsche's theories to create his novel system of knowledge/power—and that he was purposefully obtuse. Some of his feminist disciples went even further insofar as they played imaginatively with Lacanian formulations about female sexuality and infused them with the radical perspectives of Marx and Foucault.

Lacan's *Ecrits* ([1966] 1977) was translated in 1977, just three years before Elaine Marks and Isabelle de Courtivron (1980) compiled their collection of French feminist texts. They began their introduction to over fifty excerpts from militant women's works—among these women were Hélène Cixous, Simone de Beauvoir, Luce Irigaray, Monique Wittig, Catherine Clément, Monique Schneider, and Julia Kristeva—by regretting that American feminists had not had access to these provocative ideas sooner (p. ix). As liberated women, the editors felt a bond with their French counterparts, and especially with the left wing of the Movement Libération des Femmes (MLF), Psychanalyse et Politique. According to Marks and Courtivron, these women, under the aegis of Antoinette Fouque, exercised a sort of intellectual terrorism over feminist publishing after 1968 (p. 31). These French militant women's exact position was unclear: They refused to join "feminist" manifestations because they viewed them as imitations of male power; they were convinced that there can be no revolution without disrupting the symbolic order that, according to Lacan, is instituted within the individual's language and that the ensuing social relations must be disrupted (p. 33). Another group, the Féministes Révolutionnaires, whose foremost spokeswoman was Monique Wittig, was convinced it had to eschew all collaboration by men, and the lesbians in the group were certain that a lesbian position alone could withstand appropriation by a patriarchal, capitalist society (p. 33). And there were poetic and literary manifestations and a wide range of political demonstrations as well. In sum, radical women feminists espoused a revolutionary direction, defined and redefined their positions, and much of the time relied on (or brought in) Lacanian thought.

By then, French feminists already had been stimulated by the so-called structuralist movement, and they were familiar with the ins and outs of Lévi-Strauss's mediations between nature and culture, with Roland Barthes's elaborations on written and social texts, with Foucault's historical associations of power and knowledge, and with Althusser's search for a "scientific" and theoretical Marxist practice. But by the mid-1970s, along with the other Parisian intellectuals, they had more or less given up on instituting these theories as practices. However, for American feminists, who had been functioning within their own tradition and had pursued their own concrete, political agendas, these ideas provided food for new theorizing. In 1980, when the French feminists' bon mots and political savvy were being introduced in America, these ideas, for the most part, no longer played a large role in Paris. The appeal of American feminism as well was diminishing in the culture at large. And a backlash against its more extreme demands had gained strength. Hence the application of French (theoretical) radicalism was to serve as a shot in the arm, at least within the academy.

Marks and Courtivron recounted that most French feminists primarily were concerned with publicly addressing theoretical issues such as sexism, repression-oppression, Marxism, *embourgeoisement,* and the Freudian libidinal force that is said to respresent the instincts in the mind. By then, radical French feminists were split over the means of reaching their ends—via revolution, reform, or collaboration, by accepting or excluding men. Some advocated a separatist politics based on a theory of oppression in line with sex and class, others emphasized patriarchy as the first social relation and thus the primary culprit, yet others preferred to incorporate feminism into a strict class analysis. The most noted among them, the women who belonged to Psychanalyse et Politique, assumed that women's different voices emerged from their sexuality, from their personal politics, and thus rejected the less confrontational "political feminism": Accepting men within their ranks to them was too assimilationist and reformist. Thus they broke with the larger movement and became more and more sectarian.

American feminists had not been privy to these debates. They lacked the general grounding in philosophy the French routinely learn in their lycées and belonged to a more pragmatic and empirical tradition. As noted in Chapter 4, in the 1970s they organized political interest groups, managed to push through changes in divorce and child care legislation, and won many entitlements—though most of these were on the state rather than the federal level. Enterprising American women had infiltrated many institutions but had not come to dominate them.

Largely because American women, like their male counterparts, were inclined to action rather than to philosophy, their aims were political rather than philosophical or theoretical. Marks and Courtivron articulated this difference concisely in their preface:

> In France the most stimulating texts of the new feminisms are being written by women of letters, intellectuals, professors of literature and philosophy, psychoanalysts, formed by a new radical anti-bourgeois bias, steeped in Marxist culture, trained in dialectical thinking. ... [They] concentrate on the acts of reading and writing as subversive, political. ... They have assimilated ... Western philosophical and literary discourse ... have profited in varying degrees from Kojève's and Hippolyte's rereadings of Hegel, Lévi-Strauss's rereading of Saussure, Lacan's rereading of Freud, Althusser's re-

reading of Marx, Derrida's rereading of the Hegelian, existentialist, and structuralist traditions. (1980, xii)

Marks and Courtivron related the philosophical roots and cultural matrix of specific French feminist ideas to the leading male figures. Just like the male intellectuals, feminists had been influenced by Sartre's existentialism, by Michel Foucault's ([1976] 1978) new interpretations of power and knowledge, and by Gilles Deleuze and Felix Guattari's ([1972] 1977) depictions of modern society as schizoid, peopled by human "desiring machines" in "factories of desire" they cannot control (p. 1). Some of the feminists had flirted with Althusser's "scientific Marxism" and wanted to get beyond it; others had advocated academic Marxism and now turned to Nietzsche: His nihilism appealed to them as they were moving away from the (linguistically fueled) structuralism that had been delegitimated by the upheavals of 1968—which had signaled the breakdown of existing structures.

The American feminists whom Marks and Courtivron (1980) were addressing were intrigued with the esoteric pieces reprinted in their book. Unfortunately, they could reproduce no more than snippets of larger works, which meant that anyone not steeped in the intricacies of the debates had trouble understanding them properly. Most American readers were bound to misread: They were unfamiliar with the circumstances that had given rise to the French feminists' notions in the first place and did not know the reasons for the choice of these excerpts. Consequently, American feminists were bound to pick up specific notions haphazardly and were missing the context of the discussions and replacing it with their own history and polemics. Thus they could not help but ignore the internal logic of French feminism when they reflected on one or another of the clever pronouncements and applied them to their own bailiwick. Nor could they clearly distinguish between high-flown metaphors and French puns that could not but be lost in translation. And the Americans did not realize, at least at first, that the French rhetoric was heavily laced with the binary oppositions Saussurean linguistic concepts take for granted—and with Lévi-Strauss's anthropological abstractions built upon them—and that French feminists either accepted Lacan's obscure aphorisms as God-given truths or engaged in refutations of them. In sum, American feminists who started to warm to the French debates and to appropriate them to their own ends inevitably distorted and glorified them. At first, they responded to Lacan's promises of liberation and later on focused on the chauvinist elements in the theoretical underpinnings.

In order to show how and why this happened, we have to examine Lacan's "return to Freud." In addition, we have to recall that the purpose of his rereading was not only to liberate French women but to vindicate Lacan in his battles against the leading members of the (conservative) International Psychoanalytic Association (IPA).

Jacques Lacan's Ascent in Paris

In retrospect, we can say that Lacan won. But both Lacan and the Freudians in the IPA ultimately lost out to the simplifiers they all tried to keep at bay. For nearly two decades, like Freud before him but much more suddenly and dramatically, Lacan was a culture hero. But Lacan differed from Freud insofar as he did not add to psychoanalytic knowledge by means of self-analysis or by revealing his personal history. He kept his private life private, except to the extent that it would enhance his public persona. So whereas interpretations of Freud's thought—in terms of Vienna's fin de siècle mores, anti-Semitism, religion, or politics—incorporate allusions to and memories of his early life, Lacanian tenets are grounded in his novel and "corrected" understanding of Freud's texts rather than in the experiences of the young Lacan. Only since his death, after 1981, have books by a score of lapsed disciples and Anglo-Saxon academics rooted his thought in his Catholic upbringing or in his earlier immersion in surrealism (Macey, 1988; Lee, 1990; Bowie, 1991).

Among recent evaluations, Catherine Clément's *Lives and Legends of Jacques Lacan* ([1981] 1983) stands out for its direct, lively prose and for portraying Lacan's magnetic charm, his ability to attract and hold attention:

> The best of his listeners [in his seminars] knew how to recognize the moment when inspiration was about to explode. It was a marvelous spectacle: if only one side of Lacan's genius were to endure, it would undoubtedly be his genius with the spoken word. ... Yes, I loved him. Like most of my generation I was in love with an idea. Such fascination with an idea is irritating to those who do not share it. ... But this love went the way of all the others. One day you don't show up for an appointment—something else seems more important. You feel guilty. ... Decade after decade, disciples left Lacan and then began to hate him. Their attitude toward Lacan is like that of ex-Communists toward the Party. (pp. 14–16)

Lacan's fame primarily derives from these public performances. According to Clara Malraux, his seminars were social events: She and her friends would get there one or two hours early in order to get a good seat. Sometimes Lacan sat for a long time ignoring the audience, but when he started to speak, the sparks allegedly flew. Upon leaving, said Malraux, everyone remembered mostly that he had been brilliant, that he had displayed his sparkling wit and had made the most outrageous free associations to whatever subject happened to pop into his head (personal communication, 1982). He drew on his unconscious memories and incorporated these into the theoretical twists. He relished straining his listeners' ability to follow him and challenging their credulity. The seminars consisted of spontaneous (yet semiprepared) performances rather than formal lectures and were unrehearsed. And they were accompanied by gestures and intricate diagrams that contrasted spoken and heard, conscious and unconscious language—diagrams that Lacan drew on the blackboard with a flourish. The public came in droves, eager to witness spontaneous drama.

Subsequent transcriptions into written form with transliterations and elaborations by disciples inescapably have led to many diverse renditions and to disputes among the "renditioners." And they motivated others to recall that Lacan always distinguished strictly between the meaning of oral presentations and written texts. (This dichotomy itself was a larger theme *all* the structuralists addressed.) Lacan put his son-in-law, Jacques-Alain Miller, in sole charge of the transcripts of these seminars and made him his literary executor and heir as well, but that did not stop the many ongoing disputes. Problems of interpretation were bound to come up, if only because Lacan insisted that he could *not* be understood, that any reading of his text insofar as it purported to be a final reading already was a *mis*reading based on a *mis*understanding. And his substitution of *la passe*, the step that would "free" the psychoanalytic candidate from his or her supervisor, for the customary "control analysis," which was to shorten the training period, introduced new problems. But whereas the French already knew that Lacan had only replaced the difficulties intrinsic to psychoanalytic education, American acolytes often advocated Lacan's advice and his formulations of issues.

By the late 1960s, Jacques-Alain Miller and some of Lacan's feminist followers began to take him to task. In the process, they picked up the ever-present ambiguities in the seminar presentations and, most of all, the way Lacan elaborated on Freud's pronouncements on femininity, the castration complex, and the "superiority" of the penis over the vagina and the (mature) vagina over the (immature) clitoris. It did not help that by then many of Lacan's theoretical points often were reduced to attention-getting slogans and to passwords among followers—such as "the unconscious is structured like a language," "the unconscious is the discourse of the Other," or "a letter always arrives at its destination," as he stated in his much-touted seminar on Edgar Allen Poe's "The Purloined Letter" (Mehlman, 1972, pp. 39–72.)

To the extent that these phrases were rooted in Saussurean (and to a lesser extent in Roman Jakobson's) structural linguistic categories, Lacan was thought to assist in debunking the dominant language that was keeping the powerful in power. The dissecting of discourse, of the diachronic and synchronic relationships between signifiers and signifieds, and of words and language increasingly was permeating the French intellectual scene. What then could be more relevant than expanding on the unconscious content of this enterprise? Lacan's ruminations bolstered structuralism, and mutatis mutandis, structuralism enriched *la psychanalyse.* During the student uprisings of 1968, Lacan was said to have moved pyschoanalysis from the couch onto the street. In fact, by the early 1970s, Parisian intellectual life—whether assumed to be structuralist or poststructuralist—was dominated by talk of signifiers and signs, all of them pointing to and paving the road toward the Lacanian unconscious.

Clément ([1981] 1987) reported in detail on the congregation of Maoists around Lacan. After he became a celebrity, his male disciples wore bow ties like his, their female counterparts sat at his feet, and rumors about him as seducer, charlatan, and poseur started floating about (p. 18). That is why French feminism, which initially relied heavily on support from Lacan and which by the late 1970s had hit its high point, cannot be divorced from gossip about his womanizing. Nor can it be separated from the radicalism of the political agendas. After all, in his much-quoted essay "Freud and Lacan" (1971), Louis Althusser asserted that postrevolutionary society would be advanced by Lacanian psychoanalysis: It promised to help socialize infants born to bourgeois mothers into the emerging (postrevolutionary) order. Altogether, French feminists were responding to the cultural milieu they themselves increasingly were in the process of molding, and this milieu was becoming more and more Lacanian.

What, then, was Lacan's attraction? What made for the love-hate relation his women disciples developed? To what extent was the enthusiasm of the group around the avant-garde magazine *Tel Quel*—spearheaded by Julia Kristeva—responsible for French feminists' successes? In what way were they encouraged by the teaching of Lacanian psychoanalysis at the university at Vincennes and by Jacques-Alain Miller's Maoist-type leadership within it? Clearly, all of these factors converged to make for the sweep of Lacanianism, and much of its appeal was due to the wide-ranging and much publicized discussions of his tricky concepts by his feminist followers. They simultaneously both adopted and criticized Lacan's doctrines. Their lively polemics, in turn, subsequently inspired American feminists to modify and enlarge some of their own suppositions and theories in a Lacanian direction. (See Chapter 6.)

Rereading Freud

As noted in Chapter 1, Freud ended up by judging the "riddle of the nature of femininity" (1933a, p. 113) as central to all of psychoanalysis. It was the pivotal subject of the Freudians' inquiries during the 1920s. Basically, Freud postulated one libido, the masculine one, and held that children of both sexes must go through a castration complex and through the phallic phase. He also maintained that sexual differentiation is not preordained or founded in biology and that gender is not predetermined. Because both girls and boys start out with a certain amount of polymorphous perversity and initially believe that their mother has (or had) a penis, they come to accept anatomical differences before they can identify with their masculine and feminine roles. Furthermore, after declaring that "psychoanalysis does not try to describe what a woman is … but sets about inquiring how she comes into being, how a woman develops out of a child with a bisexual disposition" (1933a, p. 116), Freud suggested that his women disciples were in the best position to come to grips with this so-far-unfathomable issue. He wanted them to "explore the dark continent" and to investigate the roots of femininity. According to Lacan, their endeavors were not successful. In principle, he rejected all psychoanalytic theories based on ego psychology or object relations as too unimaginative, as too focused on reality. And he stated that the infant's first object of desire is not the breast, as Melanie Klein contended, and that Horney's concept of womb envy was simplistic and was no more than a parallel to Freud's penis envy. Both of these interpretations, he found, were perpetuating the Anglo-Saxon pursuit of ego psychology, which identifies the ego with its object. Therefore, Lacan encouraged his feminist disciples to rethink psychoanalysis by exploring the depths of their sexuality and psyche critically and to reconceptualize all of Freud's metaphors in relation to "the other."

Lacan and "Desire"

Freud likened woman to a "dark, moist and unknown" continent (1926e p. 212). As David Macey (1988) reminded us, this metaphor was widely used in Freud's time for the African continent, which was then being explored just like the woman who is about to be penetrated. Lacan too perceived "the feminine as a realm of darkness" (pp. 178–179), but Macey thought that Lacan's reevaluation of Freud could be explained by considering also, and probing into, his surrealist past and by demonstrating just how this past was replayed in his psychoanalytic theories. Macey took for granted that Lacan's imagery, unlike Freud's, was informed by linguistic oppositions between *langue* and *parole,* between levels of speech and systems of signs, and between the dual aspects of concept and sound. But Macey focused on Lacan's imagery, such as his metaphoric uses of and allusions to day and night as symbolic of "man and woman," of eyes as signifying the erect penis, and of blinding as recalling the Oedipus legend and castration. And he said that Lacan's originality was rooted in the surrealists' specifically outrageous ways of *épater les bourgeois.*

But in 1980, Anglo-Saxon feminists were not yet familiar with, for instance, such Lacanisms as " 'the obscurity concerning the vaginal organ,' [or] extensions of Freud's phallic-optical metaphors that refer to ... breaking the inviolate [vaginal] seal, and [that] supplement the old dream of penetration with a phantasy of defloration" (quoted in Macey, 1988, p. 179).

The first Anglo-Saxon to alert American feminists to Lacan's thought was Juliet Mitchell. She explained Freud's views of femininity in her introduction to *Feminine Sexuality: Jacques Lacan and the École Freudienne* (1982) and began by demonstrating that for him and his followers "the development of the human subject, its unconscious and its sexuality go hand-in-hand" (Mitchell and Rose, 1982, p. 2) and that they defined this subject differently than do most humanists (p. 5). But, unlike Macey, Mitchell integrated Lacan's theories into those of the American ego psychologists and into those of Melanie Klein, Michael Balint, W.R.D. Fairbairn, and D. W. Winnicott in England (p. 3).

Mitchell defended Freud against those who claimed that he based femininity on woman's "biological sex which then suffers vicissitudes as a result of fantasies brought into play by the girl's relations to objects" (significant others) (Mitchell, 1984, p. 272); she added that he left the door open for further investigations, and she quoted a letter by Freud to his German disciple Carl Müller-Braunschweig to illustrate her point:

> I object to all of you (Horney, Jones, Radó, etc.) to the extent that you do not distinguish more clearly and cleanly between what is psychic and what is biological, that you try to establish a neat parallelism between the two and that you, motivated by such intent, unthinkingly construe psychic facts which are unprovable and that you, in the process of doing so, must declare as reactive or regressive much that without a doubt is primary. Of course, these reproaches must remain obscure. In addition, I would only like to emphasize that we must keep psychoanalysis separate from biology just as we have kept it separate from anatomy and physiology. (p. 272)

When Lacan severed psychoanalysis from biology by equating the structure of psychoanalysis with that of language, he went beyond Freud. Moreover, as some of his critics have argued, he disengaged it from the deepest feelings of the specific analysand. Yet this very detachment also has been a source of influence, particularly on feminism. Neither Mitchell nor Jacqueline Rose, in her introduction to their book, dwelled on this factor. Rose followed Freud when she stated that "the debate on feminine sexuality must start ... with the link between sexuality and the unconscious" (Mitchell and Rose, 1982, p. 29). But she located this link in Lacan's "mirror stage" (*Ecrits I*, 1966), the fiction that determines the child's future identification: "It conceals, or freezes, the infant's lack of motor co-ordination and the fragmentation of its drives ... [and thereby] divides the child's identity into two" (p. 30). Lacan said that the infant for the first time recognizes itself in the reflection as a unified body and enters language and the social world. Therefore, Lacanians postulate this recognition as the initial locus of identity (including sexual identity) and of symbolization as well as of *misrecognition*. (Winnicott's mirror is the mother who grants an image *to* the child.) Jacqueline Rose put it well:

> Sexuality belongs in the area of instability played out in the register of demand and desire, each sex coming to stand, mythically and exclusively, for that which could satisfy and complete the other. It is when the categories "male" and "female" are seen to represent an absolute and complementary division that they fall prey to a mystification in which the difficulty of sexuality instantly disappears: "to disguise this gap by relying on the virtue of the 'genital' to resolve it through the maturation of tenderness ..., however piously intended, is nonetheless a fraud." (p. 33)

This theoretical summary was exact. But it left out the typical playfulness of Lacan's seminars and the irreverent remarks. Even at the time he decided to dissolve his École Freudienne, in 1980, he still punned, referring to himself as "je père-sévère" ("I, severe father" is a homonym of *persevere*) (Clément, [1981] 1983, p. 32). Macey (1988) was more attuned to the influences on Lacan and on his intellectual trajectory than Mitchell and Rose. And he already knew that poor translations from Freud's German texts, or even from English, into French were playing havoc with the fixing of Lacan's vivid "imaginary"—the domain of fantasy and imagination. Most Anglo-Saxon feminists did not have access to this information and thus tended to take Lacan at face value in their eagerness to put his rereadings to the service of the movement.

In their partial translation of Lacan's *Le Séminaire de Jacques Lacan, Livre XX* (1975), Mitchell and Rose left out his frilly introductions and humorous asides. The French edition of this seminar, for instance, began with "De la jouissance," and in a conversational tone he remarked, "I happened not to publish 'The Ethic of Psychoanalysis.' In those days, this for me was a form of politeness—*après vous j' vous en prie, j' vous en pire ...* [I enjoin you, I make you worse]. In time, I learned that I could talk of it a bit more" (Lacan, 1975, p. 9; my translation). Another essay in *Feminine Sexuality*, also from *Le Séminaire*, "God and the *Jouissance* of the Woman," starts with the second of three parts and thus, again, highlights the theoretical seriousness rather than Lacan's ruminations about *jouissance* and sexuality—that is, the pleasure that, when pushed to its rapturous extremes, moves "beyond" to the realm of the death instinct. In the 1970s, *jouissance* was a central ingredient of the spirited brouhaha engendered by the discourse among French intellectuals, especially between Lacan and Roland Barthes and to some extent between them and Michel Foucault and Gilles Deleuze and Felix Guattari. Of course, the transposition of Lacan's seminars to the theoretical realm (in the Lacanian manner I ought to capitalize Theoretical) may well be due to the need to confine translations to the meat of the discussions. But Mitchell and Rose's perfectly understandable omissions ultimately resulted in turning a lively and ironic Lacan into a rather ponderous Anglo-Saxon one.

Most of the commentary on the female orgasm also was more staid. Mitchell and Rose (1982), for example, did not yet dwell, as Clément had, on the fact that

> he discusses "their" orgasm as a man: with a mixture of lyricism, irritation, envy, and admiration. … "She has her own kind of pleasure (*jouissance*), 'she' who does not exist and signifies nothing. She has her own kind of pleasure about which she may know nothing, except that she feels it, and that is one thing she knows. She knows of course when it happens. It doesn't happen to all of them. … *La femme* is seeking love. As for orgasm, nothing doing, but as for love, well, about that he knows plenty! It has nothing to do with sexual intercourse." (Clément [1981] 1983, p. 64)

Such Lacanianisms were provocative and were attacked by the classical psychoanalysts as charlatanism, by philosopher Jacques Derrida as phallogocentrism, by feminists as chauvinism, and by all of them as hype. (See further on.) Still, that the general assumption underpinning Lacan's conceptualization of the phallus turned out to be erroneous is more serious. According to Macey, Lacan's presumed (theoretical) separation between the penis and the phallus had its origin in mistranslation: "The French text has *le désir de posséder un phallus* (the wish to own a phallus) for the Standard Edition's 'wish for a penis.'" However, "Freud's original German is quite unequivocal; he speaks of *der Wunsch nach dem Penis*. A phallus-penis distinction has indeed been introduced, but not by Freud. His French translator, Anne Berman, must take responsibility for the innovation. Similarly, the French reference to *le manque de la femme* is simply a free—not to say libertarian—rendition of Freud's *Penislosigkeit des Weibs*" (Macey, 1988, pp. 188–189). Was Lacan ever aware of this error? Would he have relinquished making the systematic distinction between the two had he realized that Freud did not differentiate so clearly and after he had argued so strongly that the separation between penis and phallus represents a move away from psychoanalysis's residual biologism and, by implication, allows for "replacing the notorious 'anatomy is destiny' with 'symbolization is destiny'" (p. 188)? Macey further observed:

> In *Encore*, Lacan notes with malicious glee that all his pupils have got into a muddle over the phallus. Whilst their confusion is no doubt in part a reflection of his own repressed hesitancies and contradictions, "muddle" is a superb example of litotes. Definitions of the phallus proliferate, become ever more defined, and finally cancel one another out, thus allowing a conceptual regression from the phallus to the penis. ... [Thus Serge Leclaire] in the course of a seminar at Vincennes confidently asserts: "Nowadays, no one thinks of the phallus simply as a penis," and then goes on to say that "the penis is part of the concept of the phallus. ... By 1975 Leclaire defines the phallus as, successively, a word, a letter, a symbol, a concept and a referent." (p. 189)

Macey went on to show that subsequent definitions were ever more confused: The phallus was described as a signifier, a sign, the signifer of an impossible *jouissance*, the sign of the impossible object, and as the representation of the real and the nonrepresentable (p. 190). I assume that Clément was referring to these interpretations when she maintained that some of the followers who copied Lacan's appearance, what Lacan stood for, his manner rather than his substance, were punning for the sake of punning rather than in order to convey—as he tried to—that there is no ultimate truth, that truth remains ever elusive. Still, Rachel Z. de Goldstein (1994), a psychoanalyst practicing in Argentina, explained the phallus as the essential signifier that represents the eternally desired completion and self-sufficiency that is never attainable.

Some French Feminists' Responses to Lacan

Lacan and his women disciples belonged to the same intellectual milieu: Their theories and observations were responses to, among others, those Foucault advanced in *Madness and Civilization* ([1961] 1965), *I, Pierre Rivière* ([1973] 1975), and *The History of Sexuality I* ([1976] 1978). They *all* were debating the validity and impact of Deleuze and Guattari's *Anti-Oedipus* ([1972] 1977), of the schizoid component of modern society they had postulated. Did "bodies without organs," as Deleuze and Guattari said, really replace the Freudian id? Was the breast really a machine producing milk and the infant's mouth a sucking machine coupled to it? Because social production depends on capitalist production (which Deleuze and Guattari said encompasses all the materials and energies existing within the social field), they assumed that an unconscious "libidinal economy" existed on the micropolitical level of the political one; and they speculated on extensions of Lévi-Strauss's anthropological exploits in cold (preindustrial) societies to hot (capitalist) ones (p. 1).

In that vein, Hélène Cixous and Catherine Clément, in *The Newly Born Woman* ([1975] 1986) investigated the historical roles of women sorceresses and hysterics and the general conditions fostering the marginalization of women: The sorceress heals, performs abortions, converts the unlivable space of a stifling Christianity; the hysteric unties familiar bonds, introduces disorder, gives rise to magic. Both roles, the authors held, serve *conservative* ends because *all* these women end up being destroyed; and then as now, they are controlled by beliefs in their guilt. Like Foucault, who also found that psychoanalysis (a discourse that replaced the secrecy of the confessional and transferred it to the bed) is conservative and upholds male domination, Cixous and Clément maintained that historical and cultural evolution have not made a dent: "Women's stories" are being perpetuated symbolically, and women continue to serve in the transition from one realm to another. Freud's passion for his hysterical patients, they argued, was roused by the spectacle of femininity in crisis. In Lacanian idiom, they summed up: "It is the *relations between the Imaginary, the Real, and the Symbolic* that are at stake here, ... [that] link the figures of sorceress and hysteric in the subversive weight attributed to the return of the repressed, in the evaluation of the power of the archaic, and in the Imaginary's power or lack of it over the Symbolic and the Real" (p. 9).

The authors described girls who were *bound* by convention and whose demons suddenly were being released. The headings in their book, "Signs and Marks: The Theater of the Body," "Attack, Abreaction, Expulsion," and "Attack, Celebration, Issue," are Freudian, and they quoted from his *Studies on Hysteria*. But they did so in a hyped-up, flowery idiom:

> Also bound are Emmy von N ... , Elisabeth von R ... , Katharina, Lucy— bound from all sides. With their contorted faces, sore tense muscles, and paralyzed limbs, there is no need for handcuffs at all. ... They come—phantasmic and monstrous—a toad under a rock, an enormous lizard on the stage of a theater, a mouse under a ball of wool, a bat in the bathroom— Emmy's bestiary. (Cixous and Clément, [1975] 1986, p. 11)

Interspersing their militant analyses with lurid descriptions of hysterics' antics and sorcerers' feats (as described by Jules Michelet, whose works Foucault and Barthes often quoted), Cixous and Clément expected "to break up the circus of transference" (p. 13). They quoted the crime of the (recently exhumed and much quoted) Papin sisters, who had been devoted, retiring, and exemplary servants to a mother and daughter until one day, in a fit of anger, they hacked them to pieces, disposed of the bodies, cleaned up thoroughly, and went to bed. Lacan recounted the tale in *Motives of Paranoiac Crime: The Crime of the Papin Sisters* and portrayed them as

> a mirroring couple, a double-woman who one evening is no longer able to tolerate the other couple, the master couple, proprietresses. It is an attack, in the sense one might speak of an hysterical "attack." But the murderous woman's body does not mutilate itself. Instead it turns its aggressions against the body of another woman. (p. 18)

Cixous and Clément called this gruesome historical event a real festival, another allegedly radical theme popular in the early 1970s—the heyday of the discussions among the deconstructionists around Derrida, the *Annales* (*Annales: Economies, Societés, Civilisations*) historians surrounding Fernand Braudel, and the "humanist Marxists" following Henri Lefebvre. Cixous and Clément accounted for both the witches' sabbat and the hysterics' attack as psychic mechanisms that allowed everyday rhythms to return—after they had "expel[led] the foreign body, the venom, through a violent and irksome action" (pp. 19–20); and they situated this past, as "Lévi-Strauss did, in its mythic dimension" (p. 22). Freud, the authors contended, changed the former image of childhood as bliss into its opposite, hell, and changed the hysteric's implausible tale of seduction into infantile sexuality.

Recounting the traumas of Freud's hysterical patients and reinterpreting his (and by implication Jean-Martin Charcot's and Lacan's) interpretations of their childhood traumas and their conversions into somatic (biological) symptoms, Cixous and Clément surmised that "in hysteria it is a question more of a rejection of a *perversion* [usually the father's] than of a refusal of sexuality [that is] … located in the stature of the father … at the root of a timeless, ahistorical origin" ([1975] 1986, p. 45). As noted,they employed Lacanian concepts to analyze Freud as

> the "important other person" [who] is the model for all others; he is the foundation for otherness, no longer as an important person but as a *place* in the structure of the subject, the place in relation to which the subject establishes itself in a *dependent position*. The father is the Law; the austerity of the Symbolic, the privileged force of the order, come from the looming, immemorial figure of the prehistoric father. This father is overpossessive: the perverse Law. (p. 45)

But the Lacanian father cannot tolerate "paternity in perversion," so the daughter rather than the father is blamed for having seduced him in the oedipal situation, for her infantile sexuality (Cixous and Clément, [1975] 1986, p. 47). Like Freud's patient Dora, whom he chastized for catching on to her father's infidelity with the wife of his friend, daughters always are called liars and deemed guilty—and then develop psychosomatic symptoms that turn them into the family invalids (p. 49). In the many sagas of hysterics, continued Cixous and Clément, Freud assigned the homosexual role to the feminine character with whom the hysteric "identifies" (p. 53). Ultimately, this female patient is found to resemble her predecessor, the sorceress.

Amusingly, Cixous and Clément faulted both Freud and Lacan for accepting the subjugation of women, for grounding their theories in the cultural unconscious that takes their inferior role for granted. But they praised Freud for recognizing innate human bisexuality and reiterated that "there has always been bisexuality [which, however] ... always [was] dominated by masculinity, ... [and] sequentially moved from hermaphrodite to phoenix, from the fusion of masculine and feminine to immortality" ([1975] 1986, p. 55). This formulation mirrors Foucault's language in the famous case of Herculine Barbin, a nineteenth-century hermaphrodite. She was a teacher and was sexually attracted to one of her female students. After being apprehended, she was hounded and then found guilty and forced into a sex-change operation. She had been relatively content before but never regained her equilibrium afterward (in her male reincarnation) and eventually committed suicide.

Cixous and Clément's challenging theses directly responded to Lacan and thereby helped bolster the increasing interest of the intellectual public in psychoanalysis. Moreover, unlike the Féministes Révolutionnaires, who expected to do away with the inevitable domination of women by men with the help of consciousness-raising groups and unlike those who argued for an exclusively lesbian position, Cixous and Clément ended up by exposing the patriarchal order without unduly threatening it.

Other feminists, among them Nicole Loraux and Monique Schneider, debated at great length the persistent influence of Greek myth on the roles of fathers and mothers. They too were in the Lacanian camp and asked his type of questions. They said they wanted to avoid Manicheanism and getting "mired in the [linguistic] maze of sliding strategies, of denegations and redoublings" (1984, p. 18) by moving from denunciations of feminine oppression to discussions on ways to liberate men and women from traditional roles. Loraux suggested that Mother Earth (mother of the future citizen) no longer be portrayed as feminine but as an intermediary representation that would facilitate the shift from the maternal to the paternal: "Earth, under the name of *fatherland* has as much to do with fatherhood as with motherhood" (p. 19). And she went on to show how such a formulation might facilitate political and scientific matters to be conceptualized more neutrally, in a less phallocentric fashion.

Whereas Marks and Courtivron's book introducing the previously mentioned theories is most informative, their abundance of short selections from larger arguments can be compared to a smorgasbord—which leaves the sampler satiated but ultimately dissatisfied. Although the first essay, a reprint from Simone de Beauvoir's *Second Sex* ([1949] 1960) was familiar and unproblematic, the next section, "Demystifications," by ten contributors, often mystifies. For instance, Françoise Parturier wanted to know why men "think like rabbits" and denigrate women with their raunchy, misogynous talk; treat woman as objects; separate love from pleasure; and rehabilitate the fantasies of the Marquis de Sade. Françoise d'Eaubonne perceived Catholicism as it is incorporated into the priesthood as blocking women's fulfillment because of its opposition to abortion. Benoite Groult recapped the violent, death-associated sexuality of writers like Baudelaire, the Marquis de Sade, Lautréamont and Michel Leiris to show that pornography actually channels sexuality toward the heterosexual world, which is dominated by men. Annie Leclerc argued that men masquerade as the heroes they want to be, and Claudine Herrmann maintained that woman's wish for harmony allows her to be crushed. Denise Le Dantec cautioned against the institutionalization of women's writing, and Arlette Laguiller and Madeleine Vincent warned against assuming that a feminist victory is possible within capitalist society. Other contributions focused on women writers and on utopias; and there was an entire section on manifestos and actions. All the contributions represented larger theses.

The strongest essays were by the militant French feminists who challenged Lacan. Luce Irigaray, for instance, argued that

> female sexuality has always been theorized within masculine parameters. Thus, the opposition "viril" clitoral activity/"feminine" vaginal passivity which Freud—and many others—claims are alternative behaviors or steps in the process of becoming a sexually normal woman, seems prescribed more by the practice of masculine sexuality than by anything else. For the clitoris is thought of as a little penis which is pleasurable to masturbate, as long as the anxiety of castration does not exist (for the little boy), while the vagina derives its value from the "home" it offers the male penis when the now forbidden hand must find a substitute to take its place in giving pleasure. ... Woman and her pleasure are not mentioned in this conception of the sexual relationship. Her fate is one of "lack," "atrophy" (of her genitals), and "penis envy," since the penis is the only recognized sex organ of any worth. (Marks and Courtivron, 1980, p. 99)

Were it not for this male view, stated Irigaray, the woman's pleasure in the vaginal caress would not have to substitute itself for the clitoral one; she might even experience the sex act as intrusive, especially when the man takes her only as the object of *his* pleasure. Moreover, "caressing the breasts, touching the vulva, opening the lips, ... [among other plea-sures, indicate that] *woman has sex organs just about everywhere ...* the geography of her pleasure is much more diversified, more multiple in its differences, more complex, more subtle, than [men may] imagine" (Marks and Courtivron, 1980, p. 103).

Still, concluded Irigaray, because women are *not* a class and are dis-persed over all the class structure, they have trouble organizing politi-cally in "a culture that oppresses them, uses them, cashes in on them" (Marks and Courtivron, 1980, p. 105). She then held that the indispens-able means of overcoming women's phallocentrism was to let their auto-eroticism and their homosexuality flourish at the expense of heterosex-ual pleasure (p. 106).

"Traditional" Feminists

The women in the Société Psychanalytique de Paris (SPP), of course, were much more tentative. Irigaray's suggestion that homosexuality re-place heterosexuality flew in the face of the Freudian theory that guided their practices: Since uncovering the oedipal drama of their patients was the clue to traumatic childhood incidents and the means of bringing about their cure, their feminism derived from work with patients. They focused neither on language nor on linguistic theories but on the (spo-ken) connections their patients made to the material they dug up from their unconscious. Janine Chasseguet-Smirgel, among others, applied the techniques of ego psychology when showing that the Freudian plea-sure principle and the oedipal theory were as universal as Lacan's mirroring and dissection-of-language categories.

In the introduction to her collected essays, *Sexuality and Mind* (1986), Chasseguet-Smirgel recalled the circumstances under which she had edited another collection of essays, *Female Sexuality* ([1964] 1985), and that between 1964 and 1975, when she again was asked to address the subject, she had felt compelled to point to the "perennial return" of Wilhelm Reich, who had expected to release individuals' sexual and li-bidinal energy by means of his orgone box in order to help energize the societal revolution Marx had predicted. She also spoke of the ever-recur-ring theme of "the disappearance of the father and of his function as the *separation* between mother and child, ... [including] the disappearance of the 'Ego'" (Chasseguet-Smirgel, 1986, p. 2). And she stressed that she felt she then had had to respond to Deleuze and Guattari's antioedipal ideology and to the then prevalent infatuation with Maoism and the Chinese Cultural Revolution and to its corollary, the return to nature. None of these themes, which thanks to Lacan and Miller, had become the talk of *tout Paris,* could be ignored. She recalled that at the time the prevalent *fascination* with the primitive mother had led her

> to examine the other side of the problem. In her existence a woman comes up against the very concrete fact that fear of the primitive Mother prompts men and women to control the female powers and to accord inferior status to the woman. Yet the wish to merge with Mother Nature, to abolish the Ego, to eradicate the father and his attributes and to grasp the cosmic maternal powers, leads men to compete with women, on the grounds that only men are capable of merging into the Great Whole. This rivalry prompts men to envy female powers, to denigrate them and to try to deprive women of them. (p. 4)

This very situation, stated Chasseguet-Smirgel, "conspires to cast the shadow of the 'dark continent' [of female sexuality] onto male sexuality as well" (1986, p. 9). But she did not respond to Lacan's reading of Freud's "Female Sexuality" (1931b). Instead, she pointed to the contradictions within Freud's works and to his assumptions regarding how young boys and girls learn about the existence of the vagina. She found, for instance, when rereading the case of Little Hans, that "nothing justifies Freud in assigning to his widdler (*wi-wi-macher*) an exclusively male meaning throughout the text" (p. 13); she wondered why Freud, when "on the verge of identifying the existence of the vagina at least on the preconscious level in little Hans's psyche," did not do so (p. 15) and why he did not pick up on Hans's unwillingness to accept that boys can't have babies even though he knew better (p. 16). Chasseguet-Smirgel went on to elaborate on contributions by early Freudians hypothesizing "*that the theory of sexual phallic monism corresponds not to the lack of knowledge of the vagina but to a splitting of the ego or to the repression of an earlier piece of knowledge*" (p. 16). And after extending her analysis to reexamining Freud's text on the Wolf Man, she questioned the ostensible irreversibility of male dominance. This led her to conclude that

> psychoanalytic theory does not escape this struggle between maternal and paternal law. If we underestimate the importance of our earliest relations and our cathexis of the maternal imago, this means we allow paternal law to predominate and are in flight from our infantile dependence: if we neglect the organizing effects of the Oedipus complex, which includes the experience of whole objects, of the paternal superego, of the penis, we restore the maternal primal power which, even if it does intimidate us, is an undeniable source of fascination. (p. 28)

Unlike the feminists who were following the various trendy radicalisms, Chasseguet-Smirgel, while straying into left and right fields, stayed within and enlarged the classical Freudian realm: She found it theoretically wanting and thus set out to correct it. Again, although her language was attuned to the binary linguistic theories used in her milieu, she did not rely on these alone but always brought in examples from her clinical work. This focus, of course, made her less prone to punning and metaphorical footwork and led opponents to denigrate her as conservative. Neither Chasseguet-Smirgel nor her non-Lacanian colleagues went on to publicly proclaim their feminism. But they were likely to defend feminist principles within their organization and to keep "updating" the early Freudians' theories in order to arrive at a better understanding of feminine sexuality, often using Lacanian formulations such as "the law of the father" or addressing the "phallic monism" that is said to deny the existence of the vagina.

Later, Chasseguet-Smirgel proceeded to explore the father-daughter relationship, along with problems linked to the feminine propensity to incorporate anal-sadistic components into perceptions of the paternal penis. She connected female masochism to guilt and to the revolt against an omnipotent mother rather than to the wish to become a man. She tied the girl's basic drive to become independent of the mother to the earlier work of Jeanne Lampl-de Groot (who postulated the castration complex as a secondary formation) and to that of Ruth Mack Brunswick (who held that desire for a child precedes penis envy) and Josine Müller (who maintained that the vagina is central early on), as well as to contributions by other early Freudians such as Carl Müller-Braunschweig, Annie Reich, Hanns Sachs, Ernest Jones, and Phyllis Greenacre.

At the time, Parisian intellectuals were rereading Sade. Barthes, in *Sade Fourier Loyola* ([1971] 1976) pointed to the similarity of language structure in the pervert, the revolutionary, and the saint: All three make pleasure, happiness, and communication dependent on an inflexible order. Chasseguet-Smirgel, however, set out to investigate perversions in the terms of classical psychoanalysis. She stated, for instance, that the boy's relinquishing the oedipal object may be tied to his painful recognition of his smallness and the inadequacy of his sexual organ and that the "restructuring [of the woman's psyche after giving birth] can be accomplished only by way of a re-experiencing of the oedipal conflict and with the help of this re-experience" ([1975] 1985, p. 52). And she said that "the renunciation of the oedipal object, with the dissolution of the oedipus complex, has only a relative value, and ... the bridging of the divide between ego and ego ideal is never absolutely renounced" (p. 53). Once again, she used classical Freudian theory sprinkled with Lacanian language to investigate female development.

Joyce McDougall, another prominent member of the classical Société Psychanalytique de Paris, also argued that homosexuality could not replace heterosexuality. But she postulated that it was part of every woman's psyche. She not only was influenced by the Lacanian language of her milieu but took Lacan seriously. She maintained, in *Theaters of the Mind* ([1982] 1985), that the phallus as the symbolic function of the penis takes in its intra- and intersubjective dialectic (attached to its symbolic significance) and determines psychic development (p. 44) and that the representation of the female genitals in an individual's consciousness depends on the role accorded the phallus. In fact, McDougall did not speak about feminism per se. She simply took for granted that equality of the sexes exists, and she explored how male and female sexuality become established. She assumed, along with her colleague Bela Grunberger, that the phallus is the symbol of narcissistic integrity and, along with Lacan, that it is the fundamental signifier of desire; and that as the psychic representative of desire and narcissistic completion, the *phallus* plays the same role for both sexes—although the attitude to the *anatomical penis* is necessarily different (McDougall, [1978] 1980, p. 118).

In her chapter "The Homosexual Dilemma: A Study of Female Homosexuality," ([1978] 1980), McDougall argued that

> female homosexuality is an attempt to resolve conflict concerning the two poles of psychic identity: one's identity as a separate individual and one's sexual identity. The manifold desires and conflicts that face every girl with regard to her father have, in women who become homosexual, been dealt with by giving him up as an object of love and desire and identifying with him instead. The result is that the mother becomes once more the only object worthy of love. Thus the daughter acquires a somewhat fictitious *sexual identity*; however, the unconscious identification with the father aids her in achieving a stronger sense of *subjective identity.* She uses this identification to achieve a certain detachment from the maternal imago in its more dangerous and forbidding aspects. (p. 87)

McDougall's inquiries into the genesis of "perversions" derive from her analysis of very difficult patients whose early psychic scenarios she helped them recreate and, in the process, discovered the unique psychosomatic solutions to their "psychic survival." Her straightforward writing belies the fact that her vivid, dramatic presentations of psychoanalytic cases rival those by Freud and Lacan. But her audiences tended to be smaller than Lacan's; she primarily addressed classical psychoanalysts interested in the clinical consequences of "phallic monism"—in the differentiation between attachment to the idealized mother (as in female sexuality) and in the fixation on the idealized father (as in the case of the virile woman) (Oliner, 1988, p. 178). McDougall does not have much of a public following. And her roots are in psychoanalysis rather than in feminism, in Maoism or other radical "isms," so that she does not qualify as a cult figure.

As noted, by the early 1980s radical French feminists had moved backstage. In fact, many of the militants—both men and women—had become Lacanian psychoanalysts and were seeing patients. The most prominent among them was Julia Kristeva. She had come on the scene from Bulgaria to study with Lucien Goldmann and Lévi-Strauss and had left her mark on Barthes's famous seminar on semiotics, where she introduced the work of Romanian linguist Mikhail Bakhtin. Not much later, together with her husband, Phillipe Sollers, Kristeva started the avant-garde magazine *Tel Quel*, pursued her Maoist politics, and was inspired by Lacan.

This Kristeva of the 1970s conceptualized the "science of sémanalisis" in order to "deconstruct" structuralism and phenomenology and to separate the signifying practices of Marxists and radicals from those of mass culture in terms of the unconscious experiences of individuals in the context of the social pressures on them (Kristeva, 1983, p. 44). Therefore, she approached literature and art in order to subvert the very theoretical, philosophical, or semiological apparatus and defined a signifying practice in poetic language and pictorial works. She did not directly address feminist issues, although her activities took place within the radical framework of post-1960s feminism. However, she postulated a dynamic of semiotic/symbolic dualism in language, which in turn led her to challenge "language and identity as another version of a more familiar political question: how to effect a political transformation when the terms of that transformation are given by the very order which a revolutionary practice seeks to change" (Rose, 1986, p. 148).

Still, Kristeva's interview with *psych & po* (reprinted in Marks and Courtivron, 1980) testifies to the fact that she was perceived all along as a radical feminist—even though she stated that "the belief that 'one is a woman' is almost as absurd and obscurantist as the belief that 'one is a man'" (p. 137). *Psych & po* had invited the interview to hear about the subjugation of women in China, from where Kristeva had just returned (she had visited with Lacan and a number of others). Her book, *About Chinese Women* ([1974] 1979) came out just as she was abandoning her Maoism. She stated that "other phenomena lead me to believe that the die is cast in China, for a socialism without God or man, which will accompany, at a distance, the perilous unprecedented renaissance of a new humanity that is gathering momentum here" (Marks and Courtivron, 1980, p. 241).

Some commentators held that this disappointment led Kristeva to go into psychoanalytic training; others pointed to the psychoanalytic content of her previous work and to her continuing pursuit of semiotics. However, she did not go into analysis with Lacan but with a respected member of the Société Psychanalytique de Paris. At that point she more or less left the limelight because she felt that as a practicing psychoanalyst she had to be careful not to impose her ideas, and her politics, on her patients: This could interfere with the transference (Kurzweil, 1986, p. 222). Since then, argued Rose (1986), "Kristeva has been attractive to feminism because of the way she exposes the complacent identities of psycho-sexual life" (p. 157). (See Chapter 6.)

Did French Feminism Die or Go Underground?

Even though Kristeva began to distance herself from both the feminist movement and Lacan around 1974, she continued to firmly advocate women's goals: freedom of abortion and contraception, day-care centers for children, equal pay for equal work, and so on. Her trajectory, and that of many of the less famous women, attested to the fact that after French feminism evolved, it became part of the establishment, mostly part of Lacan's following, which itself became institutionalized and inter-mingled with classical and other psychotherapeutic tendencies. Fur-thermore, the upsurge of feminism in the early 1970s was not limited to radical feminist groups but produced a groundswell that swept the en-tire Parisian educated public.

Because in France feminism and political radicalism went hand in hand and because Lacan's theories sounded more militant than they ac-tually were when translated into practice, they first were addressed by the students who came to his seminars and then by other intellectuals. That is why psychoanalysis, Marxist practices, and feminism were ex-pected to conspire in bringing about revolutionary changes. In the pro-cess, it was promised that women would become the equals of men in every sphere. And whatever changes in sexual and social practices were needed, these were to be instituted and could only be for the better in a society of equals. Parisian women—and some men—assumed this would come about with the help of structuralist theories, which were themselves indebted to Lacanian psychoanalysis. The ensuing practices did not live up to the promises of the theories, and they did not inspire enough people to follow suit. After the events of 1968, the movement lost much of its legitimacy and thus its impetus: Most of the radical leaders became writers and psychoanalysts, mothers and wives. But their spir-ited declarations and their epigrammatic formulations and flippant put-downs of masculinity, male superiority, and patriarchy continued to reflect their earlier apprenticeship with Lacan. Their animated rhetoric inspired many American feminists to expand on these theories and to explore Lacanian thought for political ends. In that respect, American feminists turned out to be as trusting as American government officials, who also took French flamboyant rhetoric at face value. Still, the Lacanian discourse was thought to offer a provocative dimension rather than a solution to the American Freudians' increasingly stale discussions. Their clinical interests, though parallel to questions of women's liberation, were for the most part in line with the aims of the First Wave of feminism. But in many of America's elite universities psychoanalytic theorizing soon dominated and thus ushered in feminism's Second Wave.

6 From American Feminism to French Psychoanalytic Feminism

During the 1970s, only a handful of American feminists did not actively criticize psychoanalysis, frown upon it, or ignore it. But women historians such as Elizabeth Fox-Genovese, Linda Gordon, Gerda Lerner, and Anne Firor Scott looked through historical archives and found that women's contributions to macro- as well as microevents in the past had been ignored; women anthropologists such as Mary Douglas, Michelle Zimbalist Rosaldo, Kathleen Gough, Louise Lamphere, and Rayna Rapp investigated the meanings and consequences of the sexual division of labor around the globe; women sociologists such as Cynthia Fuchs Epstein, Rose Laub Coser, Lenore Weitzman, Helen Hacker, and Janet Giele explored the pernicious reasons for the eternal subjugation of what used to be called the weaker sex; and women scholars in literature perused classical and neglected novels and essays by both men and women to point out again and again the shabby treatment women had been wont to receive. Among the many hundreds of professors who by then had produced a few thousand articles and books, only a tiny minority even mentioned psychoanalysis as a viable means of releasing women from their oppressed lot, and even fewer were in touch with the women psychoanalysts who were addressing these issues from *their* perspectives.

Feminist scholars who did not actively denounce the Freudians for having attempted to keep women down nevertheless assumed that they expected women to stay with the *Kinder* even when they could afford to stay out of the kitchen and away from the *Kirche*. They bore in mind that penis envy ipso facto presumed that men had something women were thought to envy; that the assumption of womb envy, or of breast envy by men, indirectly validated assumptions of male superiority. But a few feminists hoped to rid men of chauvinism and of domineering and abusive behavior by reconceptualizing the father's role (what Lacanians called the third corner of the oedipal triangle) with the help of psychoanalysis. (This issue was being debated fervently also within the Freudian milieu.) Still, a number of radical feminists such as Dorothy Dinnerstein (1976), Nancy Chodorow (1978), and Jessica Benjamin (1978) expected to adapt Freudian ideas to feminist ends: They accepted the inevitable presence of (real or imagined) fathers and argued against exclusively sociological analyses. By disregarding unconscious motivations, which tended to be associated with conservative politics and elite therapy, feminists had stayed away from the more scientific inquiries by Freudian women (see Chapter 4 and further on).

The women's liberation movement was thriving in the 1970s. Thanks to their newly raised consciousness, many American women were leading more and more successful professional and personal lives. They were prodding and influencing politics, and they were questioning and loosening the taken-for-granted community mores. All around the country, women were coming into their own. Opponents of the movement, such as Phyllis Schlafly, who themselves could not have emerged without its activities and who advocated traditional values that fostered dependency on husbands, were being publicly panned and ridiculed. For feminists had helped perfect and develop new techniques of demonstration politics and interventions for equal treatment in the workplace; they had joined—and learned from—black activists to get affirmative action policies passed by Congress; they were inventing strategies to oust the dominant, entrenched WASP elite and their old boys' networks from boardrooms, bedrooms, and clubrooms; and they were starting their own banks and mass-circulation magazines. Essentially, they were pragmatists, fighting for participation and advancement in every conceivable economic, political, and personal realm. If in their fervor they tended to project their mostly middle-class values onto the society as a whole and could not foresee that, for instance, no-fault divorces might facilitate no support for children or that equal job access for women might not provide equal pay, their overall impact changed *all* relationships between women and men.

By 1980, American feminism had turned mainstream: It had followed many twisted and roundabout paths, had taken bold initiatives, and had cleverly adjusted to political realities while influencing them and attempting to counter the backlash; and after shaping the debates aimed to stop the movement, women's issues became central to the country's politics. Advances and setbacks had initiated all sorts of intricate and crosscutting liaisons as well as tactical disagreements with the other liberation movements—black, Hispanic, gay, disabled, and their many splinter organizations. Leading feminists, all of whom by now had their followers, specific spheres of influence, and reputations, differed about tactics and preferred aims and about the direction for the movement itself. They debated whether it would be better to infiltrate the political structures or to overthrow them, to co-opt men to the cause or oust them, to advocate lesbianism in order to avoid sexual dependency or dominate their male partners. And as they argued about the best means of enacting each of these options and along the way enlisted male colleagues as well, the movement lost its unity but gained visibility. A number of feminists managed to hug the limelight, others got into the media and learned to control it, yet others wrote popular books that swept the culture. Altogether, even internal disagreements were being bent into external successes. Feminism was changing the tenor of American society, and in one way or another every American woman took note. Even the feminists' opponents, such as the right-to-lifers and the more insiduous men's groups who at the same time imitated and ridiculed them adopted the tactics perfected by feminist activists: The movement had changed mainstream institutions and discourse; it had succeeded.

Feminists in the American Academy

Like other social movements, feminism had developed its stronghold in universities around the country among students, graduate assistants, and young professors. Feminists were joined and encouraged by academic women who for many years had been given adjunct positions, who had been relegated to part-time jobs and instructorships, and who, because chained to their husbands' jobs, had been exploited. Faculty wives were rarely given tenure or promoted: Like the sediment in wine bottles, they were fated to remain at the bottom. Finally, they could vent their anger and do more with their advanced degrees than help their husbands with their research and typing. Some of them started to systematically explore the institutional reasons for women's constantly low status and the attendant disadvantages. They enlarged the feminist perspective within their own disciplines by rereading history and discovering forgotten and unpublished women authors and women's influences on famous men. And they saw to it that women students were taught a woman's approach to psychology, history, sociology, and so on. In the process, they roused their students to action, confronted college deans and presidents, and demanded posts in university administrations. In other words, they spoke up and gained political skills.

By 1980, feminists had made inroads into some of the bastions of university decisionmaking both by questioning handed-down masculine knowledge and by turning some of the expertise within their specific fields in their favor. They linked up with women in other fields by establishing national and international liaisons. Later on, these endeavors would be described as part of the First Wave of feminism, of the efforts to achieve equity, to have equal access to education and jobs, and to be remunerated on the same pay scale as their male counterparts.

Soon women were setting up women's studies courses and programs and they were creating interdisciplinary networks. Increasingly, they challenged the underlying reasons for past and present biases against women from historical, emotional, and sociological perspectives. In the process, they based their theories on biological, social, cultural, and political realities in order to explain the universal subjugation of women. The slogan "The personal is the political" had become one of the accepted battle cries of the entire American left. That many of the leaders of the 1960s student movement already were pursuing mainstream governmental and bureaucratic careers inadvertently transformed not only political debates but perceptions of both personal and societal interests. And once it was accepted that the personal is the political, anyone who dared question this premise was dismissed as "conservative" or reactionary. (That most of the few women in the natural sciences, economics, and engineering and in departments of business at first stayed out of the debates only reinforced these beliefs.)

Feminists and Modernism

In order to synthesize the proliferation of new data, of the thousands of sociological, anthropological, and psychological studies from around the globe, of factual and speculative connections, of syntheses and comparisons, feminists had to find a means of integrating this constantly expanding literature into an explanatory framework. This job entailed, among other things, a reexamination of the philosophical underpinnings of modern society as well as their replacement by nongendered thinking. Since even the most liberated men had been products of this society, it was agreed that feminist scholars had to start afresh. But to act effectively, they also had to remain within the political realm, all of whose basic assumptions they had to overturn. Thus existing theoretical and abstract formulations were useless. In the university, however, it was possible to advocate the tactics and slogans of liberation politics while affirming—without much challenge—that the personal is the political.

When feminist pacesetters acknowledged that to change society they also needed a guiding theory to advance the cause and unite its disparate factions, they realized that, in typical American tradition, they knew how to be practical but not how to construct the conceptual underpinnings. Functionalist theories were counterproductive: They inevitably incorporated the elements of male dominance and the subjugation of women. Ever since the enlightenment, modernism had been coupled to theories of progress, but neither humanists, literary figures, nor artists ever could agree on a satisfactory definition of the disparate phenomena it encompassed. To the extent that leftist theories appeared applicable, these too incorporated male biases and thus needed reworking. At that juncture, feminists started to look across the Atlantic and particularly to France. There, they discovered a wealth of explicitly radical as well as Communist texts, and linguistic and literary treatises, that purported to serve revolutionary as well as theoretical and feminist ends. Hence, it stood to reason that they would import them, however haphazardly.

Translations were slow, so that French concepts and the disputes around them were advanced piecemeal. Whereas it readily was accepted that every sign consists of two elements (a word and a thing, a signifier and a signified) and that the relation between the two is arbitrary, there was no consensus on how meaning is generated. All the so-called structuralists had taken off from Saussure's conception of, for instance, the word "tree" and had agreed that it represents a thing that evokes meanings that, in turn, invoke yet other meanings and images and that meanings and images exist in both diachronic and synchronic time. Consequently, French feminists used the structuralists' means of arbitrary interpretation and in addition were immersed in, and alluded to, the Parisians' philosophical disputes. Since Parisian esoterica are proverbially metaphoric and abound with internal jokes, it stands to reason that outsiders' explorations of French theories, hypotheses, assumptions, and strategies would lead to simplifications and misunderstandings. But then Lacan had prescribed such misunderstandings when rereading Freud. This was heady stuff. But it was tailor-made for American academics (and the feminists among them) who were looking for a theory that might explain the rapidly changing society they had helped inaugurate.

Intellectuals were trying to explain the emerging political and cultural landscape and the delegitimation of previous credos. But the new politics got its main boost in the universities with the help of feminist scholars. In the process, modernism increasingly was delegitimated. This phenomenon began in the humanities, in departments of English, French, and comparative literature. There, psychoanalytic literary criticism—which had never been dominant—had been eclipsed for some time by the New Criticism. But this formalist mode of reading was found to perpetuate male dominance and thus to block, or at least contradict, the emerging feminist understanding of the past. The New Criticism also opened an occasional door for the revaluation of the psychological criticism in the tradition of Lionel Trilling and William Phillips (Kurzweil and Phillips, 1983). But on balance, the sociological, historical, and psychosexual inquiries by the First Wave of feminists carried the day.

Altogether, notions of unconscious influences on behavior again were gaining in credibility. But these insights, it appeared, were not enough to alter women's deepest attitudes toward men. That is why a few radical women once again turned to psychoanalysis. But as they rekindled the former type of psychoanalytic investigations, they had to take account of Freud's own chauvinism and prejudices. The Parisian feminists' debates, which allegedly had shorn psychoanalysis of its traditional roots, appeared godsent and, simultaneously, introduced Jacques Lacan's re-reading of Freud by the backdoor. This is what heralded the Second Wave of American feminism.

French Leftisms, Structuralisms, and Postmodernism

In France, intellectual fashions always have had a general following, both inside and outside universities. Immediately after World War II, Jean-Paul Sartre dominated the scene: His existentialist Marxism and its fellow-traveling politics not only were favorable to the Soviet Union but were anti-American and thus were in sync with, and loosely paralleled, the anti-Americanism of the homegrown left. But with Khrushchev's denigration of the cult of personality—that is, of Stalinism—at the Twentieth Party Congress in 1956, Sartre's theories began to be questioned, along with his politics. Consequently, Parisian intellectuals started to favor a variety of so-called structuralisms (Kurzweil, 1980, pp. 227, 245).

In America, there never had been a broad *couche* of intellectuals to support political ideologies. So, when American academics cast about for a means of integrating their disparate new findings and feminists wondered why qualified women always ended up at the bottom rungs of every ladder, they were attracted to the Parisians' giddy conceptualizations. By the end of the 1970s, linguistic theories had filtered, however piecemeal, into literary debates; linguistic premises were being discussed; and sociologists and anthropologists looked to insights on culture by such figures as Claude Lévi-Strauss, Michel Foucault, and Roland Barthes. A number of Marxists, impatient with the lag between theory and the victory of the working classes, looked to Louis Althusser. *All* of these presumptions based on structuralism addressed and incorporated aspects of Lacanian psychoanalysis.

Abstract inquiries inspired by "humanistic" and "scientific" Marxism and by elements of the French structuralisms and coupled to some sort of American version of class analysis moved to the center. Soon, these "postmodern" theories became the rage in a number of elite departments in American universities—Yale, Johns Hopkins, Cornell.

Much later, Elizabeth Ermarth, in *Sequel to History: Postmodernism and the Crisis of Representational Time* (1992) defined this postmodernism as something that means different things in different contexts: In architecture, postmodernists cope with the results of early twentieth-century modernism, particularly the razing effects of Bauhaus; in philosophy and discourse analysis, partly as a result of Nietzsche's influence, it is even considered a successor to "classicism." Postmodernism supplants the discourse of representation that produced historical thinking, and postmodern "writing moves beyond the identity-and-similitude negotiations that characterize the construction of historical time and its rationalized consciousness. The tellable time of realism and its consensus become the untellable time of postmodern writing" (pp. 4–6).

In the late 1970s, Parisian intellectuals already were moving away from these inquiries. In America, however, structuralist and poststructuralist theories were being advanced almost at the same time, so that it was difficult to keep apart the avalanche of new isms—the various neo- and postmodernisms and the poststructuralisms. And most academics who could not read French were hampered by the lag in translations; they could not agree on definitions of the unfamiliar terms; they unwittingly missed the personal touches that titillated the Parisians; and many of them did not know precisely what distinguished each of these theories from the others.

When philosopher Jean-François Lyotard explained that postmodernism consisted in a certain incredulity toward metanarratives—that is, in the reduction of reality to a single meaning that no longer was credible—theories spun feverishly, and it was held by some that postmodernism itself had been replaced by post-postmodernism and post-structuralism by post-poststructuralism and by the new historicism, which sort of avoids historical specificity. Words, words, words, Hamlet would have said. But these were words that took the Freudian unconscious for granted.

Foucault's polemics around the "end of man" and the "death of the author" at first drew nothing but feminist scorn. But his exposure in his *History of Sexuality* ([1976] 1978) of nineteenth-century knowledge as an expression of patriarchal dominance inspired a bevy of historical inquiries into language and its dominating discourses and into the concomitant practices that had helped suppress women. Foucault said he wanted to free himself of the limits of linguistic structure; to distance himself from the other structuralists; and to investigate the space independent of language and grammar, of propositions and logic, and of psychology. He wanted to uncover the "archives" of thought. These archives, he stated, control the nature of our discourse and everything we express, they regulate what can be said and what must remain unsaid, and they are remembered only under special circumstances. In other words, Foucault expected to unveil the common roots of the individual and the collective unconscious. Thereby, he promised not only to undercut patriarchal authority and to guide revolutionary practices but to open a new means of inquiry into hetero- and homosexuality.

Foucault's explorations dovetailed with the Nietzschean and nihilistic formulations by his colleague Jacques Derrida, whose deconstructionist enterprise both contradicted and deepened the structuralists' and linguists' undertakings. For Derrida ([1967] 1978) not only held that play is what distinguishes living systems from dead ones but studied graphic and phonic signs as structures of differences that he said were determined by absent tracts and traces that had been erased long ago. Consequently, Derrida's followers and imitators went on to deconstruct texts. In America, however, this philosophical enterprise tended to be conceptualized more concretely and more "realistically." Eventually, complicated arguments about the ins and outs of obscure formulations—which are allegedly at the crossroads of semiology and semiotics and at the hub of all of philosophy and which are said to "abolish" history—increasingly captured the minds of conceptually oriented American humanist academics. It behooved American feminists to join in these enigmatic inquiries not only because there were increasing employment opportunities but to help in their search for the hidden elements of the pernicious aspects of chauvinism. Some of them used Derrida's framework to delve into and better understand the depth of the female psyche; others learned to master the exceedingly difficult theoretical twists and strategic turns of the linguistic dissections of discourses and embraced them to prove that women too could deal with abstractions; yet others found the deconstruction of texts a suitable method of fighting the apparently unbudgeable male establishment. Thereby, they were getting into psychoanalytic theories and language. But because their concerns were with Freudian and Lacanian texts, they often left out the fact that psychoanalysis has its roots in clinical practice based on the discourse between analyst and analysand. So, as American feminists concentrated on and incorporated the contributions of their French counterparts, they were bound to bypass those by classical women psychoanalysts.

As noted in Chapter 5, the majority of French feminists had turned to psychoanalysis after attending Lacan's public seminars. They had grown up in the same rhetorical tradition, had absorbed the intellectual polemics within their milieu, and to larger or lesser degrees had done so by jumping into linguistic and philosophical dialogues. Thus they took for granted the arguments on reading the "blank space" and on the end of man and his return, as well as the ambivalent relationship between Derrida's and Lacan's theories and their personal rivalries. They tried to mediate between them in a way that would benefit feminist goals. Inevitably, in American departments of English and of comparative literature these theories and isms were being introduced in helter-skelter fashion: Free association and arbitrariness were legitimated by the brilliance of the French masters and mistresses themselves. And because it already was taken for granted that every knowledge was relative to other knowledge and that written and spoken, historical and political, texts could be understood diachronically and synchronically and that therefore no knowledge ever could remain true, even the most implausible combinations and associations to texts were encouraged and applauded.

Shoshana Felman (1977) first introduced the new psychoanalytic feminist criticism as "literariness of psychoanalysis while psychoanalyzing literature":

> In view of this shift of emphasis, the traditional method of *application* of psychoanalysis to literature would here be in principle ruled out. The notion of *application* would be replaced by the radically different notion of *implication*: bringing analytical questions to bear upon literary question, *involving* psychoanalysis in the scene of literary analysis, the interpreter's role would here be, not to *apply* to the text an acquired science, a preconceived knowledge, but to act as a go-between, to *generate implications* between literature and psychoanalysis—to explore, bring to light and articulate the various (indirect) ways in which the two domains do indeed *implicate each other,* each one finding itself enlightened, informed, but also affected, displaced by the other. (pp. 8–9)

Theory as the potential liberator of all women and savior of the feminist movement gradually was accorded godlike status. Thereby, French psychoanalytic theory moved to the center of both literary and feminist criticism.

Kristeva's, Cixous's, and Irigaray's Extraordinary Appeal

Among the French feminists, Julia Kristeva's, Hélène Cixous's, and Luce Irigaray's ideas stood out as most relevant for the deconstructions by American literary feminists. To understand these ideas, however, they had to familiarize themselves with the French idiom—the philosophical perambulations, hypthothetical clouds, and spiritual hopes—which then had to be translated into the native vernacular. What Sandra Gilbert said in her introduction to Cixous and Clément's *The Newly Born Woman* could be said for all their works: "For an American feminist ... reading *The Newly Born Woman* is like going to sleep in one world and waking in another—going to sleep in a realm of facts, which one must labor or theorize, and waking in a domain of theory, which one must strive to (f)actualize" ([1975] 1986, p. x). The ensuing factualizations were at the root of subsequent problems and confusions.

Kristeva and Irigaray started out as nonfiction writers and Cixous as an inventor of a very special kind of (theoretical) fiction. All three were disciples of Lacan and then distanced themselves from his "phallocentrism." Irigaray became a Lacanian psychoanalyst in the early 1970s, Kristeva a Freudian one in the early 1980s, and Cixous a professor of literature. They all tried to develop plausible intrapsychic concepts that were to free psychoanalysis of its masculine bias by combining some of Lacan's ideas with those of the women psychoanalysts of the 1920s and 1930s. In *Le séminaire de Jacques Lacan* (1975), Lacan provocatively questioned whether libido is masculine and thereby put psychoanalysis at the center of the definition of feminity (p. 75). Hence he opened the floodgates for inquiries into narcissistic identification with the image of the body as an aspect of the acquisition of bodily boundaries and of psychic and sexual identity.

Already in the 1950s, Barthes had investigated the unconscious elements of writing—arbitrary choice of word sequences, vocabulary, and tone. And he focused on the fact that readers read "differently," in nonlinear fashion, and that they account for everything that *might* have been written or said by a writer in the act of putting down words. His star student, Julia Kristeva, appropriated his method of associating freely from written to social text and from historical practices to current theories. She too emphasized his playful apprehension of language and the ideas of the other intellectual gurus—Derrida, Lyotard, Foucault, Lacan. But Kristeva differentiated more clearly among the roots and development of each of their conceptions than did their American admirers.

Soon, all of the French stars shone ever brighter as they kept crossing the Atlantic. By 1980, Shoshana Felman was dividing language into "cognitive," "constative," and "performative" components. (Constative language is an instrument for the transmission of *truth* as the relation between the *énoncé* [spoken word] and its referent; "performative" refers to the field of *jouissance* [pleasure].) Felman struggled through Lacan's *Ecrits* to comprehend Freud via Lacan (Felman, 1987, pp. 5–6) and thus exemplified the type of Lacanian reading that John Lechte would characterize as typical of the French style of thinking (Lechte, 1990, p. 27). Like Kristeva, Felman expected to take account of the communicative as well as the scandalous and semiotic aspects of language (Felman, 1980, p. 28).

Altogether, the new way of reading literature, which was based on a mixture and often a mishmash of all sorts of abstractions and political and textual strategies, allowed for and flourished on the sort of connections and inferences sociological or political analysis discards as unscientific, anecdotal, and factually wrong. But because the deconstruction of texts and postmodern readings allegedly invalidated "linear" reasoning, many of their proponents heralded this activity as steps toward liberation.

In fact, Felman's essays are not particularly feminist. She did write a tribute to Lacan in *L'Arc* in the 1960s (volume 58)—where she found his intellectual peers to be more or less deconstructive and discursive and considered Lacan to be more allusive and contradictory. But the introduction of the "French" methods furthered the American debates. Jane Gallop later on argued that the psychoanalytic content of such feminist investigations "promised to save psychoanalysis from its ahistorical and apolitical doldrums" (1987, p. 126). I would say (in Derridean terminology) that psychoanalysis too was being decentered, when in *The Daughter's Seduction: Feminism and Psychoanalysis* (1982) Gallop announced that "*literature* ... is the unconscious of psychoanalysis, ... [and] literature *in* psychoanalysis functions precisely as its '*unthought*' ... [and] plays the same role (support and blind spot) in relation to psychoanalytic theory as 'the feminine' in Irigaray's reading" (pp. 60–61). Actually, Gallop advocated such theorization of psychoanalysis in order to get outside Freud's patriarchic assumptions and his construction of female sexuality as inferior to the male's.

How, then, did American feminists apply French thought, what conclusions did they draw from it, and in what way did their political interests at times subvert or even reverse the original constructions—usually for the sake of concrete, partisan ends?

Julia Kristeva's Reception in America

When Julia Kristeva first came to Columbia University in the 1970s, she taught linguistic theories based on her work in semiotics, particularly on Bakhtin. She still is one of the leading figures in semiological and linguistic circles. Her book *About Chinese Women* ([1974] 1979), though nearly forgotten in Paris, nevertheless figured prominently in the American discussions of the 1980s.

Indeed, Kristeva's feminism has peaked: Since the early 1980s she primarily has been a practicing psychoanalyst and writer. But American feminists follow closely her challenging and frequently bewildering observations: Some perceive her ideas as a boon to radical feminism; others criticize her as too accepting of the male order, as too mild or misguided; others contrast her formulations with those of other feminists; and still others restrict themselves to her trenchant comments on Chinese women.[1] Yet most of Kristeva's recent thought tends to originate at the intersection of psychoanalysis and linguistic parsing, which to-gether, she presumes derive from the special type of cooperation that can originate only in the accepting or loving communication between an analyst and her patient. She stated to Elaine Baruch (around 1982) that

> the space of freedom for the individual is love—it is the only place, the only moment in life, where the various precautions, defenses, conservatism break down and one tries to go to the limit of one's being. ... The love rela-tion is a situation where the limits between the *Ego* and the *Other* are con-stantly abolished and established. (Baruch, 1991, p. 6)

Such a focus on the personal rather than the political level inadver-tently distances Kristeva from leftist movements that tend to subsume some sort of ideologically and "politically correct" position: Her inqui-ries into feminism now are on a back burner, as she keeps advocating change predominately on the personal rather than the political level in her psychoanalytic practice. Madelon Sprengnether (1990) understood her correctly when she stated that "Kristeva's insistence on the androgy-nous nature of semiotic writing has allied her with the 'anti-feminism' of French women theorists who oppose any form of essentialism" (p. 214). To some extent this already was implied when Leon Roudiez, in his in-troduction to Kristeva's *Desire in Language* ([1977] 1980), cautioned that

> [when Kristeva] refers to the "speaking subject" one should always bear in mind that this is a split subject—divided between unconscious and con-scious motivations, that is, between physiological processes and social constraints ... [and that] the object of her investigations is no longer lan-guage (as in structuralism), or discourse (as phenomenology would have it), or even enunciation; rather it is the discourse of a split subject—and this involves her in psychoanalysis. (p. 5)

Here, Kristeva elaborates on Lacan's admonition that language always operates on two planes and also always signifies something other than what it says and invites multiple critiques of meaning within a fixed symbolic system. According to Roudiez, Kristeva accounted for the manifestations of this splitting by

> posit[ing] two types of signifying processes to be analyzed within any pro-duction of meaning: a "semiotic" one and a "symbolic" one. The semiotic process relates to the *chora*, a term meaning "receptacle," which she bor-rowed from Plato, who describes it as "an invisible and formless being which receives all things and in some mysterious way partakes of the intel-ligible, and is most incomprehensible." It is also anterior to any space, an economy of primary processes articulated by Freud's instinctual drives (*Triebe*) through condensation and displacement, and where social and family structures make their imprint through the mediation of the maternal

body. While the *chora*'s articulation is uncertain, undetermined, while it lacks thesis or position, unity or identity, it is the aim of Kristeva's practice to remove what Plato saw as "mysterious" and "incomprehensible" in what he called "mother and receptacle" of all things. ... The symbolic process refers to the establishment of sign and syntax, paternal function, grammatical and social constraints, symbolic law. In short, the signifying process, as increasingly manifest in "poetic language," results from a particular articulation between symbolic and semiotic disposition. (Kristeva, 1980, pp. 6–7)

Kristeva's generation of French feminists took its distance from Simone de Beauvoir: These feminists did not share her negative view of maternity, and their theories rejected her existentialism, which itself was derivative of Sartre's (masculine) philosophy that excluded women as subjects. They held that de Beauvoir conceived women as rational, autonomous, and self-constituting subjects and thereby underplayed the negative influence of the social repression they were exposing and fighting. But American deconstructionist feminists, who picked up also on the French women's emphases on images and constructions of the body, increasingly prided themselves on the complexities of their own postmodern readings and often chose to ignore the (historical) French context. Thus Linda Zerilli (1991), for instance, argued that de Beauvoir's representation of motherhood and female subjectivity in *The Second Sex* ([1949] 1960) "intersects with and contexts the Kristevan *mise-en-scène* of maternity," that the pregnant woman is located "on the threshold between nature and culture, biology and language," and that maternal space confounds the boundaries of self and other (Zerilli, 1991, pp. 2–3). Clearly, Zerilli did not consider that the oppositions of nature and culture, biology and language, were anathema to de Beauvoir's framework or that Sartre ([1960] 1976) and Lévi-Strauss ([1963] 1966) already had debated this issue—a debate that ended in a dead heat. But by mediating between de Beauvoir's and Kristeva's entirely different conceptualizations of the maternal body, Zerilli expected to prove that "women are more than the passive bearers of a biological process, of a species teleology" (Zerilli, 1991, p. 28). (Kristeva told me that she considers this argument nonsensical.) However, such deconstructions and associations have become the meat of the Second Wave of feminism.

Women of the First Wave as well understand Kristeva's literary intent but refuse to take it literally. Kristeva's elaborations on semiotics, however, have provided the Second Wave with a novel framework for what has turned into a cottage industry. Clearly, its proponents have refused to take seriously Leon Roudiez's warning against purely abstract speculation. Kristeva's work itself indicates that theory evolves out of practice and is modified by yet more practice. I would add, once again, that most French feminists by now have moved away from their earlier psychoanalytic conceptualizations to clinical practice. Thus Kristeva ([1981] 1989) included her views on Freud and Lacan in her primer on linguistic theories. She stated that the focus on the unconscious has proven that "psychoanalysis is inseparable from the linguistic universe, and has profoundly modified the classical notion of language" (p. 266).

But by continuing to quote Kristeva's early work, American feminists are able to make her sound more radical than she actually has become. As Jacqueline Rose (1986) commented, this phase of Kristeva's work is the least useful even though it is what she is best known for: "What happens to this maternally connoted and primitive semiotic is that it is first defined as the hidden underside of culture (we can recognise the proximity of this to the classical demonic image of femininity) and then idealised as something whose value and exuberance the culture cannot manage and has therefore had to repress" (p. 154).

Yet Gallop (1982) concluded from this passage that "a woman has nothing to laugh about when the symbolic order collapses. She can enjoy it if, identifying with the mother, vaginated body, she imagines herself thus to be the sublime repressed which returns in the fissures of the order. She can also easily die of it ... if, without successful maternal identification, the symbolic paternal order were her only tie to life" (p. 115). Gallop, who cast the female body as the site of resistance, accused Kristeva of mastering several different jargons that spring from traditional authority and of "presum[ing] to speak from the place which no one has the right to speak from" (p. 116)—that is, from the perspective of the phallic father.

Jacqueline Rose (1986) remained more judicious. She took seriously Kristeva's insistence that every element of language and every signifier be examined psychoanalytically in line with the tenets of avant-garde writing and as "the site of maximum abjection." Only at that "site," said Rose, can the "savagery" of the speaking being be heard and the pathology of language shifted (in body and letter) through clinical engagement to subjectivity and the unconscious (p. 144). In other words, only in that place can ambivalence be tolerated.

Basically, Kristeva was out to articulate the psychic processes that language normally glosses over by focusing on meaning or sense, by bridging the apparent dualism of the semiotic/symbolic division, and by transposing what goes on in the psychoanalytic process to the realm of language. Rose explained that Kristeva realized that the unconscious cannot be politicized, since this would confuse political and psychic resistance; that she gave up revolutionary politics in favor of individualistic dissidence and thereby criticized feminist ideology; and that (total) psychosexual identity carried with it the risk of wrecking all identity and of a self-blinding allegiance to psychic norms (Rose, 1986, p. 150). More explicitly, Rose stated:

> As soon as we try to draw out of [Kristeva's] exposure an image of femininity which escapes the straitjacket of symbolic forms, we fall straight into that essentialism and primacy of the semiotic which is one of the most problematic aspects of her work. And as soon as we try to make of it the basis for a political identity, we turn the concept inside out, since it was as a critique of identity itself that it was originally advanced. No politics without identity, but no identity which takes itself at its word. (p. 175)

In *The Powers of Horror* ([1980] 1982), Kristeva analyzed women's fantasies of *abjection*—a sense of extreme disgust as well as fascination—which she linked to the place femininity is accorded within culture. Janet Sayers faulted Kristeva for claiming never to have suffered personally from a sense of discrimination or from having been excluded or oppressed (Sayers, 1986, p. 172). But Rose stated that even though Kristeva never totally identified with feminism, her analysis of the formation of psychosexual identities was invaluable for feminists, so they ought not be so hard on her for investigating love as a strategy in dealing with men (Rose, 1986, p. 157). Of course, when Kristeva said that each woman must negotiate the troubled psychic waters in their interactions with men (p. 162), she was, in fact, aligned with the less radical feminists and against the militant lesbian contingent.

Janet Wolff, another Kristeva fan, showed why feminists "were inspired by [her] suggestion that avant-garde writing in late nineteenth-century France articulates the 'semiotic' (that is, the pre-Symbolic) which predates the child's entry into language and into patriarchy" (Wolff, 1990, pp. 52–53). Although Wolff's focus here was on modernism and she cautioned against simplistic notions passed off as "modernism," she pointed to Kristeva's writing as, among other things, an "escape from the confines of the predominating patriarchal culture" in her attempt to get into the prelinguistic realm, into the rhythms and pulsions of the semiotic chora (pp. 67–68, 74). Wolff too built on the Lacanian premise that the child enters into language before reaching the oedipal phase and thus approaches it from *within* the symbolic—that is, from within the patriarchic structure. Even though she criticized Kristeva's project, Wolff credited her with addressing the crucial link between language and patriarchy. On balance, she perceived her as more radical a feminist than most others.

Indeed, Kristeva's flights into the furthest philosophical-linguistic realms, into the theoretical fantasies she seems to ground in her own and her patients' subjective unconscious, legitimate her readers' own, personal associations to her works: Like the Delphic oracle, she can be interpreted in line with their needs, provided they try to cleanse themselves of their preconceived notions. Recently, Kristeva has switched to writing novels, which are, she told me, "the best way to get beyond the ideologies and to the subtle contradictions."

Luce Irigaray's Nonmasculine Discourse

Like Kristeva, Luce Irigaray assumed that every culture that considers the phallus as the signifier "produces" women who feel themselves castrated and fear the loss of their father's love. But Irigaray was more confrontational than Kristeva. And she had already criticized both Freud and Lacan in *Speculum of the Other Woman* ([1974] 1985) for underplaying the importance of the female body, for "speaking through" it rather than for it. She told Elaine Baruch that Lacan then had expelled her from the Department of Psychoanalysis at the University of Vincennes and had "put [her] into quarantine from the analytic world" (Baruch and Serrano, 1988, p. 163). According to Margaret Whitford (1991), "She was censured for being politically committed by psychoanalysts who thought that being a psychoanalyst precluded political commitment" (p. 5). After that she became truly radical and for a while aligned herself with the Communist party.

Irigaray had criticized Freud for not having paid attention to the cultural determinants of his theories, for the fact that psychoanalysis did not analyze the unconscious fantasies of its own discourse, and for the patriarchy it incorporated. Hence she said that psychoanalysis was blind to its own biases by accepting the development of little boys as the norm. And she painted Lacan with the conservative brush: He focused on the primacy of the phallus and on the transmittal of the law (culture and all this entails) from father to son. In fact, by pointing out that Lacan's mirror (the pivot of his theories of discourse, of narcissistic identification, of the imaginary ego, and of bodily autonomy) saw only that women's bodies were lacking—they have a "hole"—she challenged the until then (internally) unchallenged master.

Like Kristeva, Irigaray was trained in philosophy and linguistics. So after being ousted by Lacan she increasingly concentrated on philosophy and on radical politics. Because in France in the 1970s such politics were rather closely aligned with Communist ideology and on principle challenged state authority, Irigaray in her analyses of language and discourse proposed to alter the relation between men and women. She pointed out how differently they speak about sex; how men are more likely to use the first-person pronoun, to designate themselves as active, to deal with abstractions. Women, she found, are used to being self-effacing, to engaging in dialogue, to collaborating.

In any event, Irigaray focused on sexual difference, on the one issue she thought could save us all "on an intellectual level" (Whitford, 1991, p. 165). Answers to her questions, she thought, might produce a new age of thought and art, poetry and language, a new *poetics* and ethics. Although in her theorizing Irigaray did not spell out that she was exploring, also, the dynamics, fantasies, and so on, of lesbianism, she subsumed these questions when she spoke of a revolution in thinking that would allow for sexual difference that, in turn, would inaugurate a new society by properly addressing the relationship of art to sexual difference. At times, she linked these matters to the class struggle and to the transition to an impending era in which time and space, occupation of place and of identities, would take on as yet unknown and unfathomed shapes. At times she linked them to desire, which she said determined the alternating states of nearness and distance between lovers (p. 167). She proposed to attain this sort of rapprochement by reinterpreting Freud's notion of *sublimation* and by taking account of *female partial drives.* And Irigaray expected woman to rediscover herself by correcting how she had been depicted in history, by looking at her relation to the conditions of production rather than by looking at work itself (p. 169). Ultimately, Irigaray declared, an ethics of sexual difference cannot reduce one sex to the other. Wonder alone, she concluded, might allow for autonomy based on sexual difference, for the freedom to ally or separate, and for the uncertainty we need to get to the heart of the human mystery.

Irigaray criticized the philosopher Levinas ("Questions to Emmanuel Levinas" [Whitford, 1991, pp. 178–189]) for characterizing the feminine as the underside or reverse side of man's aspiration toward enlightenment, as its negative rather than in relation to itself, and for approaching the other's body in terms of his own needs. She said that Levinas knew nothing of communion in pleasure or of ecstasy and substituted the son for the feminine in his desire for paternity, thereby depriving the child as well. As in her other essays, Irigaray referred to the relations between living humans and God. However, I am bypassing the neoreligious dimension of her writing not only because I consider it pie-in-the-sky and fantasy but because I am concerned only with feminism and psychoanalysis. Still, insofar as Irigaray's turn to God is part of her larger theses, it either upset the scientifically oriented psychoanalysts or led them to dismiss her—even the Lacanians. The conclusion to the essay on Levinas exemplifies Irigaray's more recent concerns:

> Why, at this period of the convenant, does God suspend the link between the two most spiritual of the senses, thereby depriving men of the carnal representation of the covenant? Is this not a gesture that breaks with the more feminine cultures? The *Song of Solomon* harks back to the break and

evokes the painful separation between her who wants to be initiated in her mother's chamber, him who awakes her beneath the tree, the apple-tree where the mother is said to have conceived her, and that which takes them into the banqueting house, the chamber or the armies of the king. The two lovers are separated. (pp. 187–188)

Janet Sayers (1986) suggested, correctly, that if women were to heed Irigaray and return to her supposed preoedipal biological essence, sisterhood would be founded on an illusory basis, on that of the preoedipal child's "imaginary" experience of itself as one with the mother—hardly a sound basis for feminist struggle (p. 46). Sprengnether (1990), however, admired Irigaray's evocation of sexual difference because it "effaces the distinction between language and sexuality" (and speech) in lyrical prose full of eroticism that could be addressed to a lover of either sex or the self (p. 210). Susan Rubin Suleiman (1990) illustrated best Irigaray's notions of love as a state of being, a form of communication between women in which "binary oppositions become nonpertinent" and which may manage to avoid "the traditional male attempt to imprison the beloved woman in his rigid conception of her" (pp. 124–127).

Hélène Cixous's Appeal

Like Irigaray, Hélène Cixous suggested a rather immediate relationship between women, writing, and the body that could not but exclude men. She too started by focusing on the physical differences between men and women and declared that woman writes from her own experiences, that her libido is cosmic, that she has to speak in her own right without "becoming-a-man" (Whitford, 1991, p. 76). In *The Book of Promethea* ([1983] 1991), stated her translator Betsy Wing, Cixous

> is working to repair the separation between fiction and presence, trying to chronicle a very-present love without destroying it in the writing. … Conflation of seemingly separate fields, such as fiction and authenticity, fiction and biography, sexte/texte, person and place, person and person, subject and object, is a technique that she has frequently used to provide escape from our coded perceptions of what is 'natural.' (p. x)

In the last section of *The Newly Born Woman* ([1975] 1986), Cixous and Clément addressed their differences and thereby highlighted a central debate among French feminists. Cixous located her discourse "halfway between theory and fiction" because she distrusted the male, and thus phallocentric, discourse. Because Lacan was *master* of this discourse as well, Clément questioned whether his knowledge could be transmitted to women's discourse without compromising it. They concurred that theoretical vigilance is needed and that "the paradox of mastery is that it is made up of a sort of complex ideological secretion produced by an infinite quantity of doorkeepers" (p. 138). Yet Cixous objected to Clément's notion that the analytic act is *transmitted* through this dialogue: Accepting it ruled out the elimination of repression, particularly of those who could not enter into this (elitist) conversation and therefore into power. Postulating the French situation, where national education is centralized, hierarchically organized, and closely controlled by the state, they hypothesized that *cultural* oppression of women coincides with economic evolution and with the development of capitalism. In the process, stated Cixous, women ended up aligned with no-knowledge or with knowledge-without-power (p. 141). In Althusserian terms, she then recalled that when she had been "theoretically naive" she had felt aggressed on, under attack, because those outside "the Symbolic" always feel trapped. She implied that women have not sufficiently explored their bisexuality because "there is something in woman's libidinal organization that doesn't enjoy the discourse assuming sexual difference" (p. 146).

"I started with [Freud's patient] Dora," Cixous explained rather pompously, in yet another exchange, and first "produced a text on it" while "siding frenetically with the different characters and identifying while reading" (Cixous and Clément, [1975] 1986, p. 148). As she was theorizing about her own associations to the Dora case, she "could not keep from laughing from one end to the other, because, despite her powerlessness and with (thanks to) that powerlessness, here is a kid who successfully jams all the little adulterous wheels that are turning around her and, one after the other, they break down. ... It is she who is the victim, but the others come out of it in shreds" (p. 150). Cixous went on to make theoretical fun of the *maid in the family,* who "is everywhere," always the seductress, seduced by the boss and then eliminated for it (p. 150).

Cixous also made much of her own impeccable German, her mother's language. In *"Coming to Writing" and Other Essays* ([1977] 1991), she called it *lallemande*—the French word for German that she had spelled phonetically as a child. But having learned German while growing up in Algeria, along with Arabic and French, Cixous apparently was less attuned to the living conditions Viennese burghers like Freud took for granted: These included the ever-present maid. Yes, "she is everywhere, in all Freud's analyses ... [and] is a character who is just beginning to disappear from analyses" (Cixous and Clément, [1975] 1986, p. 150). Perhaps Cixous focused on the maid because this servant was no longer a part of every Parisian family's life. Cixous and Clément, however, were out to fault Freud for neglecting issues of class (p. 151). Thus they focused "on the servant girl that's always in the kitchen," who "appears in the notes rather than the text" but who ends up by reversing the relation between

Freud and Dora—who ultimately outfoxed him, too, by abruptly leaving her analysis (p. 153). Thereby, they contended, Dora exemplified "the hysteric who is the typical woman in all her force, and whose strength derives from her desire" (p. 154).

Cixous did not expect the revolution to happen through language. She maintained, along with Georges Bataille, that even in the class struggle the libido—desire—cannot be oppressed: "It is in the taking off from desire that you will revive the need for things to really change" (Cixous and Clément, [1975] 1986, p. 157). For desire communicates itself. In the end, Cixous moved from individual desire through language to the class struggle, which, she stated,

> does not stop. There is imagination, desire, creation, production of writing (you see I am trying to find different names for the same experiences) and then somewhere else, on another level of reality, there is class struggle, and within it, women's struggle. There are missing links in all that, which we should try to think in order to succeed in joining our two languages. Sometimes desire and artistic production anticipate class struggle in its unfolding but also, dialectically, they are fallout from it, a more or less unconscious effect, with all its mediations, unthought at the present time. A conflict so fundamental for intellectuals that it informs the totality of consciousnesses, wherever they are situated, caught in impossible contradictions, whether consciously or not, whether they lean more toward guilty conscience or toward blindness. (p. 159)

Here, Cixous not only betrays the influence of Althusser's "scientism," of Bataille's notions of artistic freedom that opens up to desire, and of Lacan's phallocentrism but expects to create a (social) space for women who will not succumb to the drawbacks of patriarchy. She vaguely intimates that this space might be on the road to homosexuality via bisexuality. American lesbian theorists picked up on her ambiguous suggestions, which, however, are beyond the scope of this book.

Years after Cixous's free-associative prose was forgotten among Parisian intellectuals, her 1977 *"Coming to Writing" and Other Essays* was published in England and the United States (in 1991). Susan Rubin Suleiman reminded us in her 1991 introduction that feminism, along with Marxism, structuralism, and poststructuralism, was no longer fashionable in Paris (p. vii). Nor was the existentialism that also nurtured Cixous when she used it to describe, for instance, "the moment [she] came to life ... [and] trembled: from the fear of separation, the dread of death ... I watched [death] wound, disfigure, paralyze, and massacre from the moment my eyes opened to seeing. I discovered that the face [mother's] was mortal, and that I would have to snatch it back every moment from Nothingness" (p. 2). Shades of *L'Être et le Néant?* Yes, but also of Lacan. Writing, she went on, manages to keep death at a distance, to win grace, to avoid blindness, to repel death and reaffirm life. Cixous "got past the walls" of being a "Jewoman" with a German mother (tongue), of growing up in Algeria without a father, of wanting to master French literature. Her passion to write allegedly emancipated her.

Still, was Cixous's fate as rare as we are led to believe—in a world where Hitler, anti-Semitism, and World War II uprooted every Jew who wasn't killed? Writing saved her, as it did Primo Levi, Jerszy Koscinski, Jakov Lind, and Clarice Lispector—the woman Cixous discovered, then taught about and cast as her double. Primarily, however, Cixous was indebted to surrealism and to Lacan: "Let yourself go, let the writing flow, … become the river, let everything go, open up, unwind, open the floodgates, let yourself roll—this could be a recipe for automatic writing, the poetic mainstay of the first Surrealist Manifesto" (Cixous, 1991, p. x). Until Cixous, Suleiman pointed out, no woman ever had written in a way that surmounted sexual difference. Like other women, Cixous too had believed that she had no right to write: She had no legitimate place, no land, no fatherland, no history of her own; she was an outsider who had to fit in (p. 15). As a young girl, she recalled, she didn't eat but consumed books instead, nourished herself on texts, on language, and "was raised on the milk of words" (p. 20). Was she anorexic, I wonder, or too taken with hyperbole?

Cixous's writing bears her out: She was raised on the *nouriture* (nourishment) of French intellectuals at a time when this *nouriture* had become especially wordy, long after the proverbial *clarté* (clarity) had been replaced by high-flown rhetoric. I don't mean to denigrate Cixous's talent. However, much original writing is done by lonely, tortured individuals such as Joseph Conrad, Emily Dickinson, Dostoevsky, Proust. Cixous got instant acclaim from a movement in the process of formation, similar to that attained by the social realists in the 1930s. So for a short time, her conversations with Clément and with other "graduates" of Lacan's seminars served as the fulcrum of Parisian feminism.

Cixous was especially inventive in mimicking Lacan-type double entendres. For instance, she "sexcused" herself, took her shameful parts in hand, questioned whether men overwhelmed by overfullness of femininity were human (Cixous, 1991, p. 35). A few pages later, she lapsed into romanticism, describing what has been discussed and argued by writers throughout time:

> The text is always written under the sweet pressure of love. My only torment, my only fear, is of failing to write as high up as the Other, my only chagrin is of failing to write as beautifully as Love. The text always comes to me in connection with the Source. If the Source were dammed up, I would not write. And the source is given to me. It is not me. One cannot be one's own source. Source: always there. (p. 42)

And so on. Is this just high-flown prose, self-indulgence, or are we learning something about femininity? Or is it her version of the death of the author theme, her positive response to Barthes and Foucault? The answer depends upon the reader's predisposition, which is as Barthes said it should be. Cixous's own disposition, updating the voice of Psychanalyse et Politique, is to repeat over and over again that males always exert intellectual terrorism and that their domination must end.

Of course, Cixous's use of Lacanian and Althusserian formulations is linked to the lofty conclusions in Freud's "sociological" works, such as "Totem and Taboo" and "The Future of an Illusion," and to Marx's *Eighteenth Brumaire* and *The Communist Manifesto*. Along with members of the other avant-garde groups that sprang up after the students had been on, and gotten off, the barricades in the late 1960s, the feminists around Cixous expected to obstruct the symbolic order, to dislocate bourgeois language, and to let their bodies be their guides.

A Number of Other French Mistresses

Catherine Clément and Monique Wittig were more explicit than Cixous by saying that a cultural revolution is dependent on a political, economic, and social one. Such a revolution, declared Clément, places high stakes on the function of intellectuals and its *anticipation* requires militant action (Marks and Courtivron, 1980, p. 131). Wittig actually rejected Cixous's and Irigaray's formulations of "woman" and of "femininity" as accepting of the ontological differences between the sexes that belong to heterosexual, bourgeois, and capitalist thinking. And she was certain that the class struggle was central to lesbian concerns:

> It is only the way that the masters interpret a historical situation of domination … for us, this means there cannot any longer be women and men, and that as classes and as categories of thought or language they have to disappear, politically, economically, ideologically. If we, as lesbians and gay men, continue to speak of ourselves and to conceive of ourselves as women and as men, we are instrumental in maintaining heterosexuality. (Suleiman, 1990, p. 131)

Clearly, such a formulation shifted into questions of tactics of lesbian and gay movements and clashed with a number of taken-for-granted American feminists' positions as well as with available and viable political means of action. Indeed, Wittig's take on the political realm inescapably was beyond the psychic realm—and beyond my topic on Freudians and feminists.

Although Toril Moi's *French Feminist Thought: A Reader* was published only in 1987, it contains articles written between 1974 and 1984.

Moi started out with a lecture by Simone de Beauvoir, "Women and Creativity," which "is marked by a disturbing tendency to accept dominant patriarchal definitions of art and artists" without mentioning that "the category of 'universality' is a concept based on male views and male experience" (p. 2). She contrasted this to Anne Tristan and Annie de Pisan's "Tales from the Women's Movement," which consisted of triumphant reminiscences of the provocative antics by radical French feminists in the late 1960s and of the ludicrous responses by the press and politicians that heralded the tortured birth of French feminism. Tristan and Pisan outdid each other in recalling their victories over and confrontations with politicians, with the "bourgeois women who merely fought for the same rights as men" (p. 35), and with those who deemed women's issues a "problem" (p. 36). That is what allegedly led them all to agree that "the main enemy ... beyond capitalism is male civilization, sustained entirely by our labor"—by our domestic and reproductive services (p. 37). But only a few of Moi's authors were directly concerned with psychoanalysis (among them were Kristeva and Irigaray).

In the section "The Politics of Difference," Annie Leclerc expanded on the consequences of women's reproductive services. She extolled the joy of childbirth, which she assumed that in their heart of hearts men envy. That is why they take pride in fatherhood: It ends up by "giving virility the taste of triumph; femininity the taste of humiliation and sacrifice" (Moi, 1987, p. 73). To make up for their deprivation, Leclerc went on, men have made women's lot painful by assigning them tasks they consider inferior and beneath their own dignity and then have treated them with contempt. If women's labor were recognized in the light of its true value instead of being seen as just arduous, exhausting, and harrowing, it would be coveted rather than what it has become: a millstone and an oppressive, intolerable necessity (p. 76). To remedy this situation, Leclerc suggested that male power values be uprooted and reduced to smithereens and that their perception of desire and misconceptions about pleasure stop consisting of *possession* alone—a pleasure that ultimately deprives men of their virility (p. 77).

Christine Delphy argued that Leclerc, in fact, was "passing from protofeminism into antifeminism" because she proceeded from actual situations in life and assumed that social organization determines values rather than the other way around (Moi, 1987, p. 81). Leclerc's circular argument, she judged, neither explained the oppression of women nor helped women understand themselves (p. 87).

In the section "Women's History," Arlette Farge stated that the origins of the debates on this topic were ideological and personal, that they were based on the idea of sexual segregation, and, as "an indispensable partner of the then thriving women's liberation movement," that they "engendered great expectations" (Moi, 1987, pp. 133–134). But the act of remembering, she continued, is impeded by the same factor, by "rewriting" this history—which either produced the forgotten heroine or the exceptional woman (p. 135). But men as well as women wrote in that mode, so that we still are in danger of remaining rooted in the existing (unquestioned) male-female relationships (p. 146).

After Elizabeth Badinter examined mother-child relations within this history, Michèle Le Doeuff maintained that women philosophers, in spite of their long oppression by male discourse, ought to recognize that only by applying the tenets of male philosophy will they be able to oust its alienating schemas and to take a position that will decipher the latent, philosophical assumptions about women (Moi, 1987, p. 182). Le Doeuff outlined how, throughout the ages, philosophers such as Pythagoras and Hegel, Comte and Sartre (with Simone de Beauvoir's blessing), have emphasized the differences between men and women and always have passed off their assumptions as rational theoretical discourse (pp. 194–197). She stated that women had not yet won the battle that would allow them to enter philosophy as equals and that this would happen only if philosophy were to become more of a collective discourse and were to recognize the necessarily incomplete character of all theorization (p. 208). Here, it is not clear whether she was speaking of philosophical thought or its professional associations.

Whereas Le Doeuff emphasized that psychoanalysis lends an extra dimension to women's sensibility and to their bent of listening to their unconscious, Sarah Kofman credited it as the only possible means of escaping the male/female trap. Kofman reinterpreted Freud's "On Narcissism: An Introduction" (1914c) by maintaining that there is a flip side to the narcissistic woman's charm. Were we to suppose that her enigmatic nature is not the "natural deficiency" Freud postulated but an affirmation of "her narcissistic self-sufficiency and her indifference," we would no longer suppose that she envies his penis but would conclude that he envies her ability to keep her narcissism in reserve and that he feels depleted for having emptied himself (into her?) of his own original narcissism (Moi, 1987, p. 212). Freud himself was trapped by women because he failed to recognize the mimetic essence of desire (p. 218) and, unlike Proust (here Kofman relied on René Girard's critical work), did not acknowledge the mythic character of narcissism (p. 219).

Conclusion

As I have noted, the dominant French discourse of the 1970s did not address feminism in as pragmatic a fashion as its American equivalent, followed a specific philosophical and rhetorical embodiment of Marx and

Freud, and by the 1980s had led many of these women to become practicing psychoanalysts and writers. When their works were inserted into American feminism, often in tandem with postmodern narratives, they provided the theoretical grist for feminist studies, as well as for the emerging gay and lesbian studies. Irigaray's *Marine Lover of Friedrich Nietzsche* ([1991] 1993), for instance, may be described as fiction or as an essay of the imagination, but it will be "theorized" in American universities and will not be read by the general intellectual.

In sum, French feminists' theories supplied much of the raw material for Anglo-Saxon feminists and in American universities ended up fueling the Second Wave of the movement. However, postmodern feminists did not simply follow the French lead but were drawn to it as a means of getting to the roots of women's repression. For instance, Nannerl Keohane, former president of Wellesley College, now president of Duke University, and coeditor of *Signs*, in her coedited reader *Feminist Theory: A Critique of Ideology* (1981), focused on the experiential aspects of feminist theory to demonstrate its nearly limitless scope:

> Its subject is women's lives, past or present, historically recorded or known only by inference, experienced in association with men of the dominant culture or with men who are also oppressed. Feminist theory reconsiders historical, economic, religious, biological, artistic, and anthropological constructs and explanations. It brings to consciousness facts of our experience as women that have hitherto escaped attention because they have not been part of, and may even have contradicted, predominant theoretical accounts of human life. (Keohane, Rosaldo, and Gelpi, 1981, p. vii)

In her eagerness to encompass and delve into the potentially drastic changes in women's consciousness, Keohane expected to analyze everything that had preceded women's recent advances, including false consciousness, from an enlightened (but not enlightenment) perspective. Moreover, she expected the flux of the evolving theory to further raise the consciousnesses of women in the movement and of those it inevitably would attract. But to "come to terms with the ideological constructs of the milieu and with the radical (male) theorists who first produced those constructs—Marx, Confucius, Freud, Saint Paul"—as well with (mistaken) feminist theory such as Simone de Beauvoir's, which "defined [women] by the male gaze, by his construct and desire"—she inevitably opened Pandora's box for both substantive and methodological reevaluations (Keohane, Rosaldo, and Gelpi, 1981, pp. vii, ix).

Within this enterprise, psychoanalytic feminism was just a fragment of a wide-ranging dialogue, and its proponents were fairly peripheral. Only three contributions in Keohane's volume cited Freud, and they did so in passing. Julia Kristeva asserted that the analytic situation showed the penis as the major referent in the "operation of separation" of the sexes (in language learning) by emphasizing the *lack* or *desire* for it (Keohane, Rosaldo, and Gelpi, 1981, p. 41) and that modern women only partially accepted Freud's theory that the desire for a child eventually replaced the desire for a penis (p. 49). Jean Elshtain pointed out that Freud had been more concerned with the "intuitive, fantastic, expressivist aspects of human experience and language than his 'scientific' American interpreters" and that his language was more "puzzling, enigmatic, full of paradoxes, irony, jokes and surprises" than that of his followers (p. 142). She chided both Dorothy Dinnerstein (1976) and Nancy Chodorow (1978) for connecting too tightly and concretely the nature of private social arrangements (which are congealed as the young child develops) and the resulting detrimental public outcomes: Dinnerstein did this by holding that "women are not allowed to speak *to* the public world" and Chodorow by recommending more collective child rearing (pp. 142–143).

Susan Griffin (1978), in her criticism of ideology and her own innermost search and in "the desire to know deeply ... the truth, the whole and compassionate being she is," quoted Freud's dictum that what seems contradictory to the conscious mind makes sense in its unconscious counterpart (Keohane, Rosaldo, and Gelpi, 1981, p. 279). Griffin, of course, made comments about all women everywhere. And she explicitly reprimanded feminists for wanting to have instant resolutions, for purposefully ignoring Freud, and for censoring anyone who disagreed with them. Altogether, she criticized this as censoring "not only [her] imagination and [her] thinking but [her] reading" (p. 279).

German feminists, as I note in Chapter 7, followed American feminists' dialogues. But on balance they were not only more sociologically but also more psychoanalytically oriented. And they had other fish to fry. Though attuned to classical psychoanalysis, they produced the type of feminism that was suited to their own milieu and that, for the most part, became a sort of updated version of America's First Wave—but with a more critical and decidedly Marxist- and Frankfurt School–oriented cast. Instead of picking up on America's Second Wave, they have focused on social and political ends.

7 Feminism in Germany

When German feminists "theorize," they do so in the "traditional" Freudian mode. Although in the former *Bundesrepublik* there now are a few Lacanian enclaves as well, these do not have much, if any, impact on psychoanalytic practices or on the larger culture. Thus German feminism is carried forth by women psychoanalysts and by their collaborators in the social sciences. (In the former East Germany, psychoanalysis was banned.) Actually, German feminism and psychoanalysis went hand in hand. At first, in the devastated postwar atmosphere, women had neither the time nor the energy to focus on feminism. The first outspoken feminist was Margarete Mitscherlich. In 1967, together with her husband, Alexander Mitscherlich, she wrote the best and best-selling work, *The Inability to Mourn* (1967), on the Germans' (unacceptable) way of dealing with the Holocaust. In their book, the Mitscherlichs explained why psychoanalysis was the only viable means for their compatriots to come to terms with their Nazi past: It alone was equipped to penetrate to the unconscious and thus able to comprehend the psychic mechanisms that had enabled some Germans to commit mass murder in cold blood and others to sit by and let it happen.

Before the Mitscherlichs embarked on writing this book, they observed their patients in the psychosomatic clinic they set up in Heidelberg in 1949 and then in the outpatient clinic they established in Frankfurt. There, they tried to penetrate to the deepest levels of their analysands' psyches in order to grasp the processes that had facilitated their active participation or passive compliance in Nazism. (The student movement of the late 1960s picked up on the Mitscherlichs' psychological focus, and the prominent German feminists of the 1980s expanded on it.) This work confirmed for the Mitscherlichs that it was necessary to expose the unconscious elements that had facilitated the adulation of Hitler and that in part were based on indulging "oceanic feelings" and passive wishes in both men and women. With the help of this liberating process, they also expected German women to come into their own and to learn to recognize the extent of their domination by men.

After 1956, the Mitscherlichs' Sigmund-Freud-Institut in Frankfurt became not only the center for applied psychoanalytic research but the meeting and testing ground for a new generation of psychoanalysts, sociologists, and psychologists. Most of the women psychoanalysts did not question the intra-institute politics that were themselves a reenactment of the patronizing, if not patriarchal, relationship between women and men in the society at large—although they did so within the Deutscher Psychoanalytischer Verein (DPV). However, a few of the women published critiques of these conditions. The emanating "politics and psychoanalysis" was fashioned neither on the radical French *psych & po* nor on the inquiries and activities endemic to the rest of French or American movements. Instead, their research as well as their political activities were in line with the Marx-Freud initiatives emanating from the native Frankfurt School. Its central protagonists, Max Horkheimer and Theodor Adorno, returned from New York after the war, and their lectures at the university drew many students; their most prominent successor, Jürgen Habermas, was one of the closest collaborators of the Mitscherlichs. He also had been a teacher of many of their younger associates, mostly sociologists and philosophers.

Consequently, it was inevitable that in their efforts to liberate women in the society at large German feminists would rely and elaborate on offshoots of this specific, theoretical and idealistic amalgam of Freud and Marx. To begin with, they tried to counter the male-oriented bias in their institute and in the university, but these efforts were limited to theory and discussions. For women rarely were appointed as more than assistants and were totally excluded from the higher academic ranks. In the Mitscherlichs' institute, some women collaborators were critical of the (mostly unconscious) chauvinistic and patronizing behavior of their colleagues (about half of whom were on the political left); they were also perceived to be guilty of the authoritarianism that Erich Fromm ([1942] 1960) had conceptualized as the source of Nazi atrocities and that T. W. Adorno had described in *The Authoritarian Personality* (1950). These women harked back to Herbert Marcuse's (1964) view of modern society as suffering from "repressive desublimation" and recalled the details of the disputes between Freud and the early feminists in order to further explore how they might go beyond them (See Chapter 2).

All in all, most of the leading German feminists not only were friendly to Freudian psychoanalysis but started out as psychotherapists or as social scientists who used psychoanalytic concepts. They expected to radically change their society by applying what they were learning in the course of their own analyses and in working with patients. Like Freud, who had generalized from dream interpretation and free association about the individual psyche and then had extended his findings to, for instance, "Totem and Taboo" (1912–1913) and "Civilization and Its Discontents" (1930a), they now aimed to generalize from their women patients to everywoman. In addition, they took note of and then expanded on the contributions by contemporary classical Freudian feminists elsewhere, such as Janine Chasseguet-Smirgel ([1964] 1985, 1986) and Joyce McDougall ([1978] 1980, [1982] 1985) in France, and bolstered some of their own points by quoting Nancy Chodorow (1978) and Dorothy Dinnerstein (1976) and selected elements from Edith Jacobson's and Melanie Klein's concepts.

Until the late 1980s, when Lacanian formulations and those by Cixous, Irigaray, and Kristeva were being translated and introduced in a few universities, these remained within the discussions of fringe groups or within small circles of psychoanalysts who were extending the debates subsumed under "psychoanalysis and literature." These linguistically based theories had no more noticeable impact on the German feminist movement than they had on German psychoanalysis—not only because the exchange of ideas across the Rhine was very slow and often proceeded via America, as I was repeatedly told when lecturing on French structuralism in the early 1980s, but because Lacan's ideas, as I have shown, were products of *his* culture and anathema to German traditions. And unlike American academics who are forever on the lookout for something new, their German counterparts prefer to incorporate what they can explain as intrinsically fitting into their own theoretical and philosophical argumentation.

Margarete Mitscherlich

Margarete Mitscherlich, who had a Danish father and a German mother, was the first German Freudian in a position to go to London after World War II in order to get psychoanalytic training. She was attracted to the First Wave of American feminism during her stay at Palo Alto in 1972–1973 and to its German equivalent when, soon thereafter, she became a friend of Alice Schwarzer (Reinke-Köberer, 1983, p. 88). Schwarzer's own feminism was inspired by Simone de Beauvoir, whom she had interviewed and befriended. Thus she was not especially enamored of psychoanalysis. But when she wanted to find out why women's sexuality is at the same time binding (*Fessel*) and loosening (*Entfesselung*), she expected that Margarete Mitscherlich might help her get to the roots of this paradox. Mitscherlich first wrote on feminism in 1975 in *Psyche*. She did so in the postwar German manner of using psychoanalysis as social critique—that is, by postulating that German women who also had been raised by German mothers and under Nazism were "sharing" the character structure of German men. They were suffering just as much from the consequences of authoritarianism, said Mitscherlich, even though it manifested itself differently due to the unequal relations between the sexes. In addition, she shared the overall concerns of the German left: vigilance against traces of fascism, goodwill toward emerging international peace and ecological movements, a general disposition to equate the evils of communism with the drawbacks of capitalism, and ever vaguer notions of a future reunification with "the brothers and sisters in the East." (This is not to say that Mitscherlich was soft on communism or expected its collapse any more than anyone else did.)

Mitscherlich's approach to feminism primarily was psychoanalytical. She was on the lookout for the emotional hang-ups that had been caused by the "fatherless society," which, together with her late husband, Alexander Mitscherlich, she had so brilliantly described. Along with him, she had exposed the psychic legacies of the Hitler regime in order to strengthen the democratic elements in the still fragile Federal Republic. But her colleagues in the International Psychoanalytic Association (IPA) for the most part have remained unaware that Mitscherlich continues to be preoccupied with "the inability of Germans to mourn their past." As she noted in 1987, "Only few Germans take time out to think of their own or their people's past. They are busy with the present and, in any event, close their eyes to the future" (p. 7). To come to terms with this past, to keep it alive, and to avoid anything resembling it, informed Mitscherlich's feminism. Still, in the early 1970s, a number of her male as well as her female disciples primarily were interested in denouncing the inadequacies of the evolving German democracy—which she kept on defending in her own, idiosyncratic fashion.

Theoretically, Mitscherlich has been attuned to what has come to be called American ego psychology, although she also has been an eclectic and often adopts formulations influenced by the Londoners' Middle Group. Certainly, her writing on clinical methods has been very much in the mainstream of classical psychoanalysis. But this is precisely why some of her Freudian colleagues have not understood the more and more militant feminist stances she has taken in her increasingly frequent and popular media appearances. They often object to her (at times explicit) politics and get upset when she does not stress, as they do, that personal neutrality is the most essential ingredient of psychoanalysis, which includes political neutrality.

In a rather direct response to the issues brought up by the feminist movement, Mitscherlich (then Mitscherlich-Nielsen) (1975) questioned Freud's assumptions about female sexuality. Because Freud formed his theoretical propositions about sexual development on the basis of the limited knowledge available to him and was guided by the unexamined ideologies of the "natural" inferiority of women, she proposed that the plethora of research on the embryology of sexual differentiation and on the physiology of sexual function of both genders be incorporated into his theories. For instance, she suggested that because in a primary sense the organization of the human embryo is female, we stop regarding the clitoris as a rudimentary penis; that we account for the fact that both genders identify first with the mother; and that we no longer assume that the clitoris must be given up for the vagina as the central zone of sexual arousal at puberty, inasmuch as research had demonstrated that vaginal orgasm was a myth. (These criticisms were close to such American Freudians as Ethel Person, Arnold Cooper, and Louise Kaplan, but they did not reach as broad an audience as Mitscherlich.) Moreover, Mitscherlich contended that the psychoanalytic theory of sexuality and of neurosis primarily dealt with the *psychic transformation* of biological-physiological givens and that, therefore, the formative power of social ideologies had been underestimated. The examination of the psychological seat of ideology, of course, was a central topic that most of the researchers at the Sigmund-Freud-Institut addressed.

The Woman Who Is Always Ready to Make Peace

By the time Mitscherlich wrote *Die friedfertige Frau* (The Peace-Loving Woman) in 1985, she had addressed all the budding young feminists. They focused on the fact that prevalent practices in the economy and in politics were based on deeply imbedded moral double standards. "Everywhere", she noted, "men's associations, fraternities, and manliness are self-idealizing; and they militate against true fatherliness—which stands for humanity, civic duty and integrity" (p. 172).

To demonstrate that women's sensibilities are more attuned to true human needs than men's, without, however, accepting the social inferiority accorded them, and to underline her solidarity with the various protest movements (mostly for peace), Mitscherlich put the students' strikes in the 1960s in the context of the students' disaffection with their fathers' generation—as she previously had done—and commented on that generation's "increasing identification with and idealization of American politics, consumerism, and their predilection to go to war" (Mitscherlich, 1985, p. 5). As the militant students went about deidealizing their parents' generation and the American victors, she went on, the women's movement gained in strength. This was due to the fact that women identified with mothers who had had to be competent while bringing them up without their fathers, who had been away at war. Mitscherlich then went through the classical psychoanalytic explanations of women's innate masochism and linked the latter to their acceptance of men's commanding power: Men expect women to be, among other things, soft (*sanft*) under specific circumstances and aggressive under others. This necessary and unquestioned adaptation, held

Mitscherlich, confers "passive power" onto them and has dire consequences. For women internalize passive aggression along with passive power, so that "whoever has power as a woman must count on being unloved ... [and then] as a woman tends to transform this underlying aggression into reproachfulness and victimization" (p. 9). The only way to get out of this double bind is for women to learn how to better deal with their feelings of guilt and to encourage their daughters to stand on their own feet."

In the second chapter, Mitscherlich wondered whether there is a difference between male and female aggression. In psychoanalysis this comes down to conceptions of the difference between strong and weak superegos, which Mitscherlich assumed induced stereotypical views of "female being" (Mitscherlich, 1985, p. 21). Still, Mitscherlich quoted Chasseguet-Smirgel's ([1970] 1971) collection on female sexuality to indicate that Germans as well were attempting to counteract simplistic applications of psychoanalytic concepts to women's concerns. Mitscherlich quoted, particularly, articles from the *Journal of the American Psychoanalytic Association* of 1976 and from *Psyche* of 1978. But none of these studies, Mitscherlich argued, went far enough. For whatever new wrinkles in their explanations, they continued to accept Freud's hypotheses about female sexuality (penis envy, true femininity, etc.) while tending to explain role conflicts as inner conflicts (pp. 22–23). Most of all, she criticized the fact that psychoanalytic theories don't take cultural forces into account. No one, not even Karen Horney or Margaret Mahler, she stated, ever paid enough attention to societal and economic influences and to the enormous impact these have on parental attitudes toward their children—the future mothers and fathers (p. 63).

To bolster her argument, Mitscherlich pointed to Erich Fromm's, D. W. Winnicott's, and Anna Freud's elaborations on the deleterious repercussions of repressed aggression, and especially to its unfolding in girls. For the most part, she supported the position of object-relations theorists and argued that only social changes will ultimately allow for the transformation in the early relations between girls and their mothers. Inevitably, only in a climate that fosters individual autonomy, she stated, will it be possible to socialize children under circumstances that create stronger superegos. For intrapsychic conflicts don't thrive in a vacuum but in human surroundings in response to unconscious and conscious parental attitudes, examples, demands, projections, and so on (Mitscherlich, 1985, p. 74).

Most psychoanalysts have blamed women's hatred of men on the defenses the helpless girl erects against her original hatred of the all-powerful mother who prohibits autonomy—including masturbation. Mitscherlich quoted the American psychoanalyst Heinz Kohut: "The development of a healthy feeling of self-worth and integration of psychic structures into a cohesive self requires the mother's admiration" (Mitscherlich, 1985, p. 99). According to Kohut, and to Mitscherlich, this self-worth evolves, also, from the child's ability to idealize and introject its parents and from the simultaneously developing safe base that alone supports the emergence of a strong superego and militates against narcissistic disorientation (p. 133). In her conclusion, Mitscherlich blamed current ailments primarily on the fact that twentieth-century societies— in spite of the changes in modes of production, and other areas and their concomitant impact on the culture—continue to be run by the very men who cannot help but go on reproducing patriarchal family and social relations. Thus it is up to women to stop them from spawning more scapegoats. They alone, said Mitscherlich, can eradicate the roots of warlike disputes by withholding their approval of them, by questioning their own attitudes, and by stopping their *Friedfertigkeit,* which means, literally, their automatic readiness to make peace. This book was not analysis alone, but a cry for action.

Other German Feminists' Observations

The best overview of the early German feminist-cum-psychoanalytic discussions appears in *Psyche* (1978, no. 32). Thereafter, during the 1980s, *Psyche* included feminist issues as part of its psychoanalytically based social criticism, and a number of collections compiled by its editors contributed to the dissemination of these concerns.

In her essay "Sexuality in Today's Psychoanalysis—A Taboo," in *Malaise in Psychoanalysis* (1983), Ellen Reinke-Köberer, for instance, took off from Freud's "Some Psychical Consequences of the Anatomical Distinctions Between the Sexes" (1925j, p. 256)—where he argues that the individal erects defenses against earlier infantile wishes to be free of unpleasant insights, especially the knowledge of childhood sexuality. After that, the individual apparently accepts that knowledge, noted Reinke-Köberer, leaving it out of all discussions, which, however, is yet another defensive maneuver. This tendency has carried over particularly into feminist and other social movements and has become part of the ongoing debate on the connections between social domination and suppression of sexuality (Reinke-Köberer, 1983, p. 88). Even within psychoanalysis, she went on, this larger issue rarely is acknowledged except in its split-off version of "female sexuality"—despite the fact that psychoanalysis is the one discipline that "possesses the methodological means to overcome this splitting by working on the defenses and the transference" (p. 87).

Waltraud Gölter (1983) examined what she called the problematic socialization of female identity, and how this identity impinges on wom-
en's writing, and on the extent to which their creativity may be determined by the earliest relations to her mother, her specific preoedipal
conflicts and their resolution, and early dependency and loss (p. 642).
After applying the usual psychoanalytic apparatus of ego psychology to
examine texts by such writers as Christa Wolf, Anaïs Nin, Marguerite Du-
ras, and less famous German writers, she concluded that female identity
is more open than its male counterpart. But this openness and the female sense of defeat, of otherness, brings about a freedom from com-
pulsive habits of thought, along with a utopian consciousness that assumes there is nothing to lose and everything to gain. Consequently,
Gölter found that those women who overcome their initial hesitations
and assert themselves often end up as fantastically creative writers.

Carol Hagemann-White (1978) scrutinized the extent to which female
protest itself can influence the definitions of what is and is not acceptable—and thus healthy—female behavior in patriarchal societies. After
rejecting Freud's prejudices much as Mitscherlich had done and criticiz-
ing the nonsensical types of dismissals of Freud that Juliet Mitchell already had taken issue with (see Chapter 6), she focused on the construc-
tive goals of the feminist movement: the insistence that fighting against
subjugation in society must advance in tandem with an increasing
awareness of personal needs and that learning to pursue this end proceeds best when coupled with a personal analysis. However, women's
analyses were found to be more difficult than men's: As women begin to
feel autonomous, their male analysts start to feel threatened by women
patients who are testing their emerging autonomy and, in the process,
expect these same women to reassure them. In other words, as such
women patients are learning not to adapt to traditional norms, their
male analysts have not yet determined how to respond to them.
Hagemann-White went on to explain this situation in terms of the thesis
Gregory Zilboorg had advanced in 1944, which focused on "strong waves
of men's hatred of women and their psychobiological basis":

> [Zilboorg] indicates that within psychoanalytic theory there is a projection
> of aggression by the threatened-castrated woman which dominates the un-
> conscious attitude of man toward woman. Before the analyst can recognize
> the psychology of the woman he first has to admit his hatred of her, be-
> cause this hatred not only distorts his own view but also determines the re-
> ality within which the woman develops. This hatred can only be rational-
> ized and denied by the conviction that woman is already castrated and not
> only after she has been debased through seduction. (Hagemann-White,
> 1978, p. 739)

Beyond reviewing the reasons for feminists' resistance to psychoanalysis (very much as I did in Chapter 3) and providing examples mostly from the American movement, Hagemann-White reiterated that psychotherapists must basically be tolerant in order to deal with the specific needs of each of their woman patients, needs that result from "ills that have been (and continue to be) forced on her concretely … [by way of] traditionally conceptualized roles that assume, for instance, that she gains pleasure by taking care of her husband and son" (Hagemann-White, 1978, p. 756). However, the women's movement, Hagemann-White then said, recently had wrought some changes insofar as it had exposed the fact that psychotherapeutic ideas of health and definitions of illness were in latent complicity with the patriarchal status quo. Karola Brede (1987), whose earlier work at the Sigmund-Freud-Institut had been on the interface between the onset of psychosomatic symptoms and their immediate psychic trigger, eventually shifted her focus onto examining and synthesizing the different ways these processes occur in men and women. Always intent on retaining a sociological view that nevertheless would remain open to the psychoanalysts' findings, she kept her finger on the feminist movement's pulse in the attempt to accelerate and strengthen it.

What Does the (German) Woman Want?

In her tribute to Margarete Mitscherlich at the conference she organized for her seventieth birthday, "Was will das Weib in Mir?," Brede (1989) stated:

> In psychoanalysis the concept of femininity emerged out of our dated, social ideas about women which, in turn, contribute to the reification of these ideas. Images of women, judgements on their actions and even the actual actions not only of women but also of men, are part of the male principle of the rejection of the female; seemingly a "pure" means of expression of the female turns out to be the opposite of the male. … Clichés of women's penis envy and of the phallic woman are proof. Can these be destroyed without leaving, or even giving up, the framework of psychoanalysis—its theory, methods and means of treatment? (p. 12)

Brede went on to postulate that women's socialization inevitably depends on the "socializable substratum" that incorporates the differences between men and women in their role behavior as well as in the structure of their innermost identities, which, in fact, relate to their anatomy. When, in addition, stated Brede while paraphrasing Adorno (1951), what is considered female is based upon the male imagination, which itself assumes the unquestioned reciprocity between the sexes, women are being debased [*herabgesetzt*] as the objects of men's desires (Brede, 1989,

p. 51). And yet, objective means that institute equality—and that upset traditional patterns of behavior and lifestyles have increased with the capitalist mode of production: Economic priorities actually are "non-sexed." Legal equality as well, although not realized, is formally assured. Why then, Brede wondered, is there no de facto equality? Are individual character structures so closely amalgamated as to foreclose a basic change? That to Freud "femininity is a riddle (*Raetsel*) is difficult to reconcile with the assumption of equality between the sexes" (p. 17). And saying that woman is handicapped because she lacks a penis and suffers from castration anxiety, continued Brede, blocks the development of a proper mode of comprehending the sexuality of the understanding subject—in this case of Freud himself. The first generation of psychoanalysts, Brede recalled, questioned the uncritical reproduction of the consequences of this theory. Horney and Deutsch, for instance, inflated the importance of (*Aufwertung*) the female genitals. But their theories were not scientifically acceptable.

In the meantime, removing taboos surrounding sexuality and the body, Brede went on, had become the basis for the many public discussions of female experiences and motives, and of their lived connections to intimacy. This had induced new insecurities and had led to increasing difficulties in communication between the sexes and to questions about whether women were not losing control over their bodies in these new types of associations over such issues as abortion, reproduction, child custody, and support. The resulting malaise, which had subsumed also women's relations to their own bodies and identification with both the envied and disdained male relations to *their* bodies, explained Brede, manifested itself in the hope that new zones of intimacy could be reestablished; but this never happened without other unexpected and unwanted consequences (Brede, 1989, p. 21). From all of this she concluded, as did Mitscherlich in the same volume, that we must continue to pose Freud's question: "What does the woman in me want?"

Maria Torok (with Nicholas Rand), at this same meeting in Frankfurt, provided an unusual answer to that question in her very specific French manner of analyzing why Freud conceptualized sexuality in the way he did: She analyzed his correspondence regarding what apparently was preoccupying him while writing *The Interpretation of Dreams* and which continued to plague him for the rest of his life. As she was reconstructing Freud's chain of thoughts, Torok elaborated on his ongoing hesitation (*Schwanken*) between seduction and fantasy and found that these two components in his theoretical scenario (*Inszenierung*) kept flowing together only to end up in oscillation. "What does the woman in Freud want?" Torok again asked in the epilogue (Brede, 1989, p. 53). She answered that woman contains both the psychic and theoretical conflict in him. For "Freud's theory makes her into a double-sided being, into a 'head of Janus,' whose fate it is to constantly revolve around two never reconcilable poles" (p. 54).

German psychoanalyst Johannes Cremerius was less tentative. He maintained that Freud never questioned his preconceived notions. For in 1932, referring to the debates with women analysts, he had declared that psychoanalysts had learned much about how woman comes into being, how she develops out of the bisexually disposed child, but that "each time an unfavorable comparison seems to come up, our women analysts have been suspicious that we, the male analysts, have not yet overcome our deeply rooted prejudices against femininity" (Brede, 1989, p. 111). Freud never corrected this position. Instead of considering the objections by Horney in 1926, by Jones in 1927, and by Klein in 1928, Cremerius reminded us, he biologized penis envy. He had done this early on when instead of blaming Wilhelm Fliess for having botched Emma Eckstein's nose operation, he had declared that her bleeding was due to her hysteria; and when Sabina Spielrein confided that she had been having an affair with C. G. Jung, he asked her whether she was not unduly expressing the hatred in herself (pp. 112–113). Later on, when Freud urged that psychoanalysts practice abstinence, he added that the lovelorn woman had to be held in check by him [*zügeln*] "so that she would give up her biological demands, and by overcoming the animal components of her ego," she could continue her analytic work (p. 114).

Because Freud would not let go of his early propositions, he had to conclude that in psychoanalytic treatment the female patient would accept that she had to either adapt or fight her analyst for phallic domination. Cremerius then showed how this dilemma first could be handled by presenting a case of his own. However, he acknowledged that he had had to begin by working on his own fear of castration by strong women. With specific types of women patients, he elaborated, the analyst must realize that he cannot simply provide a father image but has to employ male domination as part of his technique. Such an immanently analytic technique, he concluded, works to systematically get rid of instinctual drives, make them conscious, and redirect them (Brede, 1989, p. 129). Thereby, Cremerius said, it is possible to stay within the classical Freudian paradigm even as one goes beyond it, and he suggested that others join him in a research project to explore this clinical method.

During the ensuing discussion, Cremerius explained that he wanted also to explore the role his own fantasies could play in learning about the secret fantasies of a thoroughly aggressive (hostile) woman patient and to learn how such a patient would do with a woman analyst. "What happened to this patient's passive wishes?" (Brede, 1989, p. 132) asked one conference participant; "Did she develop her femininity?" wondered another. "You did not really rid yourself of Freud's concept of the phallic woman but have avoided it in your treatment," interjected psychoanalyst Mechthild Zeul (p. 137). "I find it a bit difficult to have concepts. I experience concepts as typically male," stated Mitscherlich (p. 135).

Maya Nadig, an ethnologist-psychoanalyst who has worked in Switzerland and Mexico, compared the way women become mothers and their subsequent roles in these two countries. In rural Indian societies in Central America, she demonstrated, there is little differentiation between "time" and "life," and both sexes subscribe to closely prescribed complementary relationships—practically and symbolically. Motherhood is the presupposition for an adult woman, and her child provides her with her adult status and with the accompanying privileges—her own court, her autonomy. During pregnancy, while giving birth, and afterward, she is integrated into adult women's society and given access to its rituals, taboos, and symbolic secrets by her midwife, her mother-in-law, and the other women. Everything is ordained; the new mother is taken care of by her group and by her husband; the child is close to its mother but its bond to her gradually is loosened because it "is being linked to the world as well as the group [which] also is coresponsible for its development" (Brede, 1989, p. 147). Actually, summarized Nadig in psychoanalytic terms, the Mayan tribe understands the psychic developmental phases of both the new mother and her infant perfectly and turns them into social events by resorting to prescribed behaviors and rituals. Sexuality and other drives remain on the surface, although the mother's emotional and bodily sensitivities in part are subject to ethnic taboos. Mother and child are not threatened internally but by external factors: by persons emerging from the wilderness, the evil eye, transcendental forces such as bad winds, ghosts, and so on.

Due to this socialization process, the child cannot become its mother's self-object, as it does in urban, industrial settings where families must bring up children who will become competent in the world of work. To move the child into the center of their universe, women must give up their own autonomy. After reviewing what we know from countless studies about birth in hospitals, postpartum depression, conflict between staying home and pursuing a career, and so on, Nadig concluded that we lack the transitional rituals that might better integrate young mothers and their children into the larger society without the shocks and personal decisions we know about so well and take for granted.

Ultimately, Nadig found that psychoanalytic theory had not dealt well with these larger issues, had not addressed adequately—in the requisite metatheoretical fashion—the relation of psychoanalysis to womanhood.

Even Helene Deutsch, stated Nadig, desexualized the woman's libido in relation to her child; mirrored social reality and ideology instead of uncovering it (Brede, 1989, p. 156). And extending Melanie Klein's theories, Nadig said that the mother is feared as omnipotent and intrusive and is hated and held responsible for the disturbances and lacks in mother-child relations and that some psychoanalysts went even further and blamed her for social and political conditions as well (p. 156). So did Grete Bibring and her colleagues, maintained Nadig, when they described the psychic process surrounding pregnancy (and menopause)—when they compared these events to those of adolescents in crisis—as a step toward maturity (p. 157). Winnicott, who was perceived as the most sensitive of analysts dealing with these problems, asked Nadig how "normal" or "sick," adapted or disintegrated, a mother who centered on her new-born infant was considered. Nadig responded that she perceived this question itself as a special problem in German culture (p. 158). She ended by suggesting that we need a new paradigm to deal with the basic lack of psychoanalytic theory in order to account for the culture-specific realities of women and for their subjectivity and social experiences from their own point of view—a paradigm in which the "lack of a penis" is replaced with the "lack of a culture." This might rule out exploiting women both psychically and culturally. Of course, Nadig too assumed that psychoanalysis is the road to *all* social and psychic change.

Christa Rohde-Dachser's Explications

In her brilliant and far-reaching *Expedition in den dunklen Kontinent* (Expedition into the Dark Continent) (1991) Rohde-Dachser synthesized all of the German psychoanalytic theories. She set out to go beyond every one of their explanations of what women want, what they are, what is and is not expected of them, by turning psychoanalytic theory against itself in order to reconstruct—with its own methods—what woman would be were it not for the culturally and psychologically constructed presuppositions from which neither men nor women (including psychoanalysts) so far have been able to escape. By deconstructing all revered psychoanalytic theorems, Rohde-Dachser stated, she was inevitably returning to Freud in an unconsciously aggressive act by an ungrateful daughter against her intellectual father (pp. viii–ix). In this return to the (father's?) womb, she not only was picking on Freud's initial conceptualizations of the woman as an (inferior) mirror of the male and of the Oedipus complex as rooted in *asymmetry* (of sexual differences in patriarchy) but expected to prove her thesis by quoting from Freud's works and letters and by bolstering her arguments with myriads of contemporary commentaries. In other words, she left none of the proverbial stones unturned.

To show that *all* of Freudian theory unconsciously incorporates patriarchy, Rohde-Dachser took positions on and spanned most of the American and German discussions I have scanned in this book—and more. She accepted Juliet Mitchell's anglicized Lacanian concept of the boy's heritage of the position of the father and stated that "here we see, for the first time, the basic *mechanism of projection* that is central to the perception of what is female in patriarchy" (Rohde-Dachser, 1991, p. 61); and she recapped Freud's debates with Horney and Deutsch, Jung and Jones, Sabina Spielrein and Melanie Klein, and the arguments among them, to show that none of them tried to penetrate to the mythologies based on the "myths of male domination" they themselves were incorporating into psychoanalysis (p. 25). She commented on Nancy Chodorow's benign neglect of the *father-daughter* relationship, on Dorothy Dinnerstein's characterization of the male view of women as "all-mighty goddesses or dumbbells" (p. 98), and on Christiane Olivier's view that the only means of detraumatizing the female Oedipus complex would be to have fathers take care of infants (p. 11). While citing and footnoting an international who's who among feminists and psychoanalysts, Rohde-Dachser argued with the help of minutia and particulars that the conceptualization of psychoanalysis as a method of treatment, as praxis, is part of the patriarchal bailiwick and thus unfavorable to women. And she proceeded to expose it. For the *production of the (female) unconscious* is inherent in the apprehension of this unconscious and will reproduce itself until women in psychoanalysis, with the help of an active women's movement, manage to deideologize Freud's clinical theory and learn to use it non-ideologically by means of a "feminine critique of knowledge" (p. 36).

Only by systematically untangling Freud's construction of the female and its role in the history and the theoretical grounding of psychoanalysis, Rohde-Dachser reiterated, can we possibly extrapolate their unconscious fantasies: We must reconstruct every one of the theoretically taken-for-granted defenses, projections, denials, idealizations and devaluations and the fantasies that cover up other fantasies (Rohde-Dachser, 1991, p. 59). One of the themes, based on illusions of denial, that she presented was the castration model Freud enshrined as a typical male fantasy. She demonstrated that it pictures women as devoid of (sexual or other) wishes separate from those of man: without her own genitals, sovereignty, or other valuable property; without superiority or power; and without ever voicing any objection to this state of affairs. The man's fantasy, however, his destroyed mirror image of her, imagines the *other* woman as full of independence, power, sexual organs, lust, and property and as lacking envy and never reproaching him. What would happen if this fantasy *other* woman were to emerge, to become visible? At that moment, stated Rohde-Dachser, she would threaten the man's subjectivity, his grandiose central position as the apple of his mother's or wife's eye, which now stops being his mirror (pp. 64–65). With the appearance of the *other* woman—this female subject—in his narcissistic universe, the loss of this mirror is accompanied by fear of fragmentation and rage. The wish awakens fantasies and fears that are projected onto the female subject: "She" is enraged, wants to castrate him, eat him, turn him into her son, destroy him, and so on. For Freud this was the fear of castration. For Rohde-Dachser it was the manifestation of the man's own unconscious, which Freud explained by means of the theme of bisexuality (p. 69). For specific "operations of thought" are able to reinforce "fantasies of thought" in the "scientific language of theory." The resulting (unnoticed) mythologization of scientific language appears predestined (pp. 71–72).

By drawing on literature and painting, Rohde-Dachser reinforced her theses: Frank Wedekind's opera *Lulu* (1934), for instance, exemplified the "ability of women to portray themselves as objects of men's imagination," as the "'bad' and seductive principle of femininity," as victims, and so on; the males around her suffer or kill (Rohde-Dachser, 1991, p. 116). Painters transform woman into pictures and, as in one of Edgar Allen Poe's stories, kill her in the process of painting her (pp. 102–105). Freud too, like writers and poets, dealt in metaphors. His central one, maintained Rohde-Dachser, was the ego and the id, *das Ich und das Es*— terms that in German are more concrete than in English. Sometimes this psychic apparatus appears as the model of a family drama, where "it" is the mother, the "superego" is the father, and the "I" takes the place of the son-father (p. 161). Thus Rohde-Dachser paraphrased Freud's theory: The female it (the wife) is dominated by her desires, she directs them at the I (the man); the it (she) has become "amoral," "cruel," "murderous" and dominates the I (man), of (her) servant (p. 164). And so on.

During the previous few decades, held Rohde-Dachser, the accent in psychoanalytic theory had moved from the wife to the mother, to what I have noted as the move from theories of ego psychology to those based on early object relations. Among others, Rohde-Dachser cited the following hypothesis by Chasseguet-Smirgel (1986, p. 77) to make her point:

> There exists a primary desire to discover a universe without obstacles, without roughness or differences, entirely smooth, identified with a mother's belly stripped of its contents, an interior to which one has free access. Behind the fantasy of destroying or appropriating the father's penis, the children and the feces inside the mother's body, a fantasy brought out by Melanie Klein, and, according to her, specific to the early stages of the Oedi-

pus conflict, can be detected a more basic and more archaic wish, of which the return to the smooth maternal belly is the representation. (Rohde-Dachser, 1991, p. 184)

According to Rohde-Dachser, this model represents a reality that must be destroyed. Theoretically, the model no longer epitomizes the image of the mother's belly as giving off aggression but is the goal of this aggression—as in the theme of Jack-the-Ripper in *Lulu* (Rohde-Dachser, 1991, p. 185). (Carmen is yet another favorite example that is said to demonstrate woman's masochistic desire as preparing her for her own downfall [p. 236]). Mother has become the scapegoat, in her role as "real mother," in the mother-child dyad, and as the one guilty for whatever is thought to go wrong. Psychoanalysis does offer an image of a mother who can manage *everything*—an image, alas, that is not conducive to women's emancipation (p. 215).

After dissecting the central mythic constructions of unconscious fantasies in anthropology, fairy tales, and narratives, Rohde-Dachser ended up by exemplifying female discourse via three arguments she valued most, those by Susan Griffin (1978), Nancy Chodorow (1978), and Luce Irigaray ([1977] 1985). According to Rohde-Dachser, Chodorow validated the mother-daughter relationship as the primary one, where in spite of ambivalences, emotional closeness dominates. The father remains an outsider. His maleness precludes his ability to express empathy and his feelings in the way women are prone to do. This inability lowers him in the eyes of heterosexual objects, a domain in which mother-daughter relations offer compensation. This analysis, continued Rohde-Dachser, did not differ much from Freud's theories of femininity because both were based on a view of a *primary dyadic relationship*. Instead, female emotionality somehow became the "penisequivalent" that negated Chodorow's "negative female Oedipus complex," which, ultimately, devalued the man rather than the woman (Rohde-Dachser, 1991, p. 263) and thereby remythologized Freud's theory.

Rohde-Dachser elaborated on Irigaray's commentaries and theses on phallic discourse at much greater length than I did in the preceding chapters. She emphasized that Irigaray primarily debunks patriarchal myths by focusing on the imaginary spaces of women, by trying to circumvent the patriarchal codes, by shocking people. Her reborn woman is able to be enraged, to give expression to her anger without shame, to return from her hole able to screech, explode, rant, scream, and roar (Rohde-Dachser, 1991, p. 272). Thereby, Irigaray provides a model of *legitimate* female aggression, a rebirth. Rohde-Dachser credited Susan Griffin with a similar feat: By learning to see woman "with her own eyes," she has learned to feel strong enough to stop allowing man to determine his place in the universe. This woman who has regained her own self, who is allowed to express her anger, not only legitimates the so-far-excluded femininity but gives expression to what has been banished from the patriarchal symbolic system. Hence the new range of expressions are producing a new reality as well (p. 273). But Freud's and his successors' theories, noted Rohde-Dachser, are rooted in their collective constellation of defenses against this perceived aggression, which, altogether, conceptualizes the feminine as the "container" of the negative self of the patriarchical and grandiose male subject (p. 277). Consequently, even self-reflection strengthens the male fantasy of being at the center of the universe while casting the female as his complementary object. At that point, she criticized Margarete Mitscherlich's psychoanalytic solution of the male riddle—which deals with the enlightenment of men—as a logos-derived myth for half of humanity. Reminding us that for the sphynx as well as for Jokasta the lack of self-reflection ended up in death, Rohde-Dachser stated that *"enlightenment can begin only when the male hero of the riddle responds to the question by the sphynx: Man is Man and wife, or I and you"* (p. 279).

The German Location of Oedipus

Inevitably, when comparing the German discussions on psychoanalysis and feminism to their American and French counterparts, we note that their theories are embedded in German preoccupations rooted in the recent history many Germans still have not fully faced up to. The articles and reviews in *Psyche* continue to feature contributions by Freudians from around the world, and by psychoanalytic feminists. But the German propensity to theorize and to do so with the help of logical explication of texts, with recourse to past arguments and refutations of these, and with references to a vast array of scholarship lends German feminists an air of authority that in very different ways makes both their French and American sisters seem less exacting, almost debonair. Moreover, the fact that most of these "theoreticians" are therapists as well keeps the focus on remedial socialization via the couch. Thus Karin Flaake (1992), by analyzing the many studies on mother-daughter relations by her colleagues as these relate to their attitudes to the female body, suggested that pleasurable (or unpleasurable) self-examination and subsequent acceptance during puberty of one's own body might well be the means for personal—and social—change.

Although German feminists rarely refer to the Frankfurt School, they assume—as did Horkheimer and Adorno in *The Dialectic of Enlightenment* ([1944] 1979)—that within the enlightenment the battle with the unconscious (the myth of the feminine) was subsumed (Rohde-

Dachser, 1991, p. 144). More recently, coming to grips with the Nazi past has added the need for German men as well as women to face up to their unconscious rage and aggression. So even when referring to Chodorow, German feminists do not take into account her American approach, which instead of moving from an intrinsically cultural position recommends a focus on transference and countertransference to reach the same end. In other words, whereas Chodorow (1978) criticized, for instance, Marcuse's point in *Eros and Civilization* (1955) as based on a "profoundly limited social theory and vision of liberation" that depicts women, gender relations, and generation problematically (p. 115), the German feminist Freudians no longer bother answering him; they consider him totally passé. Instead, they are out to enter the complexities of feminist scholarship around the world and to outdo it, to synthesize what their American, British, and French counterparts have done. Whereas a few German women have suggested that this habit may well be part of the German propensity to want to excel or part of an exaggerated need to win, I prefer to ascribe it to a manifestation of the Judeo-Christian, Protestant work ethic, the positive side of which has been known to turn talent into genius—from Bismarck to Hitler, from Einstein to Heisenberg, and from Marx to Freud. Moreover, when children learn throughout their schooling that they must document what they say, a commitment to substantiating their scholarship gets ingrained. Also, the Kantian tradition based on reason furthers closely argued investigative research that forecloses theories based on metaphors and on postmodern flights of fantasy—which, as we will see in the next chapter, have moved to the center in the Second Wave of American feminism. In any event, and for whatever reason, German feminism is of a piece and German feminists keep exploring psychoanalytic knowledge in the tradition of the First Wave.

8 Postmodern Feminism in America

During the 1980s, feminism expanded its base in American universities. Simultaneously, all sorts of psychotherapies were introduced there as well as in the culture to deal with social, family, and individual problems. Freudian psychoanalysts, too, applied their expertise, although their relative influence within the helping professions continuously shifted. In the universities, feminist political theory gradually moved to a structuralism without Freud; its counterpart in literary studies claimed to embrace Freud via structuralism and poststructuralism. Sociologists, for the most part, rejected psychoanalysis altogether. But with the general acceptance of feminist ideas, new theories derived from Lacanian and Freudian texts were promulgated at an ever faster rate and were imagined as a means for social advancement and as antidotes to all racism and sexism. It no longer mattered to either feminists or their detractors what psychoanalytic tenets were being championed, so that all along various "correct" versions were competing, and these included some that intermingled notions by both the first and second feminist waves.

When in 1958 philosopher Sidney Hook at a symposium in New York among philosophers, sociologists, psychoanalysts, and so-called free-floating intellectuals conceptualized psychoanalysis as a scientific theory, mostly from a metapsychological perspective (Hook, 1959, p. x) and Jacques Lacan then gave his lecture "La Signification du Phallus" in Paris, these diametrically opposed filiations from Freud remained mainly within their geographical boundaries. Americans such as Robert Waelder debated whether psychoanalysis was science or philosophy, metapsychology or therapy, while Lacan was differentiating the penis from the phallus: "Why the phallus and not the penis?" he asked. "Because the phallus is not a question of a form or an image, or a phantasy, but rather of a signifier, the signifier of desire" (Wilden, 1980, p. 187), he answered. Inevitably, Lacan had to eschew Waelder's as well as all other distinctions based on "American" ego psychology because *his* Freud primarily was rooted in theories of narcissism and the death instinct.

Here, I am not concerned with the ultimate validity of ego psychological or Lacanian theories, with their squabbles within the international movement, or even with their impact on the direction of psychoanalytic therapy but only with the effect of these unassimilable and contesting systems of psychoanalysis on American feminism. Clearly, Lacan's metapsychological assumptions and his high-flown theories are even less clinically testable than those of the ego psychologists. But many American Freudians as well have held that their psychoanalytic therapy is more of an art than a science insofar as it is based on the rapport between an analyst and his or her analysand.

In spite of the fact that each patient's history is unique, by discovering the "rational" elements in the irrational unconscious, psychoanalysts have established a common denominator; each of them knows of hundreds of patients of dozens of psychoanalysts who have been helped by "inductive" therapy. However, when divorcing psychoanalytic language from therapy, we are dealing with another, though related, enterprise. All psychoanalysts differentiate between clinical theory and metatheoretical generalizations from it while simultaneously updating them both to stay in line with the insights they are gaining from work with patients. In the clinical process, they all listen carefully to the language of their patients and continually reflect on the ongoing psychic dynamics. But Lacanians pay more attention to specific spoken words than do ego psychologists, who tend to listen just as much to the content of these words and to the context of the communication, to what is said, left out, expressed in bodily movements, and so on. These differences, in turn, feed into the theories.

Moreover, the Lacanian concepts that were introduced into American feminism also contained responses to Parisian intellectuals' preoccupations, to their (often idiosyncratic) responses to a variety of Marxisms, which their proponents had begun to question by the time they reached American universities. These extrapsychoanalytic presumptions were indigenous to Parisian intellectual life and there were being understood and responded to in terms of fundamental political and epistemological issues. When inserted into the American milieu, they could not be anything but interesting new theories that had to be learned, absorbed, or refuted. As such, they were the grains of sand in the oyster. Some academics expected these grains to turn into valuable pearls, others considered them irritants. But few of them dealt with the fact that while crossing the Atlantic, Lacanian theory had become rootless.

However, feminists on the lookout for better ways of explaining the everlasting disadvantaging of women in the social realm hoped to find some sort of answers in Lacan's freewheeling formulations. Lacan's conceptions of the unconscious as structured by language and his reliance on metaphors and alliterations were particularly open to gender-related conceptualizations in elite departments of literature. In addition, the new way of reading also challenged hermeneutic analyses and psycho-analytic interpretations by such literary critics as Lionel Trilling, whom some feminists already were discarding as passé, as belonging to "patri-archy."

But as this Second Wave of feminism was gaining ground and the new feminist theory was taking hold, its foreign and abstract language re-moved it more and more from the feminists-in-the-street. Furthermore, many of the devotees' contributions were in the postmodern realm (see Chapter 6), so they frequently were being supported by postmodernists outside feminism. This debate itself divided professors into so-called postmodernists and traditionalists in spite of the fact that no one ever precisely defined these terms. Gradually, postmodern feminists who, among other things, purported to have some sort of link to Lacanian psychoanalysis primarily were speaking to the converted and the soon-to-be-converted, to students working on their graduate degrees. And in the capitalist mode, one of the things they denounced, they wrote myri-ads of esoteric books their publishers were eager to sell and to commis-sion.

The French Incursions

As noted in Chapter 6, the French influence on literature and feminism coincided with debates about manifestations of postmodernism, with Derrida's deconstructions (which themselves were deeply embedded in Nietzschean nihilism), with pseudo-Lacanian rhetoric, and with inter-pretations of Foucault's bold and paradoxical, revisionist history. The Parisian debates on Oedipus and anti-Oedipus themselves kept altering not only in response to intellectual fashions but to the rise and fall of specific intellectual stars. When these debates were transplanted to American universities, older and outdated concepts along with newer ones were also imported and were superimposed on and adapted to America's own intellectual dilemmas. And as abstract theories sup-planted the prevalent pragmatism, the French flair—which has its own seductive attraction—as well entered American academe. So, whereas before, American professors, just like President Truman, had not be-lieved what they couldn't see, they became less and less inclined to insist on empirical evidence.

Psychoanalysis, of course, had been hampered all along because ana-lysts had been unable to demonstrate its cures concretely and incontro-vertibly. Its insertion into American medicine led psychoanalysts to cast it as a scientific practice that led to substantive questions by "real" doctors as well as by humanists in the universities. Therefore, when the controversies between the proponents of ego psychology and the Lacanians began to emerge in the literature, these too became legitimate subjects for the psychoanalytic feminists' debates. For instance Jane Gallop questioned some American feminists' assumptions by commenting on encounters among Freudian and Lacanian luminaries (which are discussed in the preceding chapters of this book). She accused feminists of too familial interpretations of power relations (1982, p. xv). For example, she found Mitchell guilty of ad hominem arguments, of being locked into an exchange with the feminists she tried to transcend, and of doing so in fanciful prose (p. 5). But by introducing Lacanian concepts along with the multilevel polemics among him and his dissenting disciples, Gallop herself was being too fanciful for American feminists not yet privy to Lacanian discourse and *tournures de phrases.* (She referred to the tactics by the First Wave of feminists, tried to preserve unity within the movement, and wanted to confront the male establishment shoulder to shoulder.)

By 1987, however, Gallop had become a "French" feminist and reminded her colleagues, correctly, that in the early 1970s American feminists were impatient with psychoanalytic interpretations and dismissed them as "phallic criticism" and as perpetrating patriarchy (Gallop, 1987, p. 125). She went on to say that the reversal came about because "feminism has assured the link between psychosexuality and the sociohistorical realm that connects it to major political and cultural questions … [and] promises to save it from its ahistorical and apolitical doldrums" and because French poststructuralist thought, Lacanian psychoanalysis, and Derridean deconstructions provided a "new viability" for American feminist criticism (p. 126). Gallop then went on to observe that this type of feminist criticism had become a growth industry due to writers such as Irigaray, Cixous, and Kristeva and due to Lacan's and Derrida's influence that was "at once feminist, psychoanalytic and highly literary" (p. 127). Of course, she was on target. But she failed to explain that this new feminist literary criticism no longer incorporated its intimate contact with therapeutic elements. And she might have recalled that psychoanalysis had addressed political and cultural questions and women's liberation since its very inception. Yes, Nancy Chodorow (1978) did introduce object-relations theory into the feminist framework and questioned the sociohistorical conditions of mothering, but Gallup ignored, as Chodorow did not, that the early Freudians had done so as well (see Chapter 1).

More recently, Kaja Silverman (1992) pointed out that Ellie Ragland-Sullivan (1986), along with, for instance, A. G. Wilden, Frederic Jamieson, and Jacqueline Rose, also held that "the phallic signifier does not denote any sexual gender [or] superiority" (Silverman, 1992, p. 84). Jane Gallop, however, she went on, "use[d] a misprint in the 1966 edition of *Ecrits* as the occasion for fantasizing about an 'epicene' phallus" (p. 84). Basically, if the definite article "le" had not been replaced by the feminine "la," Gallop's theory that "the signifier 'phallus' ... might be either feminine or masculine" disintegrates, and, I would add, so do the attendant readings and elaborations of the castration complex, of fantasies, and so on (1984). Of course, Silverman's scrutiny comes after the fact, after Lacan's linguistic flights of fancy had set the course for both French and American feminists.

But false gods too are able to invigorate the imagination. And French rhetoric did offer a road to theories of the literary unconscious, which some of the Second Wave feminists supplemented with ingredients of Peircean philosophy, which others peppered with Frankfurt School critical theory, and which yet others based on Hegelian and Marxist formulations and promises. The arguments of these inwardly oriented essays were extremely difficult to follow and thus often were perceived as exceedingly deep and consequential. And they elicited erudite and provocative discussions at meetings of the Modern Language Association (MLA) that captivated new adherents. Ultimately, feminist literary theorists were talking to each other about differences and *différances,* although it was not always clear when, and how, they were differentiating between men and women and among women. They attracted wide attention when it became apparent that some of the more outrageous statements were meant to fuel the political arm of gay liberation. (However, the arguments between "gay" and "straight" feminists are peripheral to this book.) In this context, it was nearly forgotten that psychoanalysis itself is based on dynamic and unconscious human development and on the acceptance of bisexuality.

Ten Years of Postmodern Feminism

By the end of the 1980s, in addition to producing the many monographs explaining sexual difference from myriads of perspectives, a number of Second Wave feminists assembled books of readings that presented the central themes of the new enterprise in all its aspects. The most comprehensive collections are by Françoise Meltzer (1987), Teresa Brennan (1989), Ellie Ragland-Sullivan and Mark Bracher (1991), Nancy Fraser and Sandra Lee Bartky (1992), and Judith Butler and Joan Scott (1992).[1] Together, they cover the main arguments within this field. Despite the wide range of their contributions, these authors shared at least some of the postmodern assumptions. Thus their texts are taken out of their historical context, which means that, to a greater or lesser degree, they tend to lose their relation to history, to the connections of specific ideas of the milieu that gave rise to them. Moreover, postmodern theorists, though making much of the subjectivity of actors, have problems in accounting and allowing room for the living, active subject. For even when addressing fiction that, as it were, springs from the unconscious of the inventive writer, they depersonalize the subject simply by theorizing about it. Hence the politics of postmodern feminism, though expounded in these texts, are artifacts rather than viable means of action. Only in a narrow sense, insofar as it has begun to take over parts of the university, can this enterprise be deemed "political."

Françoise Meltzer in her *Trial(s) of Psychoanalysis* (1987) offered a representative sample of the enigmatic, double-punning, and personal fashion so typical of the new psychoanalytic feminism. Her references were not to Derrida and Lacan alone but to all those like-minded scholars who thought of psychoanalysis as "not only an economy which is hydraulic (mirroring the nineteenth-century physics from which it springs), but has as well an economy of seepage" (p. 1). Essentially, Meltzer argued that with his science of the unconscious, Freud was not truly scientific, tried to explain too much and did so all at once, and got away with it because beneath every unconscious association that surfaces there always is yet another one ready to pop out. Although she was not wrong, she did not tell us anything new. For what Meltzer called "seepage" was called free association by Freud, was attributed to the inner dynamism of the artist by Otto Rank, and was understood to be "also the esthetic form assumed by the self-awareness of an age" by Erich Heller (1983, p. 73). However, unlike Derrida, neither Freud, Rank, nor Heller, had Derrida's ([1967] 1978) grammatological deconstructions at their disposal. So they could not yet find, as Meltzer did, that "once psychoanalysis has discovered itself, what it then again proceeds to discover around it is always itself" (Meltzer, 1987, p. 2). Nor could they proceed to perceive it as

> a Subject which sees itself as omnipresent, omniscient, and without a center—precisely the terms in which God has been described. ... The unconscious takes the place of the Judeo-Christian God [that] ... reveal[s] itself in fleeting moments and fragments, thereby suggesting its fullness and totality; and it would have "other" intellectual enterprises be only apparent totalities which are revealed through psychoanalysis alone to be "really" incomplete because they exist without recognizing the unconscious and its mother, psychoanalysis itself. (p. 2)

Basically, Meltzer's contributors differentiated themselves from their psychoanalytically informed predecessors by their remoteness from clinical concerns, their abstract language, and their academic allegiance: (1) Lacanian and Derridean terminology was de rigeur; (2) psychoanalysis in its relation to literature was discussed as Subject versus Object, as master versus slave, or as the reverse; (3) psychoanalytic criticism no longer derived from the works of literature themselves but to a greater or lesser degree from comments by others on these works, particularly those within the postmodern fold; (4) other French gurus, mostly Foucault and Barthes, were appealed to and quoted, but less in their original, critical form or intent than in the use of their texts for the production of new, seductive texts; (5) In the process, these French puns frequently were taken more seriously than their authors intended, and at face value; (6) the American literal followers' puns and their *explications des textes* were as much the meat of their own free associations as were those of their French "masters" and (in case of the feminists) "mistresses."

Meltzer questioned Shoshana Felman's effort to "understand the 'and' between these two fields" in her edited collection of essays, *Literature and Psychoanalysis: The Question of Reading: Otherwise* (1977) (Meltzer, 1987, p. 2). Felman maintained that a "real *dialogue*" between the two fields must take place outside the Hegelian master-slave dialectic; Meltzer accused her of once again falling into the totalizing teleology of psychoanalysis (p. 3). And she went on to argue that because psychoanalysis takes this position in relation to all other disciplines, it must be put back into its place, must become once again the object of study rather than the all-consuming master subject of inquiry (p. 5). When telling of an encounter she had with a peremptory psychoanalyst who assumed he had the definitive understanding of Baudelaire, an encounter in which this man put her down by psychoanalyzing her rather than responding to her criticism, her outrage seemed justified and her questions were apt. However, her postmodern analysis was incomplete if only because she ignored that this type of limited, frequently simplistic, literary criticism by practicing psychoanalysts had been disparaged all along; and that invoking the *erasure of difference* between *modes of thinking* is simply the imposition of a new idiom on old problems. (In another essay she got into Freud's failure to discuss Descartes's three dreams—which allegedly led to *his* theories.)

Basically, I am not asserting that "traditional" psychoanalysis has solved all—or even many of—its problems. However, by continuing to explore their patients' subjective psyches, practicing (Lacanian and classical) psychoanalysts stay in touch with the internalized realities of these patients, so that the theories they then derive address the problems of living people rather than of dead texts—if only because they keep watching these subjects. Thereby, they hold on to (personal) history—with a small "h"—in the making. Of course, insofar as they address politics, such politics are indirect and personal and cannot lead to a Marxist-type societal liberation. Instead, these psychoanalysts assume that the personal emancipation of a large mass of individuals who in the course of their therapies have been freed of neurotic and other inhibitions that distort reality may ultimately create the "good" society we would prefer. In other words, they assume that neither Marx's nor Freud's larger promises can be realized but that personal psychoanalysis or therapy may be a viable step in that direction.

Meltzer's collection primarily focused on applications of psychoanalysis to feminism and on former renditions by some Freudians that now are outdated. Dominick LaCapra, for instance, after a lengthy and somewhat tedious review of the many interpretations of Freudian transference and the underpinnings in reality or fantasy of the seduction theory (including Jeffrey Masson's indictment of Freud as opportunistic or fraudulent) agreed with the French psychoanalysts Jean Laplanche and J.-B. Pontalis that the seduction theory "is not an alternative to the Oedipus complex but an adumbration to it" (Meltzer, 1987, p. 20). He then picked up on the rereading by Nicolas Abraham and Maria Torok of Freud's study (1976) of the Wolf Man, whose multilingual and seemingly outlandish analysis "presumably parallels the 'new rhetoric' of the unconscious itself" (p. 22). (Two more contributions in this collection by Maria Torok, one with Abraham and the other with Nicholas Rand, further elaborated this thesis.) From here, LaCapra moved on to the recent theoretical criticism that no longer takes its Freud "straight" and reminded us that Freud did indeed always experience the necessary tension between dealing with his patients in a one-on-one situation and generalizations from it to his social criticism (p. 27). He then suggested we try to build yet another bridge between Marx and Freud, this time with assistance from Emile Durkheim and Max Weber (p. 35) and from Foucault's investigations into the connections between normality and pathology in both individuals and society.

LaCapra suggested we look at the question of psychoanalysis and history in terms of "binding" and "unbinding" cultural processes, as Freud did. Basing himself on an Althusserian "theoretical" reading of the institution of the family, which in turn was based on Lacan's rereading of Freud, he ended up advocating the application of critical reflection that avoids strictly binary oppositions based on Saussurean linguistics to questions of normality and pathology. Were Freud alive, he would certainly agree with LaCapra that sociocultural judgments are better arrived at when analyzed with the help of the transference as a means of critical reflection. This transference may ultimately overcome the tendency to conformity.

Arnold Davidson, in "How to Do the History of Psychoanalysis," focused on Freud's *Three Essays on the Theory of Sexuality* to address the historiography of science. After a detour through Foucault's complex method of discursive practice (which incorporated the philosophies of his teachers Gaston Bachelard and Georges Canguilhem), Davidson connected Freud's deliberations on sexual perversions to those by his medical contemporaries, such as Paul Moreau (de Tours) (*Des aberrations du sens génésique*, Paris, 1880), Richard von Krafft-Ebing (*Text-book of Insanity Based on Clinical Observations*, Philadelphia, 1904), Havelock Ellis, Albert Moll, and his own French mentor, Jean-Martin Charcot. Frank Sulloway (1979), among others, already had argued that Freud was attuned to the science of his day but that his roots were in science and he had become a "biologist of the mind."

Still, by rebottling their former knowledge in French complexities, American scholars learned an array of new skills that sometimes sent them back to the classical philosophers they probably had rejected while in graduate school: These provided further intellectual fertilizer for the concepts they were getting immersed in. And this recycling enlarged the terrain of the disputes around Freudian lore, including the disagreements about the origins of "drives" and "instincts" (both component ones and sexual ones) and the problematization of "perversion." Ultimately, concluded Davidson, "Freud's hesitations and ambiguities … are not the result of some deconstructive indeterminacy or undecidability of the text but are rather the consequences of the dynamics of fundamental change" (Meltzer, 1987, p. 63).

In "The Struggle of Psychiatry with Psychoanalysis: Who Won?" Sander Gilman, a professor of German literature and psychiatry, reiterated the historical controversies on whether psychoanalysis was "scientific," placed these debates within the assumptions and prejudices prevalent in Freud's Vienna and into the literature relevant to the subject, and then offered the reasons that in America psychoanalysis was inserted into medicine. The French Marxist Ernesto Laclau argued for a new "post-Marxism" that would be based on a "classical Marxism similar to what Heidegger called a 'de-struction of the history of ontology'" and thereby expected to transcend concepts of class, capital, and so on. Primarily, Laclau focused on where Marxism *broke* with Enlightenment tradition (Meltzer, 1987, p. 142); here, his thoughts conceptually parallel Althusser's perceived "theoretical break" in Marx's philosophy (what Marx wrote before *The German Ideology*, the so-called work of the transition) and his subsequent "scientific theory." Neither Laclau nor the rest of the contributors to this volume focused primarily on feminism, although they summarized and increasingly took for granted the terminologies of deconstruction and the Lacanian concepts they all subsumed. Among these, the only one that so far had not been mentioned was intertextuality, which literary scholar Michael Riffaterre defined as "the perception that our reading of a text or textual component is complete or satisfactory only if it constrains us to refer to or to cancel out its homologue or intertext" (p. 214). He then explained that recovering the (unexpressed) intertext is not analogous to recovering the unconscious but is only a guide to the repressed: It is "a mimesis of repression" (p. 214).

Clearly, Meltzer chose the contributors to this volume because they represented a variety of postmodern approaches. The last essay, by Jean Starobinsky (pp. 273–286), for instance, centered on a quote by Freud of Virgil, on interpretations of Freud's motives for this citation, and on its repercussions on psychoanalysis and postmodern criticism. Other contributors addressed more concrete topics such as voters' rights, welfare policies, and issues of race and class. But none of the contributors pretended to directly influence the political system. Instead, they mimicked Roland Barthes's clever observations in *Mythologies* ([1957] 1972) and in *Barthes by Barthes* ([1975] 1977): They tried to dazzle and shock, to make the author part of his or her work and text, and to celebrate outrage and nonconformism. Thus they were cheered and applauded. But Freud and his followers had scandalized and offended their compatriots just as profoundly and, at times, had indeed influenced their culture. (See Chapters 1 and 2.)

Teresa Brennan's *Between Feminism and Psychoanalysis* (1989) was based on fifteen international seminars at Cambridge University. They centered on "the status of the Lacanian 'symbolic,' sexual difference and knowledge, the bearing of essentialism on feminist politics, and the relation between psychical reality and the social" (p. 1).[2] Among the participants prominent in America were Gallop, Moi, and Irigaray, as well as Lisa Jardine, who expounded on Lacan's "Politics of Impenetrability," Alice Jardine, who presented the short- and long-term dilemmas of being a *radical feminist intellectual, teacher, and writer* (p. 82), and Margaret Whitford, who reread Irigaray in order to argue for "the creation of a powerful female symbolic to represent the *other* against the omnipresent effects of the male imaginary" (p. 121). Gayatri Chakravorty Spivak, an early advocate of deconstruction, held that even though this theory itself is unable to found a politics, it could help make the in-built problems of political programs more visible by applying an existential Derridean position to these issues (pp. 206–223).

Ellie Ragland-Sullivan and Mark Bracher's (1991) collection offered strictly Lacanian interpretations: All of these were by individuals who in one way or another had done a "stage" with Lacan or with one of his disciples. In her introduction, Ragland-Sullivan stated that Lacan's teachings were central to all their concerns and that "each essay sheds a bit more light on [his] innovative theories of what language is and what a subject is" (p. 1). Thus, Jacques-Alain Miller (pp. 21–35) questioned the ado about language, and after elaborating this theme via historical and present-day examples of the relationship between a sign and what it designates, he likened the "benevolent neutrality" of the psychoanalyst to the Zen master, who also teaches his pupils that language does not refer and does not describe, in order to understand, "this vacuousness of reference" (p. 33). Henry W. Sullivan addressed the role of desire in human evolution in light of "a Lacanian *episteme*," which, once more, was an elaboration of the "Saussurean cut" in a linguistic epistemology (p. 37). He ended up by reaffirming that "language, in [its] fifth dimension is phallic cause and effect, has the power to move mountains and has indeed done so in every corner of our planet" (p. 47). Ragland-Sullivan's essay "The Sexual Masquerade: A Lacanian Theory of Sexual Difference" was yet another reiteration and reinterpretation of Lacan's *Le séminaire.* She "corrects," for instance, Jacqueline Rose's interpretation by means of a textual analysis and essentially denounced feminists (among them Irigaray and Cixous) who "lump Lacan together with Freud as an enemy of the female sex and share the view that he was anti-woman, a phallocrat, a man who is derogatory of women" (p. 53). As Ragland-Sullivan informed us toward the end of her introduction, all these essays focused on the burden of language in our times and on the ways in which "truth can open up only through our misrecognition of the thing—the object *a*—that embodies our impossible *jouissances*" (the edge of pleasure that is beyond our grasp, in the realm of the death instinct) (p. 16). Yes, each new artistic creation, like the end of each analysis, produced an invention, a "new symptom." But again I must add that Otto Rank had already reached this conclusion in 1905.

Judith Butler and Joan W. Scott's *Feminists Theorize the Political* (1992), as the title indicates, primarily was concerned with the applications of postmodern theoretical analyses to explore new avenues of discourse that might create a feminist "political imaginary" (p. xiii). Toward this end, the authors subdivided the contributions into "Contesting Grounds," "Signifying Identity," "Subjects Before the Law," "Critical Practices," and "Postmodern Postscripts." Psychoanalytic ideas entered only peripherally into implications of previous and suggested Freud-Marx syntheses and politics—in Joan Scott's references to the link between "experiences" and language as "the importance of 'the literary' to the historical project" (p. 34)[3] and in arguments that picked up on the psychoanalytic feminists' postmodern discussions surveyed in previous chapters of Scott and Butler's book.[4] However, none of these essays in any way offered new means of understanding the link between Freudians and feminists, which is the aim of the present book.

Nancy Fraser and Sandra Lee Bartky, in *Revaluing French Feminism* (1992), invited feminist theorists to comment. American feminists essentially argued with and against French deconstructive and psychoanalytic formulations:

> In each case the critic surveys a large body of difficult and often elusive theoretical writing; she reconstructs the French theorist's principal line of argument, identifies the evidence and assumptions on which it rests, and assesses its cogency ... [and] presuppos[es] that the point of feminist philosophy is to change the world, not merely to theorize it, [but to] ... question its present usefulness for feminist practice. (p. 5)

Dorothy Leland (Fraser and Bartky, 1992, pp. 113–135) expressed disappointment in Julia Kristeva by arguing that she surrendered to political pessimism because she was too faithful to Lacan and to his dictum that the phallocentric symbolic order is not susceptible to change. She attributed this weakness also to Irigaray. Both of them, stated Fraser, "accept the Lacanian assumption ... that 'patriarchal representations ... exhaust the entire symbolic dimension that mediates experience'" (p. 12). Diana Meyers (pp. 136–158) addressed questions of women's agency. She held that "gender dichotomies subvert both Chodorow's valorization of traditional feminine capacities and Jane Flax's more circumspect synthesis of traditional male capacities with traditional feminine ones" (p. 137). Kristeva, while trying to overcome these handicaps, according to Meyers, revived "the sentimental ideal of maternal devotion to the sinister forces of destruction that she ascribes to women's unconscious" (p. 151). In her essay "Essentially Speaking" (pp. 94–112) Diana Fuss masterfully quoted the basic points every one of the American gurus of feminist psychoanalytic (and nonpsychoanalytic) theories had made.[5] She defended Irigaray by arguing that her "fearlessness towards speaking the body has earned for her work the dismissive label 'essentialist'" (p. 94).

These intricate and convoluted polemics, though displaying much learned lore, especially Irigaray's essay on Greek philosophy that preceded Fuss's (Fraser and Bartky, 1992, pp. 64–76), included mention that Irigaray "has been criticized by both psychoanalysts and materialists alike"—an indication, I would add, that these theorists take for granted their ongoing rootedness in both Freud and Marx. All in all, Fraser and Bartky were not as concerned with revaluing French feminism as with its American hybrid—which has abandoned its French origins for doctrines that respond to American esoteric, in-group discussions rather than to Parisian ones—and with the shift of the center within the Second Wave of American feminism from "straight" to "gay." However, this shift coincided with the increasing inroads that Second Wave activists were making into the culture.

Consequently, the discussions increasingly invoked political strategy. Judith Butler (Fraser and Bartky, 1992, pp. 162–176), in the essay based on her book *Gender Trouble* (1990), accused Kristeva of describing the semiotic as a poetic-maternal linguistic practice that "seems to accept rather than contest the inevitable hegemony of the Symbolic," that is, the paternal order (p. 163). She went on to argue that Kristeva's poetic language breaks the incest taboo and as such verges always on psychosis (p. 169), that her "heterosexual poet-mother suffers interminably from the displacement of the homosexual cathexis," and that "for women, heterosexuality and coherent selfhood are indissolubly linked" (p. 169). In her concluding article (pp. 177–194), Nancy Fraser was even more explicit: She preferred the pragmatic concept of discourse to the structural model of language for feminist politics (p. 185) because it allows us to focus on power and inequality (p. 186). She found that Kristeva's "semanalyzing" of poetic language in the 1970s, which was aimed at uncovering psychic traces of Fascism and Stalinism in human subjects, "alternate[d] essentialist gynocentric moments with anti-essentialist nominalist moments" (p. 190). Fraser judged Kristeva's "semanalyzing" as equally useless for feminist politics. Clearly, literary theory had turned into a special branch of (political) theory. Its roots are in an obscure discourse that eschews practical politics—and that its French originators denounce or disclaim—and have been forgotten. Or have they sunk into the cultural unconscious?

In her introduction to *Femininity and Domination* (1990), Sandra Lee Bartky already had surveyed her own progression of (feminist) concerns: Her earliest essays (between 1979 and 1982), she recalled, "were attempts to articulate the profound experience of personal transformation" in response to "consciousness-raising" (p. 1). As her own self-understanding evolved, she kept examining the damage women suffer in patriarchal culture and the individual consciousness this culture ends up producing in "the embodied consciousness of a feminine subject" (p. 1). Bartky explicitly attempted to (phenomenologically) synthesize Marxism and feminism because she was convinced that gender (and racial) oppression cannot be understood in isolation from class oppression (p. 3).

I too believe in class analysis and would agree that (in the manner of the First Wave of feminists) class analysis may help construct a more just society. However, Bartky went on to state that "the women's movement has receded before a growing tide of conservatism" and that "the fashionable poststructuralist attack on the kind of 'totalizing' theory Marxist and socialist feminists were trying to construct in the days of the Marxism-feminism debate is ... a symptom of the same political malaise" (Bartky, 1990, p. 3). This facile political jump, I believe, not only contradicts the fact that feminism has become mainstream but also that this reality flies in the face of Bartky's own analysis: For her conclusions do not follow from her own investigation. (Betty Friedan [1992] also attacked all that.)

Actually, the Marxism-feminism debate, even though inordinately influential in graduate seminars, did not reach the majority of women around the country. But the consciousness-raising by feminists of the First Wave *did* alter the relationships to the men in their lives and social practices. Some of the women who felt that pressure-group politics were going too far shifted from voting for Democrats to voting for Republicans; others objected to notions that rejected men. None of them, however, were particularly aware of poststructualist theory, which "accused" them of and "excused" them for their false consciousness. Of course, Bartky was not the only one to confuse university politics—which *did* move to poststructuralism but not to conservatism—with the politics of the country that elected Ronald Reagan and George Bush. But such confusions appear to be necessary ingredients of the theory. How else could she prove that

> whatever pertains to sexuality ... will have to be understood in relation to a larger system of subordination; [and that] the deformed sexuality of patriarchical culture must be moved from the hidden domain of "private life" into an arena for struggle, where a "politically correct" sexuality of mutual respect will contend with an "incorrect" sexuality of domination and submission. (Bartky, 1990, p. 45)

Basically, Bartky maintained that feminists have attributed sadomasochistic fantasies to male-dominated culture instead of allowing themselves to act on their fantasies, including the "kinky" ones. According to other feminists, such sexual tastes challenge the sexual norms of the bourgeois family (Bartky, 1990, p. 48) and, I may add, those of the more straightlaced heterosexual feminists as well. Here, of course, the theories touch the political advocacies whose center, as noted, increasingly shifted to provide the foundations for gay and lesbian politics and for other victim-related causes. (These issues, however, are yet another subject.) In the process, psychoanalytic terms occasionally were invoked, but the bedrock of psychoanalytic clinical practice was totally ignored.

Bartky occasionally referred to psychoanalysis, for instance, when she cited Ethel Spector Person, who "suggested that the relationship between sexuality and identity is mediated not only by gender but by what she calls the 'sex-print,' ... [in] 'an individualized script that elicits erotic desire'" (Bartky, 1990, p. 58). In her essay "Narcissism, Femininity and Alienation," Bartky did rely on psychoanalysis directly to bolster her notions of alienation and self-estrangement. After recounting Freud's basic ideas in "On Narcissism" and Helene Deutsch's expansion on them (see Chapter 2), she went on to Simone de Beauvoir's existential concept of "situation" as her preferred explanation for women's persisting narcissism, of the stranger who inhabits her consciousness, who is *herself* (p. 38) and who, in turn, reflects her society's demands for a beautiful body and for beauty in general. To dealienate themselves from the expected femininity, Bartky concluded, women will have to "struggle against that excessive, damaged, and debilitating narcissism which now holds sway" (p. 42). She forgot, however, that de Beauvoir, like Sartre, basically rejected the Freudian unconscious and that the existentialist unconscious—which more or less wafts into consciousness—already was a popularized version of the Freudian concept and is devoid of clinical, developmental observations.

A Few "Classical" Freudians' Contributions

Since Second Wave feminists dismissed most scholarship other than their own out of hand as traditional or conservative, it stands to reason that classical Freudian feminists compiled their own selection of readings. They differentiated themselves from the postmodern feminists by keeping their feet planted in psychotherapy, or at least by keeping their fingers on its pulse. Toni Bernay and Dorothy W. Cantor's *The Psychology of Today's Woman: New Psychoanalytic Visions* (1986) presented a representative sample. Like other feminist theorists, they challenged "the deficiency model of psychoanalytic feminine identity" by beginning with a reassessment of traditional and new visions of feminine psychology and by looking into the situations of contemporary women in society and in the therapeutic relationship (p. 3). Helen Block Lewis (pp. 7–35) started out by showing that Freud's most enduring contribution to our understanding of sex differences comes from his insight into the conflicted feelings about these differences as they arise from every individual's primary process transformations. She concluded, after citing some of the feminist literature, by stating that she evaluated contemporary changing sex roles in relation to how they fostered affectionateness and morality. Eleanor Galenson, in "Early Pathways to Female Sexuality in Advantaged and Disadvantaged Girls" (pp. 37–48), reported on her study of girls from disadvantaged families, where, she found, "the mother assumes a definitely sadomasochistic quality early in life," which later on "the girl appears to replicate" (pp. 47–48).

Toni Bernay focused on the aggression, assertiveness, and achievement versus the former dependence, passivity, and submission of the feminine ego ideal and on theories that might prove helpful to women when facing the complexities of modern life (Bernay and Cantor, 1986, pp. 51–79). Whereas Bernay juxtaposed Winnicott's conceptions of the environmental mother (she is loving and benign) to Gilligan's concepts of a moral ethic of responsible caring, Judith Jordan and Janet L. Surrey (pp. 81–104), after overviewing classical, psychoanalytic theories, investigated why it is that women who view themselves as caretakers have trouble bringing caretaking to bear on themselves (p. 100). They concluded that new models of development and maintenance of self-images—of identity, motivation, and structures of the self—are needed and may assist therapists to build on woman's innate capacity without decapacitating her. Other contributions dealt with the psychological effects of mother's work on herself, her daughter, and other family members; with changing attitudes toward reproduction; with views of marriage and divorce; and with the myriads of women's symptoms and attitudes in relation to therapy—whether with male or female psychoanalysts. In sum, they generalized from their own and their colleagues' hands-on experiences.

Some classical psychoanalysts, and the feminists among them, at times extended their theories to literary works—particularly by paralleling changes over time in patients' symptoms and ego identification to literary creations—and to their authors. For instance, clinical psychologist Katherine Dalsimer, in *Female Adolescence: Psychoanalytic Reflections on Literature* (1986), compared female adolescence in five works of literature—*Member of the Wedding, The Prime of Miss Jean Brodie, Romeo and Juliet, Emma,* and the *Diary of Anne Frank*—by focusing on the adolescent's search for new relationships at the moment when both rivalrous and sexual oedipal passions threaten to be reawakened. Dalsimer investigated how these new experiences bring individuals into synchrony with wider segments of their society. Because puberty stirs new fantasies based on earlier identifications with the mother, she found that girls redefine their "inner presence" as they move into adulthood.

Louise Kaplan, in *Adolescence: The Farewell to Childhood* (1984), went back in history to trace adolescence from ancient Greece through Darwin's and Rousseau's views to Freud's in order to unravel the connections among psychological, sociological, and social transformations that have affected adolescents (p. 185). Spanning and distinguishing among historical epochs, she discovered that teenagers all along have longed for intimacy: This longing has been as pervasive as the wish to restore commitment to the family life they inevitably rejected while growing up (p. 331). From her explicitly developmental perspective, Kaplan ended by generalizing, in classical Freudian fashion, to humanity, to the human instinct of aggression, and to self-destruction.

Kaplan's subsequent book, *Female Perversions: The Temptations of Emma Bovary* (1991), exposed the myth that perversion is the province of males alone and demonstrated that female perversions parody feminine models of submission and purity. She advanced her argument in a language accessible enough to have won her converts outside the academy. In fact, Kaplan's insights fueled the internal arguments among both heterosexual and lesbian theorists. Kaplan never mentioned Foucault or Lacan. Nevertheless, she admirably described the background of perversions in family and church and the attendant reasoning about male and female sexuality and gender differences by Flaubert's doctors, who hovered around Madame Bovary.

Just like these doctors, Kaplan began, the medical profession still boxed aberrant sexual behaviors into lists and categories. She went on to say that except for sexual masochism, where the ratio of males to females in cited cases was about twenty to one, less than one percent of the cases cited had concerned females (Kaplan, 1991, pp. 7–8). This was so because "what makes a perversion is a mental strategy that uses ... a social stereotype of masculinity and femininity in a way that deceives the onlooker about the unconscious meanings of the observed behavior" (p. 9). Thus Kaplan felt that perversions derive much of their emotional force from gender role identity, from "socially normalized gender stereotypes of femininity" (p. 14), which in turn are based on an unconscious scenario or fantasy (p. 16). After deciphering the unconscious motivations of fetishism and transvestism, sexual masochism and sadism, exhibitionism and voyeurism, pedophilia, zoophilia and necrophilia, and the origins of these practices in childhood experiences and fantasies, Kaplan demonstrated that the driven quality of these rituals— which their practitioners tend to experience as manifestations of special powers—are due to rigidity and conservatism, to the need to hold terrorizing, personal demons (including death wishes) at bay (p. 42). She demonstrated her familiarity with French feminist ideas as well:

> A penis is an anatomical part. A phallus is a fictitious genital, a symbol of power, and it is a fact that traditionally, in most societies, those with penises have the power, a power associated with an erect penis and its sexual performance. Males, however, are not inherently phallic and females are not castrated beings—except in the eye of a beholder who is reacting to a genital difference the way a child does. By equating one anatomical part, the penis, with a phallic power and other anatomical parts, the vagina and clitoris, with a castrated vulnerability, psychoanalysts were reflecting the power structures and gender stereotypes of their social order. (p. 79)

Finally, Kaplan noted that trouble arises not from the unconscious meanings of the *phallus* but from a social order that assigns power only to those possessing the anatomical penis and from the meanings that accrue to the resulting differences (p. 195). Thus perversion is a psychological strategy aimed at repressing childhood traumas and disguising shameful and forbidden cross-gender wishes, which, in fact, exist in both men and women. Female disguises, however, are based on stereotypes of normal femininity (rather than masculinity) and never have been recognized as perversions. One of these is exaggerated attention to parts of the body—plucking facial hair and undergoing cosmetic surgery, starving oneself to the point of anorexia nervosa, mutilating oneself—that persists beyond the disorganizing physical and emotional experiences of adolescence (p. 379).

Kaplan's radical revisions of Freudian theory from a clinical perspective had much in common with the work of some of her French counterparts. Along with Dalsimer and some others, she stayed in touch with the French discussions of literature and artistic creation. But Kaplan's and Dalsimer's types of analyses continue to adhere to ego psychological precepts. Followers of Lacan, however, have tended to emulate his renowned "deconstruction" of Edgar Allan Poe's tale in his "Seminar on 'The Purloined Letter'" (Mehlman, 1972, pp. 38–72). Language, represented by the purloined letter, Lacan maintained, confers power upon whoever possesses it—the minister, the queen, Dupin. In line with Saussurean linguistic theory, Lacan held that "the creator's unconscious memories ... with his complexes," *excluded* Poe's person from the text; that is, he was "replaced" as the *signifier.* By heuristically separating the narration of the drama from the conditions of its narration, he reconstructed and reinterpreted the scenes, the protagonists' motives for action, the maneuvers, the guile, and so on, on separate levels. He divided the drama by scenes. In the first scene, in the queen's boudoir, she received the compromising letter she must hide from the king. Minister D., noticing the queen's distress, replaced the letter with one of similar appearance—a maneuver the queen watched but could not prevent. In the second scene, in the minister's office, the minister succeeded in fooling the police but not the deceitful and mysterious Dupin, who ultimately stole the letter—which also was the object of deceit and counterdeceit.

Some French classical Freudians wanted to know what Lacan was saying and therefore occasionally went to his seminars or to the public events arranged by his disciples. And those who did not, in addition to living in the midst of structuralist, deconstructionist, and poststructural concepts, heard about Lacan from patients on their couches—some of whom had been treated by Lacanians. Essentially, their critiques were of the clinical aspects of his theories. They responded to the fact that Lacan saw his patients for short sessions only and was arbitrary in his treatment of them and that his reputation was based on his public performances rather than on his casework. And because he did not write up his cases systematically, these could not be scrutinized in terms of either diagnoses, techniques, or results. Nevertheless, a number of Parisian classical Freudians were attracted to a few of Lacan's clinical concepts and thereby broadened the debates within their association and, eventually, their own practices.

Rachel Z. de Goldstein (1994), an Argentinian Freudian, pointed to the Lacanian concepts that filtered in. She emphasized that Lacan "does not follow Freud, [but] accompanies him, as he stated in his "Seminar I: 'The topic of the Imaginary'" and that he focused strongly on his patients' language in his attempt to better penetrate to their ever elusive unconscious. Lacan also resuscitated Freud's concept of drive (it is on the frontier between the mental and the somatic, as the psychical representative of the stimuli originating from within the organism reaching the mind ... in consequence of its connection with the body [Freud, 1915c, pp. 121–122]). In addition, Goldstein reminded us that Freud distinguished clearly between *Instinkt* and *Trieb*. When Parisian classical Freudians pondered this point, they gradually focused more thoroughly on the family triad in their practices rather than on the mother-child dyad.

Moreover, Lacan moved Freud's concept of desire to the center. Its connection to the *objet-petit-a* and to the moment of castration (when the imaginary and narcissistic relationship between mother and child is dissociated) puts it beyond the realm of what is recoverable in memory. Thus it is said to endure only in the realm of the symbolic: It is not representable and remains "uncanny," although it may return as nostalgia. In sum, Parisian classical Freudians kept rejecting Lacan's clinical practices but little by little began to address Lacan's seductive theories—which had, as it were, inundated the culture—at first by approaching popular subjects such as books on the Marquis de Sade and then by paying more attention to the early role of the fathers of their patients than they otherwise might have done.

For instance, Janine Chasseguet-Smirgel, in *Creativity and Perversion* (1984), questioned "phallic monism." She focused, among other things, on the psychological dynamics of Sade's fantasies of transsexuality and adultery and how interchangeable erotogenic zones were related to his pleasure in transgression (p. 3). Sade wanted to break the barriers separating man from woman, child from adult, mother from son, daughter from father, brother from sister, and to separate the erotogenic zones from one another; he set out to create an undifferentiated, *anal* world full of endless and repetitive taboos, and sacrilege. This anal-sadistic universe of confusion and homogenization, according to Chasseguet-Smirgel, constitutes an imitation or parody of the genital universe of the father (p. 11). By defining perversion as pathological rather than as sexual deviance, she further argued that Caligula, who was brought up among the troops and had witnessed tortures and executions, gluttony and adultery, had been conditioned to cruelty in early life. Her focus on perversion now led Chasseguet-Smirgel to reinterpret Freud's *clinical* narratives of Little Hans, and of the Wolf Man, in relation to their oedipal wishes and the concomitant narcissism. She concluded that "phallic monism is a means of healing a part of the narcissistic injury, ... [stemming from] the child's helplessness [which largely is determined by] the biological factor [that] establishes the earliest situation of danger and creates the need to be loved" (p. 53).

Joyce McDougall, in "The Homosexual Dilemma: A Study of Female Homosexuality" ([1978] 1980, pp. 87–139), also leaned on some of Lacan's rereading of Freud when she explained female homosexuality as a compromise formation of the conflict between one's individual and sexual identities (see Chapter 5). This formation, she said, may occur in relation to a mother who perceives her daughter as a rival, may be wrought with parental conflicts, and then may be complicated by the unconscious violence the reaction against such predicaments may cause. The sense of identity may be expressed in depersonalization when threatened by real or psychic separation; violence by men may be feared because the father is despised and denigrated rather than desired or idealized (in the oedipal stage); and the mother is likely to be cast as the unobtainable ideal, even by the father. McDougall brilliantly outlined the ins and outs of the problems inherent in the analysis of homosexual women. She depicted the homosexual relationship as triumph over both mother and father (though different in each patient) and concluded that such analyses may or may not lead to the abandonment of homosexuality, depending partly on whether such abandonment is a matter of choice rather than compulsion and whether abandonment would lead to more stable relations with parents and partners.

Unquestionably, Chasseguet-Smirgel's and McDougall's spotlight on perversions was a way of advancing the cause of feminism and of "decriminalizing" homosexuality. Still, in their focus on psychosexual development rather than on discourse and language, they do assume that sexuality is developed rather than inborn. This question, which increasingly preoccupied American feminist theorists who were involved in the political sphere, was a point of contention. That may be, at least in part, why the clinically oriented Chodorow incorporated Chasserguet-Smirgel's finding that sexual monism results from repression or a splitting of the ego ([1974] 1989, p. 181). Kaplan too shared most of Chasse-guet-Smirgel's and McDougall's theoretical assumptions. She won brief acclaim for her *Female Perversions: The Temptations of Emma Bovary* (1991) but then could not hold the attention of women in the political movement. But practicing psychoanalytic feminists did not urge political action, as did the "theoretical feminists" who discussed "perversion": Their inquiries increasingly have been carried out in the context of gender studies and gay and lesbian studies.

In American postmodern feminism, the articulation of differences, transgressions, and the subversion of identity are challenging entrenched heterosexual norms and often have called for concrete, political action such as demonstrations and changes in the legal system. But contemporary American feminists differ from their French predecessors insofar as they—unconsciously—incorporate beliefs in the historical determinants of Marxist practice and assume political outcomes that, in France, have been abandoned or have been relegated to the realm of the "imaginary." But there, Lacan's spotlight on the father as the head of the family *has* had its impact on clinical practice by putting more emphasis on "the third element," that is, on the triadic relationship of mother, father, and infant as determining its future social and psychic position and development.

The Radicalization of Sexual Difference

By the end of the 1980s, the radicalization of American feminism, for the most part, took two different (though not always separate or distinguishable) directions. Intent on changing basic social values, the gay movement staged political events and advanced provocative, radical theories. In order to influence and institute these ends, political theorists extended their hypotheses to advocate changes in laws affecting child care, abortion, health insurance, and welfare that would permanently ensure the institutionalization of a new (and more liberal) set of values.

Certainly these changes already were being foreshadowed in "On 'Compulsory Heterosexuality and Lesbian Existence': Defining the Issues," an essay by Anne Ferguson, Jacquelin Zita, and Kathryn Pyne Addelson in Keohane, Rosaldo, and Gelpi (1981). The essay's authors were described as "the first lesbian-feminist theorists to suggest a reconstruction of the concept *lesbian*" (p. 149). The authors' definitions did not derive from psychoanalysis but from behavior: A lesbian is a woman who is bonded to women, who is attracted to other women, who is sexual exclusively in relation to other women, and who chooses women to support and nurture her. Both Ferguson and Jacqueline Zita expanded on the writer-poet Adrienne Rich's notion of the "lesbian continuum" and on the commonality that links lesbian existence to its location within compulsory heterosexuality, and they found that this notion fails to sort out "successful existence" from "mere victimization." Instead, Ferguson suggested a "strategy through which lesbian existence becomes a political concept suitable for our own times"; this existence, stated Kathryn Pyne Addelson, is countercultural, although she acknowledged that some groups do engage in effective political battle (pp. 187–188).

Cass Sunstein's (1982) much-reprinted reader *Feminism and Political Theory* reveals that feminism became a major issue for political scientists and philosophers as well, that political battles were also waged within these disciplines, and that the growing concern with interdisciplinarity added to the conceptual confusions between feminist theory and political assumptions. In his introduction, Sunstein stated that Freud's explorations of the topic had been notoriously inadequate but that Michel Foucault might be up to the job (p. 10). Beyond that, he twice referred to Freud in passing, and he mentioned that moral philosopher and psychologist Carol Gilligan accepted a neo-Freudian account of early childhood based on Chodorow's ideas of mothering. Altogether, Sunstein introduced some of the political consequences of feminist theory, such as issues of justice and rights and controversies over abortion and prostitution—all of which are beyond the scope of this book.

In sum, in universities feminist political theory moved to a structuralism without Freud at a time when feminist literary theorists claimed to embrace Freud via structuralism and poststructuralism. But for sociologists, as noted in Chapter 3, differences in gender always have been a major subject of study, and sociologists—though in the forefront of the feminist movement in the 1960s—did not take to psychoanalysis. Still, Christine L. Williams, in *Gender Differences at Work* (1989), used a psychoanalytic approach in her comparative study of male nurses and female recruits in the Marine Corps in order to probe the depth of gender identification. Following Chodorow, she assumed that females continue throughout their lives to identify with their mothers, and following Robert Stoller, she presupposed that men as well retain a sense of femininity that they have to renounce later on (p. 13). Williams noticed that male nurses went to a lot of trouble to carve a special niche for themselves that they then defined as masculine but that women marines felt they could maintain their femininity in any job they were assigned to. This study illustrates the consequences of our process of gender socialization and the asymmetry of childhood experiences—which Williams said that psychoanalysis alone can tap into in order to uncover the hidden motives and unconscious desires that inform her sociological study (pp. 14–15). Maybe because psychoanalytic investigations such as this one ultimately illustrate what we know—although over time changes may be registered—and cannot be directly action- or policy-oriented, sociologists rarely undertake them. Clearly, structuralist feminist criticism lends itself even less to such concrete, empirical ends.

More Adaptations of French Psychoanalytic Feminism

The many formulations on differences between males and females and on the roots of gender, and their interdisciplinary thrust, were, of course, the essential ingredients and texts American feminist theorists relied upon as they split over which discourse or language to "privilege," which "strategy" of speech or social facts to favor, or whether to examine the relationships among power, language, and meaning from the point of view of the signifier or the signified. Ultimately, these concerns became rarified enough to leave behind the French feminists' setting altogether: French theorists' words and rhetoric were applied in order to create new academic endeavors and enrich existing ones. As noted, the center of the discourse shifted from women's liberation to lesbian feminism and then to textual analyses of prejudice against gays and lesbians. And because theory was imagined to bring about social change, it was assumed that it would manage to cure every manifestation of sexism and racism.

Moreover, as these theories attracted more and more followers, publishers looking for profits encouraged this "postmodern" enterprise. For instance, Cornell University Press started an entire series entitled Reading Women Writing. Some of these volumes were psychoanalytically oriented. Thus Biddy Martin (1991) presented Freud's disciple Lou Andreas-Salomé as "a writer, thinker, and lay analyst who spent the greater part of her life among the cultural and intellectual elites ... [and made her mark] on the basis of her liaisons with famous men" (p. 1). She depicted Andreas-Salomé as both intellectual and seductress, as a woman who allegedly "entered a discursive and social universe in which gender polarity was essential" (p. 3) and whose "construction of femininity did not challenge the ultimate fact of sexual difference on the presumption of heterosexuality head on ... [because] affirmative femininity, free of competitiveness and *ressentiment,* exposed man's lack and his need, but also reassured him, protected him from the threat of direct challenge" (p. 5). Martin quoted profusely from the usual sources of postmodernist feminism, especially from Michel Foucault, Jane Gallop, and Luce Irigaray, and maintained that Andreas-Salomé "enjoyed a privileged place among her male colleagues and associates," did not identify with feminists, and "conceived and enacted positions other than oedipal ones, [in] her efforts to imagine and to perform the oxymoron of feminine individuality" (p. 22). (When Chodorow interviewed the surviving 1930s psychoanalysts in the early 1980s, she found out that they all had assumed themselves to be feminists [Chodorow, (1974) 1989, pp. 199–218].)

Andreas-Salomé's analysis with Freud, said Martin, "displaced the hierarchical gender divide and inevitable appropriation that had characterized other pedagogical exchanges, other all-too-conventional scenes of seduction." In François Roustang's familiar formulation, she had found a "father" who "granted her her own desires, her own name, and her own ability to think without requiring the renunciation or the murder of the father" (Martin, 1991, p. 196). Yet in spite of her subsequent friendship and correspondence with Freud and the other major psychoanalysts, Andreas-Salomé could not "completely escape the discursive constraints of phallic law" (p. 198). Ultimately, Martin concluded that Andreas-Salomé "structured her relationship to Freud, as she structured her relationships to other important (male) figures, in such a way as to return them and herself to a fundamental bisexuality" (p. 230), and her "woman appears to include 'masculine' activity within a more universal femininity, within the spirals of an autotelic, unrepressed feminine unfolding" (p. 232).

In their foreword to Patricia Elliot's *From Mastery to Psychoanalysis* (1991), the Cornell series editors cast her as still another one of the psychoanalytic feminists who "desire to develop a critical theory of the gendered subject" (p. ix). Anchored in Lacan's four fundamental discourses (mastery, bureaucracy, hysteria, and analysis) and dissecting the *earlier* theories of Juliet Mitchell, Jacqueline Rose, Dorothy Dinnerstein, Nancy Chodorow, Luce Irigaray, and Julia Kristeva, Elliot was said to have developed a "particular method of theorizing gender as the object of transformation" (p. 3), based on "the relationship of subjectivity and power in advanced capitalist societies" (p. 5) and on their reading of Lacan's multiple discourses.

Elliot quoted François Roustang at the head of her concluding chapter: "What distinguishes madness from theory is precisely that theory is recognized as fiction" (Elliot, 1991, p. 230). She then went on to say that the different feminist discourses emphasize the collective process of theorizing gender (p. 231). She was perturbed by Mitchell and Rose, and even more so by Dinnerstein and Chodorow, for being sympathetic and deferential to psychoanalysis, "as if some desire for certainty lurked in the background" (p. 232). And she found that "Kristeva's [desire] is not immune to the danger of inverting itself into a discourse of mastery," although Kristeva somewhat safeguarded against it (p. 234). In defense of Elliot, I must add that she cautioned against generalizations and against assuming that she had found the "Truth" (p. 240); but unfortunately, neither she nor any of the other postmodern feminists have endorsed Roustang's point that the theory itself is a fiction.

Tentative Conclusion

I am raising questions about these activities because I find that the analysis of feminists' written texts is not a good substitute for empirical investigation no matter how carefully and tentatively it may proceed and that such inquiries foreclose their authors' subsequently developing views, their changes of mind. Moreover, neither Foucault nor Lacan, whose formulations are implicit in most of these conceptualizations of desire, allowed their open-ended and dynamic ideas to be pinned down.

As I noted, Kristeva has moved away from these disputes and from theory to writing novels. The study of inequalities due to race and gender, and to class, all along were the purview of sociologists and anthropologists (and not of their explicitly Marxist contingent alone): Empirical findings led some of them to construct relevant theories of social dynamics. The raw material of the literary theorists, however, was culled from writings by a very select number of its members. Yes, just as in the past, feminist critics have examined these works in relation to their authors' lives and times. But after Foucault and Barthes (and in a narrower fashion Lévi-Strauss as well) held—however briefly—that the author does not exist, that he or she is just a product of the surroundings, some American feminist critics took such pronouncements seriously. And they continued to do so for nearly twenty years after Foucault declared that authors had to be brought back in.

Because theoretical premises were infused with Jacques Derrida's deconstructionism and were subsumed under a number of ill-defined (and parallel) theories of postmodernism, it soon was taken for granted that *all* knowledge is relative and that ultimately one knowledge is as good as any other. This premise did not distinguish between tested facts and imaginative assertions; hierarchies were abolished and many of the deconstructivists thus considered their radical, political stances as intrinsically moral. Soon, people who questioned either the content or the methods of their analyses on *any* grounds were being dismissed as conservative and intellectually wanting. To get out of the resulting polarization within academic departments and the rarified debates, some academic administrators began to advocate interdisciplinary programs. Primarily, these were to reintegrate the multiplicity of specialties that had evolved over the years. But because overall these esoteric theories no longer made sense to an ever broader range of students, their content often was simplified in the effort to be fair and to further democratic values.

In the political realm, American psychoanalysts such as Stephan Frosh (1987) got into the fray more directly when they felt increasingly marginalized and, to "defend" themselves, held that they too could contribute to political change—either by entering the postmodern discourse or by trying to disprove one or another of its psychoanalytic assumptions. In a way, when postmodern theorists (whether male or female) argue that because nothing in our world any longer makes sense, their theories as well don't have to make sense in the "traditional" manner, they resemble the child that accuses its mother for not loving it because it was naughty and then goes on being naughty.

Some sociologists and anthropologists, and other social scientists, who noticed that their empirical findings did not prove the theories they had been relying on also looked to those advanced by the literary theorists. Others were impressed by the conceptual intricacies. And some classical analysts began to introduce Saussurean tenets into their discussions of literature. Eventually, the confusion among theories—which by then incorporated one or more Freudian tenets—and social practice was total. But this intellectual anarchy could be defended theoretically: French structuralist theory and psychoanalysis had shown that time and space in the human mind are neither chronological nor static. Postmodern notions accepted the ensuing confusion of realms and theorized these as intrinsic elements of the postmodern condition.

With the installation of this type of reasoning, the shift from the feminist politics of the First Wave was justifiable. Thereby, homosexuality, which Freud had explained as part of natural development, was being politicized. But this politicization now was being separated from psychoanalytic therapy, and the confusion went beyond the theoretical feminists' discussions, so that there ensued a total jumble between theory and practice. In academe, the Second Wave of feminism now claimed to speak for all the disadvantaged constituencies. Most academics would not condone or turn the other cheek to racial or sexual prejudice. But some of them did react against the theoretical esoterica. Ultimately, this endless embroidery about what Freud and Lacan really meant was incomprehensible to most students. However, to the extent that this postmodern, feminist discourse came to dominate humanities departments, which increasingly hired feminist theorists, it became counterproductive to the education of the majority of students.

Historically, I believe, the postmodern Marx-Freud syntheses have run their course. Ultimately, they did not hold up, and they are too complex for dissemination by the media. However, the proponents of postmodern psychoanalytic feminism initiated many studies that in themselves are harmless but that, finally, have detracted us from investigating our nearly insuperable social problems in a truly nonideological and productive way.

Conclusion

Julien Benda, in *La trahison des clercs* ([1927] 1928), called attention to a new phenomenon, the subordination of scholarship and speculation to personal commitment or political interest. Although the translation into English, "the treason of intellectuals," is not quite correct, it conveys Benda's thesis: Treason is committed when scholars or writers set themselves up as a spiritual militia of temporal interests. Rulers always have tried to use *clercs* to further their own ends, to advance the interests of the state, noted Benda. But in the past, he concluded, writers and scholars did not *themselves* offer their services to a political cause. Instead, they expected to expose the seeds of tyranny and superstition by the use of reason. Max Weber reaffirmed this ethical principle when in "Politics as a Vocation" ([1919] 1946), he argued that even though he had strong political commitments, he had no right to impose these on the students in his classrooms or to judge them because of theirs.

As for the university, it follows from Benda's and Weber's warnings that it should be preserved as a neutral space for open debate, that neither police nor thought police should intrude. Since the end of the Middle Ages, the tradition of the university as a protected space for free speech and a refuge from persecution by authorities had been sacrosanct. Over the years, a variety of causes and movements—some legitimate—gradually have eroded this custom. Now, some people presuppose that education for democracy consists of politicization and that the university is the location par excellence to achieve this end. Psychoanalysts as well as feminists are among them.

Benda's book had been nearly forgotten by the time of World War II. But the reverse of his thesis gained credence, namely that scholarship would influence politics. That was when the confusion of scholarship with political commitment inadvertently received a somewhat peripheral boost from the émigré psychoanalysts who were getting established within American psychiatry. As I have noted in this book, psychoanalysis, studies of authoritarianism (T. W. Adorno, et al. [1950]),[1] field theory (developed by Kurt Lewin [1948]),[2] and the growing assumption that all social ills would be eliminated with the help of psychotherapy inevitably took for granted that psychoanalysis could (and should) explain political behavior.

Around 1945, both American government officials and intellectuals were already acting on the belief that the proper applications of psychoanalysis might help alter the personality structures of the German population. It was assumed that psychoanalysis held the secret to personal happiness and success, that it legitimately could (and had to) shift from personal to societal issues and from clinical theory to clinical practice, and that the spread of its practices itself would heal the rifts and contradictions within cultural-societal and theoretical-clinical issues. At that time, the academy rather suddenly was transformed into an arena for mass education as the war veterans started to get their government-funded higher education. The resulting confusion between education and politics, however, was not appropriately addressed. The population at large always had veered from envy of successful entrepreneurs to believing that they too would hit the jackpot. The notion that the discovery of individuals' unconscious conflicts would bring out the "gold" within themselves led to the belief that with a college education individuals could achieve whatever they wanted. (In its current and popular version this quest has become coded as finding out "who I am.")

Feminists and feminist movements have functioned within this context. At the turn of the century, most American feminists belonged to the northern or the southern upper classes and supported the downtrodden: They had helped to abolish slavery and enact women's suffrage, and they propped up poor immigrants and exploited workers. With few exceptions, they expected to change the structures of American society, but even when they called for action, they did not do so from a knowledge of Marxism, although their socialist ideals were in line with its reformist version. Nor did many feminists ever join the Communist party. Instead, the female equivalent of Horatio Alger, the destitute working boy who became a millionaire, kept alive the widespread belief that hard work and practical guile would extend not only the Western frontier but the horizon of each woman and each worker. These credos were reinforced by the implementation of John Dewey's pragmatic and educational philosophies with their emphasis on the consequences of ideas and beliefs.

Few critical American academics employed a Marxist analysis—although such sociologists as David Reisman and Nathan Glazer pointed to the alienation of working people to what they called "other-directedness," and C. Wright Mills used a class analysis in his put-down of American society. They did so not because they had read Marx but because they were observing American society critically, as Chicago sociologists George Herbert Mead, William Graham Sumner, Charles Horton

Cooley, and Thorstein Veblen had done before them. (Ironically, the participants of the recent liberation movements do not recall that Veblen described their activities as belonging to the conspicuous consumption of the leisure class within American democracy and described them as driven to good works by the guilt their success had brought on.)

During the student rebellions of 1968, New Left radicals, along with their feminist constituents, denounced psychoanalysis (together with its "deviant" offsprings) as conservative and elitist and ignored the fact that the earlier and "deviant" émigré Freudians such as Erich Fromm, Erik Erikson, and Wilhelm Reich, had introduced the Freud-Marx syntheses that were to revolutionize modern society. (As noted, in Germany and France, Marxism had fueled the student uprisings—along with feminist theory.) The 1960s feminists dismissed Freud as an old-fashioned patriarch mired in Austro-Hungarian traditional thinking, as an agent of women's repression. And as more and more students joined in efforts to destroy "the system," it turned out that it was easier to alter traditional family structures—and sexual mores—than those of the whole system and easier to challenge traditional authority than to do away with entrepreneurship, that is, capitalism.

In the process, administrators responsive to the new climate guilelessly allowed the protected status of universities to erode and, as Benda and Max Weber had warned against, permitted the invasion of its traditionally neutral space. And when politics on campuses took violent forms, the iron rule of keeping out police was broken: In the name of safety campus officials inadvertently assisted the rapprochement between their own authority and that of the state. It was just a matter of time before the scholarship of politics and the politics of scholarship merged. But by then, the confusion over who was a scholar, an intellectual, an academic, or an activist had become total, and definitions as well were made in keeping with one's position on the political spectrum.

Whereas psychoanalysis remained more or less on the couch, "the unconscious" became everyone's property. And the formerly dormant feminism that was stirring in middle-class psyches began to flourish in the universities and then spread to the political realm. The influences of academic feminists reached government agencies—with the help of affirmative action policies—and gradually began to move into the sources of power, much as C. Wright Mills described the process in relation to the military-industrial leaders in *The Power Elite* (1956).

The resulting amalgam of education and politics, which now was immortalized in the slogan "The personal is the political," provided a favorable climate for all liberation movements, including the feminist one. Weber had questioned whether the achievement of worthwhile ends ever could justify questionable means to these ends, but the fact that his sociology was being labeled conservative somehow led scholars to underplay, or forget, his distinctions. Self-righteous and dedicated fervor started to take the place of rational debates.

* * *

The interrelationship of psychoanalysis and feminism has been rocky. I have sketched the ups and downs of their affinities and disputes since Freud's time—when his women followers began to apply psychoanalysis in order to alter the social consequences that follow from women's ability to bear children. For even though the repercussions that originate in women's exclusive capacity to give birth had been challenged before, psychoanalysis offered a tool that would reach women's psychic roots in order to change them by penetrating to what was thought to be the innate motivations that, throughout time, had kept women from achieving status and opportunities equal to men's.

I have noted that Freud's earliest female disciples were emancipated women who, like the men around them, were drawn to psychoanalysis's potentials to liberate through its method of explaining the differences between the sexes—through looking at biological, psychological, and social factors all at once. These outspoken women were the men's match, and in their contributions they often outdid their male colleagues. They were practicing feminists as well as socialists at a time when socialism was popular and was making political strides and psycholanalysis promised to become its psychological arm. Freud's women expected to be in the forefront of the impending "society of equals" and to help eradicate distinctions of class and gender. In fact, the radical promises of psychoanalysis continued to fuel the psychoanalytic movement, and Freud as well as most of his followers paid lip service to its associated causes long after they had lost their revolutionary fervor.

All social movements tend to be created by enterprising idealists and to die when their goals are fulfilled or begin to appear unattainable. Yet within the psychoanalytic movement, feminists at various times continued to invigorate the social promises. As we noted, Karen Horney and Helene Deutsch contributed to feminism as they began to develop their personality theories in the 1920s and as they elaborated on them as social theories in the 1940s. In the 1970s and 1980s, primarily in France and America, feminists reached back to some of their concepts. But each of these bursts of psychoanalytic feminism was different, and each time psychoanalysis was eyed from different angles.

Throughout the century, psychoanalytic therapies, in spite of temporary setbacks and new reincarnations, also grew by leaps and bounds, as did a bevy of national and international organizations. And Freudian women, just like their male colleagues, were extrapolating from their own experiences and insights to improve their theories. Despite the chauvinism of some of the male members, women advanced within the organization. However, feminism was not their central concern. Also, whenever they were being treated as second-class members within the Freudian fold, they were aware that some male psychoanalysts were in the same boat. This type of inequality was based on whether they had medical degrees or were deemed to have been fully analyzed and was cross-sexual and specific to the American milieu. Still, the resulting theoretical divergences splintered the Freudian movement, and feminists outside psychoanalysis borrowed from all of the existing factions and from earlier women psychoanalysts.

In the 1920s, women psychoanalysts objected to Freud's supposition that boys' and girls' (unconscious) psychic growth paralleled one another; and they emphasized the consequences of the distinctive treatment that arose from social attitudes that assumed inherent differences. In the 1940s, their focus increasingly shifted to the social fabric that helped engender and support these differences. But then, women psychoanalysts in their work with patients, for the most part, supported the liberation of the individual women they had on their couches. This "privatization," which proceeded apace with the marginalization of Freudian theory even as the society was buying into the therapeutic ethos, resulted in a general amnesia about the beginnings of Freudian therapy in the American public and among feminists.

I noted that in the late 1960s the upsurge of feminism was accompanied by anti-Freudian bias even though sex-typing had been perpetrated just as much by all social scientists and was permeating all social strata: Boys were dressed in blue and girls in pink; boys were not expected to cry but girls were; boys were assumed to breeze through advanced algebra, which allegedly was beyond the comprehension of girls; and so on. Still, *all* feminists remained baffled when the analysis of sex-typing did not eradicate it. That was when they started to cooperate with feminist psychoanalysts, who for some time had been reexamining the unconscious elements that induce women to buckle under to men's blustering and boasting, to men's dominating public and private life, and to mothering their daughters the way their mothers mothered them.

By then, feminists had helped establish laws that mandated equal access to education and jobs. The women's movement (in step with black liberation) had succeeded. This is not to say that the unconscious obstacles to equality had been removed, that women could have rested on their laurels, or that they could have ignored the backlash they now had to fight. However, this First Wave of feminism had every reason to feel victorious and to observe with satisfaction that a society that a few years before had had no more than 3 to 5 percent of women lawyers and doctors now had around one-third; and that women had penetrated Wall Street and corporate headquarters, even if only a few of them had as yet reached the top ranks.

The Second Wave of feminists gained their stronghold in the universities and assumed that they were at one with their predecessors. True, many of the main players were the same: They had joined the movement to heighten feminist consciousness in colleagues and students but got restless when progress appeared to be halted, when the movement lost its unity. Some of them primarily supported disadvantaged groups, others proposed radical solutions based on a variety of theoretical orientations, yet others advocated that feminists forgo (sexual) relationships with men; some concentrated on instituting feminist practices around the world.

The reverberations from the international women's conferences they organized, in turn, strengthened the movement and exposed American feminists to the fact that compared to women in other countries, they were indeed liberated. In the process, they were also being exposed to French feminism and to Jacques Lacan's idiosyncratic "rereading" of Freud. Whether they responded to his anti-Freudian or his anti-American stance, to the fact that the writings by his female disciples appeared to have liberated them (even though, as the French knew, quite a number among them had been his lovers), or to the intellectual challenge these theories themselves presented is a moot issue. In fact, the transposition of Lacanian and French feminist thought (especially of Julia Kristeva, Luce Irigaray, Hélène Cixous, Janine Chasseguet-Smirgel, and Joyce McDougall)—along with new interpretations and elaborations of history, philosophy, and literature by, among others, Michel Foucault, Jacques Derrida, Louis Althusser, and Roland Barthes—inspired what I perceive as the Second Wave of American feminism.

By the time most American academics (including feminists) came upon the French intellectual scene, their predecessors' theories had peaked in Paris. The creators and champions of these theories had grown tired of the hidden structures that failed to emerge, especially when they realized that they were heading into blind alleys; empirical realities did not correspond to expectations. Nevertheless, Americans were intrigued by the novel promises to revive the radical movements that by then appeared to have become shopworn and uninspired. In the past, attempts to mesh the revolutionary components of Marxism with those of psychoanalysis had been rather haphazard and, in the long run, unsuccessful. In its French and so-called postmodern incarnation (which does away with historical and qualitative distinctions and facilitates *all* free associations to conscious and unconscious phenomena that are said to give vent to as yet unexplored components of the imagination), psychoanalytic feminism got a new start in America, mostly in departments of literature in elite universities. From there it spread to other disciplines—the social sciences and humanities—and to other institutions around the country.

When the proponents of this new "Theory" extrapolated from literary texts to radical, sociological theories and to the contradictions between state and civil society and, like Foucault, predicted yet another historical break based on the new knowledge arising from the changes in the social fabric, they increasingly assumed that theory and practice were one and the same thing. In their enthusiasm, some generalized from the changes within universities to the society: Women held more and better positions and they supposed that "the proletariat" did too. Others assumed (with Marx) that "history" was progressing, and yet others were so busy organizing postmodern meetings that they lost sight of other orientations.

Of course, the lines between the First Wave and Second Wave of feminism were blurred: Interest-group politics moved into the universities, and theoretical feminism and disciplinary politics moved outside via professors turned consultants and the media. And whereas the psychoanalytic feminists of the First Wave did not function primarily in the academic arena, it became the Second Wave's stronghold. Yet neither feminists nor other postmodernists managed appreciably to reorder or improve existing inequalities. What, in fact, both feminist Waves did was help change the general sensibility about sexuality. This opened the way to gay and lesbian liberation, that is, to further psychopolitics, which is yet another topic. Classical Freudian feminists (and male psychoanalysts) outside the university also added their expertise to concerns about health care and psychiatry, to training social workers and psychologists. Unavoidably, their "classical" theoretical approaches, particularly object-relations theory and questions of transference and countertransference, came to be included in the discussions (Kernberg, 1993).

As long as extraneous political ends did not overshadow the psychoanalytic feminists' theories, they kept their exploratory and speculative vitality. During the First Wave of feminism they helped initiate the changes that guaranteed equal opportunity of access to jobs and education. But when the radical doctrines introduced by the Second Wave of feminism replaced simple, liberating rhetoric with a pseudopolitics in order to get rid of "a system of male dominance," of "heteropatriarchy," of the existing "sex-gender system," and of "phallocentrism," they went beyond the ongoing and often excellent scholarship by women historians and social scientists. Some women formed separatist groups; others based their theories on wild speculation rather than research; still others assumed that because "the Word" is central, their plays on words and on categories of words were what psychoanalysis is all about. Yes, the philosophical bent and volatile, high-flown verbosity of French women's literature, and its rationalism (overlaid with mythological content), lent American imitators a certain amount of prestige. But for all postmodern feminism's flair, it was being practiced quite narrowly and inconsistently. Thus Julia Kristeva, for instance, recently was accused of "incorrectness" for including in her studies such traditional figures as Michelet and Montesquieu, Voltaire and Rousseau, although her "transgressions" were forgiven in the name of sisterhood (personal communication, 1991). But the French feminists were flexible enough to pay homage to Sartre even as they discarded his existentialism in order to bring in Lévi-Strauss and Barthes. And they could, however grudgingly, appreciate Simone de Beauvoir as their liberated mother while disavowing—often by discounting first-hand observations—that she had played second fiddle to her companion. How else could they follow in the footsteps of the "second sex" while assiduously striving to become the first one?

The current disjuncture between French and American feminism was apparent, for instance, in Lisa Jardine and Anne M. Menke's (1991) interviews with the fifteen "most prominent" women writers and in the provincial questions they posed to them. When asked, for example (an "American" question), whether French feminist writers expected to be included in the twentieth-century canon, some answered that notions of a literary "canon" were hopelessly passé, were meaningless in an age dominated by a high-tech media culture, and belonged to sociology rather than literature. (These women "demonstrated a strong resistance not only to the notion of the 'canon' itself ... [but] wondered why anyone would want to be in it" [p. 7].) They also said that the construction of sexual difference through ideas of the feminine and the masculine might be more crucial than a metaphysical category of "women" (p. 6). Monique Wittig, whose contribution also was the conclusion to that book, said that she did not think of herself as any more of a lesbian writer than a woman writer (p. 195). This response appears to be a rejection, by implication, of the Second Wave of American feminism, which, among other things, espouses "sexual politics" and at times the exclusion of men.

The original success of the American feminist movement, it seems to me, was followed by a decline after the takeover of the Second Wave, when theories purporting to push for equality of the sexes began to move into arcane theories and to subvert democratic principles in the name of equality and when it started to be taken for granted that men do not deserve a hearing or academic jobs because they have been heard all along. The French appear to know that to achieve feminist ends through questionable means, or through any type of dubious intellectual strategy, can end only in undermining each woman's own and cherished authenticity. Furthermore, to be against everything deemed "traditional"—whether this is classical psychoanalysis, the use of historical chronology, so-called "privileging" (a favorite word) of heterosexuality, or the refusal to value what has come to be called male thought—often subverts the ultimate ends of feminism, of genuine equality in every realm. By overly politicalizing their aims, some feminist theorists, and the psychoanalytic theorists among them, have exemplified the dangers Benda warned against: They have become a spiritual militia. Thereby, they have lost much of their legitimation. Of course, I am here referring to the extremists who assume that feminist theory, that is, theory per se, imparts authority to their lofty, rhetorical endeavors.

In fact, upon looking up "theory" in the thesaurus, I find that it may be defined as "explanation" or "speculation"—a number of pegs below the sublime heights to which some of its pedestrian proponents have elevated it. Moreover, by assuming that these theories belong in the political realm, extremists have shifted them from literature to sociology, from the realm of imaginative speculation to the real world. There, the application of theories, as the founder of sociology, Auguste Comte, stated, is in trouble because all of society cannot be used as a laboratory for speculation. Comte himself, as we know, solved this dilemma by turning sociology itself into a religion. Some of the feminist theorists of the Second Wave have wavered between transforming feminism into a "secular" religion and transforming society into a huge laboratory. The fact remains that the liberation of women lies not in theories but in practical solutions.

In this book, I have tried to illuminate the symbiotic relationship between psychoanalysis and feminism, and I have traced the recurrent and altering ambivalences among their practitioners throughout this century. I also have observed the pitfalls in the conspicuous "theorizing" of the recent feminist movements, which, via academic advocacy, has helped to impose what has come to be known as "political correctness." Therefore, I suggest that we replace abstract and unbridled rhetoric with more concrete—and less flighty—theories based on painstaking research that remains anchored in empirical realities and that, it is hoped, will deflate some of the more extreme views and replace them with a confident but more modest self-awareness.

Notes

Chapter 1

1. The others are "War Neurosis in Women" (1915), "A Case of Female Foot Fetishism, or Rather, Shoe Fetishism" (1916), "The Middle Child" (1921), "Psychoanalytic Findings About Women" (1921), "The Importance of Family for the Fate of the Individual" (1923), and "The Libidinal Structure of Family Life" (1924). Recently, MacLean and Reppen (1991) wrote a biography, *Hug-Hellmuth: Her Life and Work*.

2. In this book I am not getting into the theories that were discarded, mostly because these, for the most part, were not picked up by later feminists. In addition to Jones's contributions, Jeanne Lampl-de Groot's "The Evolution of the Oedipus Complex in Women" (*International Journal of Psychoanalysis* 9:332–345) bears mentioning.

Chapter 2

1. Recently London psychoanalysts Pearl King and Riccardo Steiner published the proceedings of these controversial discussions.

Chapter 3

1. C. Wright Mills's *The Sociological Imagination* (1959) was the first salvo.

2. In *Women's Estate* (1971) Mitchell asked feminist questions from a Marxist perspective. Therefore, her book is peripheral to my present focus on psychoanalysis alone.

Chapter 4

1. For instance, none of Annette Kuhn and AnnMarie Wolpe's eleven contributors in *Feminism and Materialism* (Routledge & Kegan Paul, 1978) refer to Freud, and only one mentions Althusser's article "Freud and Lacan" (p. 40). None of Nona Glazer-Malbin's ten contributors in *Old Family/New Family* (Van Nostrand, 1975) referred to psychoanalysis, although Glazer-Malbin noted Americans' predilection to use the individualistic approach of Freud's followers and detractors (p. 12). In Jo Freeman's *Women: A Feminist Perspective* (Mayfield, [1975] 1979) by thirty contributors, Freud's theory of penis envy is challenged—briefly—three times and is postulated once as in agreement with existentialism. Martha Blaxall and Barbara Reagan, in their thirty presentations in *Women and the Workplace* (Chicago University Press, 1976), do not cite Freud or psychoanalysis in the index, although there are a number of vague allusions and refutations in the text.

As we know, most authors of articles in collections have written books or monographs before being asked to contribute their thoughts to scholarly readers. Thus it should be clear that the marginalization of Freudian thought from the feminist movement was fairly complete.

2. The sociologists Fred Weinstein and Gerald M. Platt, in *Psychoanalytic Sociology: An Essay on the Interpretation of Historical Data and the Phenomena of Collective Behavior* (Johns Hopkins University Press, 1973), although questioning Freud's explanation of female behavior, did not add to the debates on psychoanalytic feminism.

3. I too was intrigued with Foucault's formulations of the institutionalization of knowledge/power and presented a paper, "The Use of Foucault's Theories for Feminists," in 1977. However, I subsequently decided not to submit it for publication because, ultimately, empirical data did not support the theory.

Chapter 6

1. In Kelly Oliver's recently edited book, *Ethics, Politics, and Difference in Julia Kristeva's Writing* (Routledge, 1993), the focus is on Kristeva's evolving project, in which she tries to "link ethics and negativity [in order] to steer between tyranny and delirium" and to avoid both conformity and perversion (p. 1).

Chapter 8

1. I am leaving out Elizabeth Wright's edited dictionary, *Feminism and Psychoanalysis* (Basil Blackwell, 1992), which is too inclusive, and all the readers that don't directly deal with psychoanalysis, such as Linda S. Kauffman's *American Feminist Thought at Century's End: A Reader* (Blackwell, 1993). Other books, as well, are left out: Shoshana Felman and Dori Laub, *Testimony: Crises of Witnessing in Literature, Psychoanalysis, and History* (Routledge, 1992); Jane Flax, *Disputed Subjects: Essays on Psychoanalysis, Politics and Philosophy* (Routledge, 1993); Lisa Appignanesi and John Forrester, *Freud's Women: Family, Patients, Followers* (Basic Books, 1992).

2. Here, I am not including Teresa Brennan's *The Interpretation of the Flesh: Freud and Femininity* (Routledge, 1992) because it is a (competent) survey of the discussions since Freud and thus goes over some of the territory my present book is covering.

3. Scott was quoting comments by Karen Swann at a colloquium at Wesleyan University on January 19, 1991 (p. 40).

4. This is especially evident in Ruth Ley's chapter, "The Real Miss Beauchamp" (pp. 167–214), in Drucilla L. Cornell's "Gender, Sex, and Equivalent Rights" (pp. 280–296), and in Chantal Mouffe's "Feminism, Citizenship and Radical Democratic Politics" (pp. 369–384).

5. Diana Fuss's *Inside/Out: Lesbian Theories, Gay Theories* (Routledge, 1991) goes beyond the topic of my current discussion.

Conclusion

1. Together with both émigré and American academics who had been attracted to the Marx-Freud syntheses of the Frankfurt School, Adorno conducted

extensive interviews and then analyzed these in order to construct a scale of authoritarianism.

2. Lewin (1948) stated, for instance, that in Germany, for most persons, a political or even a scientific disagreement seemed to be inseparable from moral disapproval.

References

Abraham, K. [1920, 1922] 1974."Manifestations of the Female Castration Complex." In Strouse, *Women and Analysis*, pp. 109–135.

Abraham, N., and Torok, M. 1976. *Le verbier de l'homme aux loups*. Paris: Aubier-Flammirion.

Adler, A. [1912] 1922. *Über den nervösen Charakter*. Munich: Bergman.

Adorno, T. W., et al. 1950. *The Authoritarian Personality*. New York: Norton.

_____. 1951. *Minima Moralia*. New York: Norton.

Althusser, L. 1965. *Pour Marx*. Paris: Maspero.

_____. [1965] 1971. "Freud and Lacan." In *Lenin and Philosophy and Other Essays*. London: New Left Books.

Bart, P. 1974. "Ideologies and Utopias of Psychotherapy." In Roman and Trice, *The Sociology of Psychotherapy*, pp. 9–57.

Barthes, R. [1957] 1972. *Mythologies*. New York: Hill and Wang.

_____. [1975] 1977. *Roland Barthes by Roland Barthes*. New York: Hill and Wang.

Bartky, S. L. 1990. *Femininity and Domination: Studies in the Phenomenology of Oppression*. London: Routledge.

Baruch, E. H. 1991. *Women, Love and Power: Literary and Psychoanalytic Perspectives*. New York: New York University Press.

Baruch, E. H., and Serrano, L. J. 1988. *Women Analyze Women*. New York: New York University Press.

Beauvoir, S. de [1949] 1952. *The Second Sex*. New York: Vintage.

Benda, J. [1927] 1928. *The Treason of the Intellectuals*. New York: William Morrow.

Benedict, R. 1934. *Patterns of Culture*. Boston: Houghton Mifflin.

Benjamin, J. 1978. "Authority and the Family Revisited; or A World Without Fathers?" *New German Critique* 13:35–58.

_____. 1988. *Bonds of Love: Psychoanalysis, Feminism, and the Problem of Domination*. New York: Pantheon.

Bernay, T., and Cantor, D. W., eds. 1986. *The Psychology of Today's Woman: New Psychoanalytic Perspectives*. Cambridge: Harvard University Press.

Bowie, M. 1991. *Lacan*. Cambridge: Harvard University Press.

Brede, K., ed. 1987. *Befreiung zum Widerstand*. Frankfurt: Fischer Verlag.

_____, ed. 1989. *Was will das Weib in mir?* Freiburg: Kore Verlag.

Brennan, T., ed. 1989. *Between Feminism and Psychoanalysis*. London: Routledge.

Butler J., and Scott, J. W., eds. 1992. *Feminists Theorize the Political*. New York: Routledge.

Chasseguet-Smirgel, J. 1984. *Creativity and Perversion*. New York: Norton.

_____.[1964] 1985. *Female Sexuality: New Psychoanalytic Views.* London: Karnak Books.

_____. [1975] 1985. *The Ego Ideal.* New York: Norton.

_____. 1986. *Sexuality and the Mind: The Role of the Father and the Mother in the Psyche.* New York: New York University Press.

Chesler, P. 1972. *"Lesbians": Women and Madness.* New York: Harcourt Brace Jovanovich.

Chisholm, D. 1992. *H.D.'s Freudian Poetics: Psychoanalysis in Translation.* Ithaca, N.Y.: Cornell University Press.

Chodorow, N. 1978. *The Reproduction of Mothering: Psychoanalysis and the Psychology of Gender.* Berkeley: University of California Press.

_____. 1989. *Feminism and Psychoanalytic Theory.* New Haven: Yale University Press.

Cixous, H. [1977] 1991. *"Coming to Writing" and Other Essays.* D. Johnson, ed. Cambridge: Harvard University Press.

_____. [1983] 1991. *The Book of Promethea.* Lincoln: University of Nebraska Press.

Cixous, H. and Clément, C. [1975] 1986. *The Newly Born Woman.* Minneapolis: University of Minnesota Press.

Clément, C. [1981] 1983. *The Lives and Legends of Jacques Lacan.* New York: Columbia University Press.

_____. [1978] 1987. *The Weary Sons of Freud.* Bristol, England: Verso.

Cohen, M. B. [1966] 1973. *"Personal Identity and Sexual Identity."* In Miller, *Psychoanalysis and Women,* pp. 155–182.

Dalsimer, K. 1986. *Female Adolescence: Psychoanalytic Reflections on Literature.* New Haven: Yale University Press.

Deleuze, G., and Guattari, F. [1972] 1977. *Anti-Oedipus: Capitalism and Schizophrenia.* New York: Viking.

Derrida, J. [1974] 1976. *Of Grammatology.* Baltimore: Johns Hopkins University Press.

_____. [1967] 1978. *Writing and Difference.* Chicago: Chicago University Press.

Deutsch, H. 1930. *"The Significance of Masochism in the Mental Life of Women."* *International Journal of Psychoanalysis* 11:48–60.

_____. 1944. *The Psychology of Women,* vol. 1. New York: Grune & Stratton.

_____. 1945. *The Psychology of Women,* vol. 2. New York: Grune & Stratton.

_____. [1924] 1974. *"The Psychology of Women in Relation to the Functions of Reproduction."* In Strouse, *Women and Analysis,* pp. 147–161.

Dinnerstein, D. 1976. *The Mermaid and the Minotaur: Sexual Arrangements and Human Malaise.* New York: Harper & Row.

Eissler, K. 1960. *"The Efficient Soldier."* In W. Muensterberger and S. Axelrad, eds., *The Psychoanalytic Study of Society.* New York: International Universities Press, pp. 39–97.

Elliot, P. 1991. *From Mastery to Psychoanalysis: Theories of Gender in Psychoanalytic Feminism.* Ithaca, N.Y.: Cornell University Press.

Elshtain, J. B. 1981. *Public Man, Private Woman: Women in Social and Political Thought.* Princeton: Princeton University Press.

Endleman, R. 1981. *Psyche and Society.* New York: Columbia University Press.

Erikson, E. H. 1950. *Childhood and Society.* New York: Norton.

———. 1959. *Identity and the Life Cycle,* vol. 1 of *Psychological Issues.* New York: International Universities Press.

———. [1968] 1974. "Womanhood and Inner Space." In Strouse, *Women and Analysis,* pp. 291–340.

Ermarth, E. D. 1992. *Sequel to History: Postmodernism and the Crisis of Representational Time.* Princeton: Princeton University Press.

Felman, S., ed. 1977. *Literature and Psychoanalysis: The Question of Reading: Otherwise.* Yale French Studies, no. 55/56.

———. 1980. *Le scandale du corps parlant: Don Juan avec Austin ou la séduction en deux langues.* Paris: Seuil.

———. 1987. *Jacques Lacan and the Adventure of Insight: Psychoanalysis in Contemporary Culture.* Cambridge: Harvard University Press.

Felman, S., and Laub, D. 1992. *Testimony: Crises of Witnessing in Literature, Psychoanalysis, and History.* London: Routledge.

Ferenzi, S. 1955. *Final Contributions to the Problems and Methods of Psychoanalysis.* Michael Balint, ed. London: Maresfield Reprints.

Ferguson, A., Zita, J. N., and Addelson, K. P. [1980] 1981. "On 'Compulsory Heterosexuality and Lesbian Existence': Defining the Issues." In Keohane, Rosaldo, and Gelpi, *Feminist Theory,* pp. 147–188.

Figes, E. 1970. *Patriarchal Attitudes.* London: Faber & Faber.

Firestone, S. 1972. *The Dialectic of Sex.* New York: Bantam.

Flaake, K. 1992. "Die Beziehung zwischen Müttern und Töchtern." *Psyche* 46, no. 7:642–652.

Flax, J. 1990. *Thinking Fragments: Psychoanalysis, Feminism, and Postmodernism in the Contemporary West.* Berkeley: University of California Press.

Foucault, M. [1976] 1978. *The History of Sexuality I.* New York: Pantheon.

Fraser, N., and Bartky, S. L. 1992. *Revaluing French Feminism: Critical Essays on Difference, Agency, and Culture.* Bloomington: Indiana University Press.

Freeman, D. 1983. *Margaret Mead and Samoa: The Making of an Anthropological Myth.* Cambridge: Harvard University Press.

Freeman, J. [1975] 1979. *Women: A Feminist Perspective.* Palo Alto: Mayfield.

Freud, A. [1936] 1966. *The Ego and the Mechanisms of Defense,* vol. 2 of *The Writings of Anna Freud,* pp. 1–181. New York: International Universities Press.

Freud, S. 1895d. "Studies on Hysteria." Standard Edition (S.E.) 2:37–59.

———. 1900a. *The Interpretation of Dreams.* S.E. 4–5.

———. 1905d. "Three Essays on the Theory of Sexuality." S.E. 7:123–245.

———. 1912–1913. "Totem and Taboo." S.E. 13:1–161.

———. 1914c. "On Narcissism: An Introduction." S.E. 14:69–102.

———. 1915c. "Drives and their Vicissitudes." S.E. 14:109–140.

———. 1916–17. "Introductory Lectures on Psychoanalysis." S.E. 15:3–239; 16:243–476.

———. 1917e. "Mourning and Melancholia." S.E. 14:237–258.

———. 1918a. "The Taboo of Virginity." S.E. 11:191–208.

———. 1923b. "The Ego and the Id." S.E. 19:1–66.

———. 1925j. "Some Psychical Consequences of the Anatomical Distinctions Between the Sexes." S.E. 19:243–258.

_____. 1926e. "On the Question of Lay Analysis." S.E. 20:177–258.

_____. 1927c. "The Future of an Illusion." S.E., 21:3–56.

_____. 1930a. "Civilization and Its Discontents." 21:57–145.

_____. 1931b. "Female Sexuality." S.E. 21:223–243.

_____. 1933a. "New Introductory Lectures on Psychoanalysis." S.E. 22:1–182.

_____. 1939a. "Moses and Monotheism." S.E. 22:3–137.

_____. [1935] 1971. "Letter to Carl Müller–Braunschweig." *Psychiatry* 34 (August):328–329.

Friday, N. 1977. *My Mother/Myself.* New York: Dell.

Friedan, B. 1963. *The Feminine Mystique.* New York: Norton.

_____. 1992. "Our Party." *New Republic,* October 5, pp. 16–20.

Fromm, E. [1942] 1960. *The Fear of Freedom.* London: Routledge and Kegan Paul.

Frosh, S. 1987. *The Politics of Psychoanalysis.* London: Macmillan.

Gallop, J. 1982. *The Daughter's Seduction: Feminism and Psychoanalysis.* Ithaca, N.Y.: Cornell University Press.

_____. 1987. "The Mother Tongue." In Meltzer, *The Trial(s) of Psychoanalysis.* pp. 125–140.

Gilligan, C. [1982] 1993. *In a Different Voice: Psychological Theory and Women's Development.* Cambridge: Harvard University Press.

Goldstein, R. Z. de. 1994. "And Then: Why Lacan." Ballard Lecture, Columbia University Institute of Psychoanalysis, March 1.

Gölter, W. 1983. "Zukunftstüchtige Erinnerung: Aspekte weiblichen Schreibens." *Psyche,* 37, no. 7:642–668.

Graf-Nold, A. 1988. *Der Fall Hermine Hug-Hellmuth: Eine Geschichte der frühen Kinder-Psychoanalyse.* Munich: Verlag Internationale Psychoanalyse.

Greer, G. 1971. *The Female Eunoch.* London: Paladin.

Griffin, S. 1978. *Woman and Nature.* New York: Harper & Row.

Hagemann-White, C. 1978. "Die Kontroverse um die Psychoanalyse in der Frauenbewegung." *Psyche* 32:733–763.

Hale, N. G., Jr. 1971. *Freud and the Americans.* London: Oxford University Press.

Hartman, G. H. 1978. *Psychoanalysis and the Question of the Text.* Baltimore: Johns Hopkins University Press.

Hartmann, H. 1944. "Psychoanalysis and Sociology." In *Essays in Ego Psychology.* New York: International Universities Press, pp. 19–36

_____. 1950. "The Application of Psychoanalytic Concepts to Social Science." In *Essays in Ego Psychology,* pp. 90–98.

Heller, E. 1983. "Observations on Psychoanalysis and Modern Literature." In Kurzweil and Phillips, *Literature and Psychoanalysis,* pp. 72–84.

Hook, S., ed. 1959. *Psychoanalysis, Scientific Method and Philosophy.* New York: Columbia University Press.

Horkheimer, M., and Adorno, T. W. [1944] 1979. *The Dialectic of Enlightenment.* Frankfurt: Fischer.

Horney, K. [1922] 1924. "On the Genesis of the Castration Complex in Women." *International Journal of Psycho-Analysis* 5:50–65.

_____. 1935. "The Problem of Feminine Masochism." *Psychoanalytic Review* 12, no. 3:241–257.

_____. 1937. *The Neurotic Personality of Our Time.* New York: Norton.

———. 1939. *New Ways in Psychoanalysis.* New York: Norton.

———. 1943. *Bulletin #3: American Journal of Psychoanalysis.* New York: Committee on the War Effort.

———. [1926] 1974. "The Flight from Womanhood: The Masculinity-Complex in Women as Viewed by Men and Women." In Strouse, *Women and Analysis,* pp. 171–186.

Hug-Hellmuth, H. 1911. "Analysis of a Dream of a Five and a Half Year Old Boy." *Zentralblatt* 2 3:122–127.

Hughes, J. M. 1989. *Reshaping the Psychoanalytic Domain.* Berkeley: University of California Press.

Irigaray, L. [1974] 1985. *Speculum of the Other Woman.* Ithaca, N.Y.: Cornell University Press.

———. [1991] 1993. *Marine Lover of Friedrich Nietzsche.* New York: Columbia University Press.

Janeway, E. 1971. *Man's World, Woman's Place.* New York: Morrow.

Jardine, A. A., and Menke, A. M., eds. 1991. *Shifting Scenes: Interviews on Women, Writing, and Politics in Post-68 France.* New York: Columbia University Press.

Jones, E. 1927. "Early Development of Female Sexuality." *International Journal of Psychoanalysis* 8:459–472.

———. 1933. "The Phallic Phase." *International Journal of Psychoanalysis* 14:1–33.

———. 1955. *The Life and Work of Sigmund Freud,* vol. 2. New York: Basic Books.

———. [1953, 1955] 1957. *The Life and Work of Sigmund Freud.* New York: Basic Books.

Kaplan, L. 1984. *Adolescence: The Farewell to Childhood:* New York: Simon & Schuster.

———. 1991. *Female Perversions: The Temptations of Emma Bovary.* New York: Doubleday.

Kardiner, A. Karush, A., and Ovesey, L. 1959. "A Methodological Study of Freudian Theory, Part III: Narcissism, Bisexuality and the Dual Instinct Theory." *Journal of Nervous and Mental Diseases* 129:215–220.

Kauffman, L. S. 1993. *American Feminist Thought at Century's End.* Cambridge: Blackwell.

Keller, E. F. [1991] 1993. "Making Gender Visible in the Pursuit of Nature's Secrets." In Kauffman, *American Feminist Thought at Century's End,* pp. 189–198.

Keohane, N. O., Rosaldo, M. Z., Gelpi, B. C., eds. 1981. *Feminist Theory: A Critique of Ideology.* Chicago: Chicago University Press.

Kernberg, O. 1992. *Aggression in Personality Disorders and Perversions.* New Haven: Yale University Press.

King, P., and Steiner, R. 1991. "The Freud-Klein Controversy." *New Library of Psychoanalysis,* no. 11: 1941–1945.

Klaich, D. 1974. *Woman + Woman: Attitudes Toward Lesbianism.* New York: William Morrow.

Klein, M. 1932. *The Psychoanalysis of Children.* London: Hogarth Press, 1975.

———. [1926] 1975. "The Psychological Principles of Early Analysis." In *Love, Guilt and Reparation and Other Works 1921–1945.* London: Hogarth Press, pp. 128–138.

_____. [1928]. 1975. "Early Stages of the Oedipus Complex." In *Love, Guilt and Reparation and Other Works 1921–1945*. London: Hogarth Press, pp. 186–198.

_____. [1937] 1975. "Love, Guilt and Reparation," In *Love, Guilt and Reparation and Other Works 1921–1945*. London: Hogarth Press, pp. 303–343.

Klein, V. 1945. *The Feminine Character: History of an Ideology*. Chicago: University of Chicago Press.

Kristeva, J. [1974] 1979. *About Chinese Women*. New York: Urizen.

_____. [1977] 1980. *Desire in Language*. New York: Columbia University Press.

_____. [1980] 1982. *The Powers of Horror: An Essay in Abjection*. New York: Columbia University Press.

_____. 1983. "Mémoires." *L'Infini* 1:39–54.

_____. [1983] 1987. *Tales of Love*. New York: Columbia University Press.

_____. [1981] 1989. *Language the Unknown: An Initiation into Linguistics*. New York: Columbia University Press.

Kurzweil, E. 1980. *The Age of Structuralism: Lévi-Strauss to Foucault*. New York: Columbia University Press.

_____. 1984. "The Uses of Psychoanalysis in Critical Theory and Structuralism." In J. Marcus and Z. Tar, eds., *Foundations of the Frankfurt School of Social Research*. New Brunswick, N.J.: Transaction, pp. 273–287.

_____. 1986. "Interview with Julia Kristeva." *Partisan Review*, no. 2:216–229.

_____. 1987. "Macro and Micro Structures in Psychoanalysis." In J. Alexander et al., eds., *The Micro-Macro Link*. Berkeley: University of California Press, pp. 237–254.

_____. 1989a. "Psychoanalytic Feminism: Implications for Sociological Theory." In R. Wallace, ed., *Feminism and Sociological Theory*. Newbury Park, Calif.: Sage, pp. 82–97.

_____. 1989b. *The Freudians: A Comparative Perspective*. New Haven: Yale University Press.

Kurzweil, E., and Phillips, W., eds. 1983. *Literature and Psychoanalysis*. New York: Columbia University Press.

Lacan, J. 1966. *Ecrits I*. Paris: Editions du Seuil.

_____. 1971. *Ecrits II*. Paris: Editions du Seuil.

_____. 1975. *Le séminaire de Jacques Lacan, Livre XX: Encore 1972–1973*. Paris: Editions du Seuil.

_____. [1966] 1977. *Ecrits: A Selection*. New York: Norton.

Laing, R. D. 1965. *The Divided Self*. London: Penguin Books.

Langer, W. 1972. *The Mind of Hitler*. New York: Basic Books.

Lechte, J. 1990. *Julia Kristeva*. London: Routledge.

Lee, Jonathan S. 1990. *Jacques Lacan*. Amherst: University of Massachusetts Press.

Lévi-Strauss, C. [1963] 1966. *The Savage Mind*. Chicago: Chicago University Press.

Lewin, K. 1948. *Resolving Social Conflicts*. New York: Hayer.

Lowenstein, R. 1957. "A Contribution to the Psychoanalytic Theory of Masochism." *Journal of the American Psychoanalytic Association* 5:197–234.

Lyotard, J. F. 1986. *The Postmodern Condition: A Report on Knowledge*. Manchester: Manchester University Press.

Macey, D. 1988. *Lacan in Context*. London: Verso.

MacLean G., and Rappen, U. 1991. *Hermine Hug-Hellmuth: Her Life and Work.* London: Routledge.

Mahler, M. S., Pine, F., and Bergman, A. 1975. *The Psychological Birth of the Human Infant: Symbiosis and Individuation.* New York: Basic Books.

Marcuse, H. 1955. *Eros and Civilization.* New York: Vintage.

_____. 1964. *One-dimensional Man.* Boston: Beacon Press.

Marks, E., and Courtivron, I., eds. 1980. *New French Feminisms.* Amherst: University of Massachusetts Press.

Martin, B. 1991. *Women and Modernity: The (Life)Styles of Lou Andreas-Salomé.* Ithaca, N.Y.: Cornell University Press.

McDougall, J. [1978] 1980. *Plea for a Measure of Abnormality.* New York: International Universities Press.

_____. [1982] 1985. *Theaters of the Mind.* New York: Basic Books.

Mead, M. 1935. *Sex and Temperament in Three Primitive Societies.* New York: William Morrow.

Mehlman, J. 1972. *French Freud: Structural Studies in Psychoanalysis.* Yale French Studies, no. 48. New Haven: Yale University Press.

Meltzer, F., ed. 1987. *The Trial(s) of Psychoanalysis.* Chicago: Chicago University Press.

Miller, J.-A., ed. 1982. "Au lecteur." *Ornicar?* no. 25:1, 4.

_____. [1975] 1988. *The Seminar of Jacques Lacan, Book I: Freud's Papers on Techniques, 1953–1954.* New York: Norton.

_____. [1978] 1988. *The Seminar of Jacques Lacan, Book II: The Ego in Freud's Theory and in the Technique of Psychoanalysis, 1954–1955.* New York: Norton.

Miller, J. B. 1973. *Psychoanalysis and Women.* London: Penguin.

Millet, K. 1970. *Sexual Politics.* New York: Doubleday.

Mills, C. W. 1956. *The Power Elite.* New York: Oxford University Press.

Mitchell, J. 1971. *Women's Estate.* New York: Pantheon.

_____. 1974. *Psychoanalysis and Feminism.* New York: Pantheon.

_____. 1984. *Women: The Longest Revolution.* New York: Pantheon.

Mitchell, J., and Rose, J., eds., 1982. *Feminine Sexuality: Jacques Lacan and the École Freudienne.* New York: Norton.

Mitscherlich, A. [1963] 1969. *Society Without the Father.* New York: Harcourt, Brace and World.

Mitscherlich, A., and Mitscherlich-Nielson, M. 1967. *Die Unfähigkeit zu trauern.* Munich: Piper.

Mitscherlich, M. 1985. *Die friedfertige Frau* (The Peace-Loving Woman). Frankfurt am Main: Fischer.

_____. 1987. *Erinnerungsarbeit: Zur Psychoanalyse der Unfähigkeit zu trauern.* Frankfurt am Main: Fischer.

Mitscherlich, M., et al. 1983. *Das Unbehagen in der Psychoanalyse: Eine Streitschrift.* Frankfurt am Main: Qumran.

_____. 1992. "Die Beziehung zwischen Müttern und Töchtern." *Psyche* 46, no. 7:642–652.

Mitscherlich-Nielsen, M. 1975. "Psychoanalyse und weibliche Sexualität." *Psyche,* 29:769–788.

Moi, T. 1987. *French Feminist Thought: A Reader.* Oxford: Basil Blackwell.

New York Psychoanalytic Society. Various years. *Minutes of the Society.* Archives.

Nunberg, H., and Federn, E. 1962; 1967; 1974. *Minutes of the Vienna Psychoanalytic Society,* vols. 1–3. New York: International Universities Press.

Oliner, M. 1988. *Cultivating Freud's Garden in France.* New York: Jason Aronson.

Oliver, K., ed. 1993. *Ethics, Politics, and Difference in Julia Kristeva's Writing.* New York: Routledge.

Parsons, T. [1964] 1970. *Social Structure and Personality.* New York: Free Press.

Quinn, S. 1987. *A Mind of Her Own: The Life of Karen Horney.* New York: Summit Books.

Radó, S. 1933. "Fear of Castration in Women." *Psychoanalytic Quarterly* 2, no. 3:425–475.

Ragland-Sullivan, E. 1986. *Jacques Lacan and the Language of Psychoanalysis.* Chicago: Chicago University Press.

Ragland-Sullivan, E., and Bracher, M. 1991. *Lacan and the Subject of Language.* New York: Routledge.

Reiff, P. 1963. *Freud: The Mind of the Moralist.* New York: Viking.

———. 1966. *The Triumph of the Therapeutic.* New York: Harper & Row.

Reinke-Köberer, E. 1983. "Sexualität in der Psychoanalyse heute—Ein Tabu." In *Das Unbehagen in der Psychoanalyse.* Frankfurt: Qumran, pp. 86–92.

Rich, A. 1976. *Of Woman Born.* New York: Norton.

Rohde-Dachser, C. 1991. *Expedition in den dunklen Kontinent.* Berlin: Springer Verlag.

Roman, P. M., and Trice, H. M. 1974. *The Sociology of Psychotherapy.* New York: Jason Aronson.

Rose, J. 1986. *Sexuality in the Field of Vision.* London: Verso.

Rubin, G. 1975. "The Traffic in Women: Notes on the 'Political Economy' of Sex." In R. Reiter, ed., *Toward an Anthropology of Women.* New York: Monthly Review Press, pp. 157–210.

Safilos-Rothschild, C. [1969] 1972. *Toward a Sociology of Women.* Lexington, Mass.: Xerox College Publishing.

Sartre, J.-P. [1960] 1976. *Being and Nothingness* and *The Critique of Dialectical Reason.* London: New Left Books.

Sayers, J. 1986. *Sexual Contradictions: Psychology, Psychoanalysis, Feminism.* London: Tavistock.

———. 1991. *Mothers of Psychoanalysis.* New York: Norton.

Sedgwick, E. K. 1990. *Epistemology of the Closet.* Berkeley: University of California Press.

Segal, H. 1979. *Klein.* London: Fontana.

Sherfey, M. J. [1966] 1972. *The Nature and Evolution of Female Sexuality.* New York: Random House.

Silverman, K. 1992. "The Lacanian Phallus." *Differences: A Journal for Feminist Cultural Studies* 4, no. 1:84–115.

Smith, J. H., and Kerrigan, W., eds. 1984. *Interpreting Lacan.* Yale University Psychiatry and the Humanities Series, no. 6. New Haven: Yale University Press.

Sommers, C. H. 1992. "Sister Soldiers." *New Republic,* October 5, 1992, pp. 29–33.

Sprengnether, M. 1990. *The Spectral Mother: Freud, Feminism, and Psychoanalysis.* Ithaca, N.Y.: Cornell University Press.

Stimpson, C. R., and Person, E. S. 1980. *Women: Sex and Sexuality.* Chicago: Chicago University Press.

Stoller, R. J. [1972] 1973. "The Bedrock of Masculinity and Femininity: Bisexuality." In Miller, *Psychoanalysis and Women,* pp. 273–284.

Stone, L. J., and Church, J. 1957. *Childhood and Society: A Psychology of the Growing Person.* New York: Random House.

Strouse, J., ed. 1974. *Women and Analysis: Dialogues on Psychoanalytic Views of Femininity.* New York: Viking.

Suleiman, S. R. 1990. *Subversive Intent: Gender, Politics, and the Avant-Garde.* Cambridge: Harvard University Press.

Sullivan, H. S. 1972. *Personal Psychopathology: Early Formulations.* New York: Norton.

Sulloway, F. J. 1979. *Freud, Biologist of the Mind: Beyond the Psychoanalytic Legend.* New York: Basic Books.

Sunstein, C. R., ed. 1982. *Feminism and Political Theory.* Chicago: Chicago University Press.

Thompson, C. 1943. "'Penis Envy' in Women." *Psychiatry* 6:123–125.

Thompson, N. 1987. "Early Women Psychoanalysts." *International Review of Psycho-Analysis* 14:391–407.

Turkle, S. 1978. *Psychoanalytic Politics.* New York: Basic Books.

Veblen, T. V. [1899] 1953. *The Theory of the Leisure Class.* New York: Mentor Books.

Weber, M. [1919] 1946. "Politics as a Vocation." In H. Gerth and C. W. Mills, eds., *From Max Weber: Essays in Sociology.* New York: Oxford University Press, pp. 77–128.

Westcott, M. 1986. *The Feminist Legacy of Karen Horney.* New Haven: Yale University Press.

Whitford, M., ed. 1991. *The Irigaray Reader.* London: Basil Blackwell.

Wilden, A. 1980. *System and Structure: Essays in Communication and Exchange.* London: Tavistock.

Williams, C. L. 1989. *Gender Differences at Work: Women and Men in Nontraditional Occupations.* Berkeley: University of California Press.

Wolff, J. 1990. *Feminine Sentences: Essays on Women and Culture.* Berkeley: University of California Press.

Wright, E. 1992. *Feminism and Psychoanalysis: A Critical Dictionary.* London: Basil Blackwell.

Young-Bruehl, E., ed. 1990. *Freud on Women: A Reader.* New York: Norton.

Zerilli, L. M. 1991. "A Process Without a Subject: Simone de Beauvoir and Julia Kristeva on Maternity." Paper presented at Rutgers–Newark, November 11.

Zilboorg, G. 1944. "Masculine and Feminine: Some Biological and Cultural Aspects." *Psychiatry* 7:257–296.

About the Book and Author

Twenty years ago, few observers would have foreseen that some feminists would once again turn to Freud. But in recent years, the adoption by American feminists of French concepts—especially the ideas of Lacan—has led to new approaches in feminist theory and psychology. This book traces the intellectual history of the interaction between feminists and Freudian thought, charting the essence of psychoanalytic theories through the years to show specific notions were adapted, readapted, and discarded by successive generations of feminists.

Edith Kurzweil, a sociologist, is University Professor of Social Thought at Adelphi University. She is the author of *The Age of Structuralism: Lévi-Strauss to Focault* (1980); *Literature and Psychoanalysis,* coedited with W. Phillips (1983); and *The Freudians: A Comparative Perspective* (1989), among other books. She is editor of *Partisan Review* and frequently writes on cultural issues.

Index

222 / *Index*